A PHILOSOPHY OF FREEDOM

Also by Lars Svendsen and published by Reaktion Books:

Fashion: A Philosophy
A Philosophy of Boredom
A Philosophy of Fear

A Philosophy of Freedom

Lars Svendsen

REAKTION BOOKS

Published by
Reaktion Books Ltd
33 Great Sutton Street
London EC1V ODX, UK

www.reaktionbooks.co.uk

First published in English 2014

English-language translation by Kerri Pierce
© Reaktion Books 2014

This book was first published in Norwegian in 2013 by Universitetsforlaget AS
under the title *Frihetens filosofi* by Lars Fr. Svendsen
Copyright © Universitetsforlaget 2013

This translation has been published with the financial assistance of NORLA

Printed and bound by TJ International, Padstow, Cornwall

A catalogue record for this book is available from the British Library

ISBN 978 1 78023 370 3

Contents

The really important kind of freedom involves attention, and awareness, and discipline, and effort, and being able truly to care about other
people and to sacrifice for them, over and over, in myriad petty little
unsexy ways, every day.

David Foster Wallace

Foreword

Freedom's existence can appear to be self-evident. It is a fundamental component of our human identity, of what separates us from other animals. Basically, it is up to you whether you want to read this book. You can continue reading or you can put it down and do something else instead. The choice is yours. Except in certain special situations, we largely have the ability to decide whether or not to do something, according to what we deem best. Freedom, however, has a political framework as well. For example, a government authority might conceivably decide that the book's content is threatening and forbid you to read it. As its author, I could be jailed for expressing such thoughts. Ultimately, the question of why you should read the book hinges on the role it can play in how you choose to lead your life.

This book is a defence of freedom. It is directed at those who argue that freedom is incompatible with a scientific worldview, as well as at those in the political arena who are willing to sacrifice freedom for the sake of a seemingly higher purpose. The two issues are addressed in the context of each other. Freedom, after all, is a multi-dimensional phenomenon, from its ontological and metaphysical to its political or personal aspects. As a result, one major point of departure for this book is simply the idea that many of the difficulties we face in understanding freedom spring from the blending of diverse freedom concepts. For example, we might use a political freedom concept to explain personal freedom or vice versa. It was, therefore, important for me to write a broadly conceived book in which I could attempt to understand how freedom concepts on many different levels are related to and deviate from each other. In this sense, the potential originality in this book is more the result of its overall conception than of its individual components. At the same time, I believe I make several new contributions along the way in terms of my interpretation and critique of various philosophies and theories.

This book has been a relatively long time in the coming and its character has changed several times during that process. It is about a third of the size I had originally intended. Over the course of the project, however, it became clear to me that much of what I had planned to address was superfluous in terms of my goals for the project. The first part of the book in particular has been pared down; much of the natural-sciences-oriented content is gone. The reason for this is simple. Though recent neurophysiological research has certainly turned up much that is relevant to freedom's problematic, I still chose to cut that section down to a minimum because advances in the field happen so quickly that whatever I might write would soon be outdated. My argument, however, does not rest upon specific neurophysiological findings. Instead, freedom's political dimension clearly emerged as the book's focus. It is here, in my opinion, that the most pressing problems surrounding freedom can be found today.

Obviously this is not an *exhaustive* freedom study. A work on that scale would be impossible to write. Indeed, every theme the book touches upon could easily have its own volume. The breadth of philosophical literature on freedom, furthermore, is so extensive that it is hard to imagine anyone getting through more than just a fraction of it. Many readers will certainly note the absence of lengthy discourses on the concepts of freedom belonging, for example, to Thomas Aquinas, Spinoza, Kant, Schelling and Sartre. Undoubtedly, these philosophers approach freedom in very interesting ways. However, trying to include everything one considers interesting is a luxury ill-afforded anyone seeking to finish a book. Instead of providing general accounts of various individual philosophers' theories of freedom, I have chosen to take portions of different philosophers' theories and use them to produce something of my own. What I have set out to write here is not a social or philosophical history of freedom; nor does it offer a systematic account of all the different approaches to freedom found in contemporary philosophy.[1] That project would fill several volumes and about 90 per cent of it would be devoted to what I consider dead-end discussions. In the foreword to *A Philosophy of Evil*, I wrote that I had never dealt with a subject whose source material was so overwhelming. After having written a book on freedom, I can only say that, by comparison, tackling the literature on evil seems to be a relatively tame undertaking. Indeed, more philosophical works have probably been written on freedom than any other subject. The bibliography at the end of this book consists of nearly 350 titles, and that is only a minor part of what I actually went through in writing the book, and only a small fraction of the collected literature itself. I have to agree here with Daniel Dennett's observation that numerous philosophical works on freedom of will are so technical in character that, unfortunately, they are only of aesthetic interest. While one can certainly marvel at their technical brilliance, they fail to address the *actual* problems to which the subject gives rise.[2] And yet Dennett and I would disagree on what those actual problems are. As I see it, Dennett is too reductive and, as a result, suffers from a problem deficit. That is to say, he simply rationalizes pressing issues away. On the other hand, Dennett would argue that I simply waltz right out into the very metaphysical quagmire from which he has tried to rescue us.

In this book, I have only tried to cover the literature that I judged to be the most relevant to my purposes; my references direct the reader to other works across the field. Different authors, of course, would have selected different texts, and would, for example, have devoted more space to John Rawls's theory of justice, which in my opinion no longer offers fresh insights. Instead, I consider Amartya Sen's approach to be a more productive path. In this context it is worth remarking that even though Rawls's *Theory of Justice* is notably the most discussed, celebrated and criticized work in political philosophy since its publication in 1971, it has not had much of an impact on actual politics – which Sen's work, in contrast, has done. However, a thorough explanation of all the theoretical choices I made along the way would take up far too much space. Suffice it to say that this book could have been many times as comprehensive as it ended up being, and there are countless ancillary questions that could have, and perhaps should have, received thorough treatment. However, my ambition was to try and write the most coherent possible narrative of the fundamental ontological and anthropological questions surrounding freedom as I moved through freedom's political aspects and on to personal freedom's domain.

At the same time, this book has ended up being less accessible than most of my previous works and, despite the above, a good deal more comprehensive. Some parts are written in a more 'analytical' style than many of my earlier books, which often have a more 'Continental' flavour. This should not be taken as a philosophical *volte-face* on my part. I am trained in both disciplines and do not consider the apparent contrasts between the two to be all that critical. Instead I regard both traditions as part and parcel of a philosophical toolbox from which I select the implements best suited to a particular theme. Some of the numerous subjects the book addresses warrant more 'analytical' tools, others more 'Continental' – and most a combination of the two. As I see it, the most important philosophical divide is not the one found between 'analytical philosophy' and 'Continental philosophy', but rather the one between a philosophy that wants to assume a useful place in our lives and a philosophy that does not have this ambition. However, that is a subject for another discussion.

Introduction

In the novel *Walden Two* (1948), the psychologist B. F. Skinner depicts a rural society whose members work the earth and collectively raise their children. They lead a comfortable existence characterized by free time in abundance, which they devote to arts, crafts and science. The community's founder, Frazier – who acts as Skinner's mouthpiece in the novel – insists that the inhabitants' harmonious existence is enabled by the fact that they have been conditioned since childhood to want and choose only what they can have and do. Behavioural therapy has so influenced their actions, conduct and emotional life that they have neither the desire nor the will to deviate from the smallest detail of Frazier's vision for their lives. As a result, Frazier insists that Walden Two is 'the freest place on earth', since no one, either by force or threat, is compelled to do anything they do not want.[1] On the contrary, all the inhabitants can do exactly as they please. There are no jails in this society, since Frazier's will does not need punishment to enforce it. When a philosopher named Castle visits Walden Two, however, he objects that the inhabitants are only apparently free, because although they can do whatever they want, they have no ability to influence *what* they want. Their will is fully determined by causes over which they have no control. In effect, they have been brainwashed. Frazier takes this protest with devastating calm. He admits that the inhabitants are indeed subject to a strict determinism, for they do not have the 'deeper' freedom of will that philosophers argue all men possess. At the same time, he insists that such free will, which implies a person may also choose what he wills, is pure illusion. Therefore the inhabitants of Walden Two have simply secured happiness without missing out on anything else in life.

If Frazier (and Skinner) are correct, the consequences for our viewpoint on humanity, on what it means to be human, would be severe. For example, would there be any rational reason to hold the inhabitants of Walden Two accountable for their actions or to praise them when they do right? Let us imagine that another rural community, Walden Three, is located right next to Walden Two, and that Frazier's brother, Niles, is its founder and head. Niles is a social anthropologist and psychologist, and he is fascinated with Colin Turnbull's book on the Ik society, whose members present a stark contrast to all that is humanly decent and moral.[2] Niles sets out to create a similar society – and he succeeds. From a moral point of view, Walden Three's inhabitants are really nothing more than malicious assholes. Like the inhabitants of Walden Two, moreover, the members of Walden Three can do exactly as they please. Both groups are strictly determined to want what they want, and they act in accordance with these desires. The question then becomes: do we have any grounds to praise the members of Walden Two and condemn the members of Walden Three for good and bad behaviour respectively? It appears that we do not, at least no more so than we have for morally praising Fido, a dog, for being friendly and morally condemning Rex, another dog, for being vicious. And yet, the irrationality of morally condemning a dog for being what it is, and for acting in keeping with that canine character, should be obvious. A dog cannot be held responsible for its nature. In our example, the same would be true of the inhabitants of Walden Two and Walden Three, who have been shaped by Frazier and Niles to be exactly what they are. It seems they are just as determined and morally unaccountable as Fido and Rex.

At this point, we have lost all moral standards by which to judge human behaviour. It seems that the only possible conclusion to draw is that people just are the way they are and this determines how they act. As such, there does not seem to be a compelling reason to burden anyone with a normative requirement – a requirement, that is, stating that people *should* act in certain ways rather than others – any more so than a vicious dog or a tile that happens to tumble off a roof and strike a passer-by on the head. Yet is that really the case? Or is Frazier's philosophical opponent, Castle, right when he claims that freedom has a deeper dimension that Frazier fails to take into account? Does another alternative exist where people can essentially be considered to be as determined as Frazier describes, but can nonetheless be held accountable for their actions?

Let us assume that Frazier is correct in his viewpoint on humanity. In that case, he is also subject to this truth. Can we, therefore, persist in saying that it is morally wrong or right for Frazier to create Walden Two? Must this kind of deterministic universe necessarily be nihilistic, or can it hold moral values as well? In a universe where everything simply is what it is, where Frazier can only do X and not Y, there seems to be no room for moral evaluations, such as: it is morally wrong for Frazier to do X. Good and evil cannot exist in a world where everything is as it is and nothing more; norms simply have no place. In a deterministic universe, there is accordingly no moral distinction between a sadistic killer and his victim. They are both living out their nature, end of discussion. However, a world lacking all moral distinctions would be uninhabitable.

Walden Two is a strictly regulated society. The inhabitants have a shared set of values. The question then becomes: can a society be considered free when no other alternative exists? As I will attempt to demonstrate in later chapters, autonomy and pluralism are closely connected, which means that Frazier is completely wrong in his assertion that Walden Two is 'the freest place on earth', simply because no one, neither by force nor threat, is made to do anything against his will.[3] Frazier believes that he has found the optimal way of life. However, what if some of the inhabitants of Walden Two should happen to think otherwise? Frazier would perhaps say that they *cannot* have other thoughts because their indoctrination has proven so total. At the same time, we might imagine that the visitor, Castle, brought a number of books with him in his luggage, and that without Frazier's knowledge he stashed them in Walden Two's library. These books hold accounts of different ways of life, and it is conceivable that after reading them, some inhabitants find that they want to try out different lifestyles. How would Frazier deal with these people? It is difficult to imagine that he could do anything but implement general coercive measures, which means that Walden Two in no way lives up to the ideal of 'the freest place on earth'. These subversive elements, who happen to prefer other ways of life, could not be allowed the opportunity to influence others in Walden Two. Instead, they would have to be forcibly deported, jailed or eliminated, and Frazier would be compelled to introduce censorship into the community by removing all 'harmful' books from the library. Value pluralism, after all, is the greatest threat to Walden Two's existence. As a result, freedom in Walden Two is a deceptive entity, since it presupposes that every door remains closed but the ones chosen by Frazier, the apparently good-hearted dictator. Walden Two is Skinner's vision for a paradise on earth, and in one excursion I will attempt to demonstrate why such paradisiacal concepts are, in reality, recipes for political catastrophes.

The debate between Frazier and Castle illustrates that 'freedom' will always be a controversial idea. It is not that freedom has a large number of opponents; it it is just that freedom concepts are simply so varied and irreconcilable. We can, perhaps, say that there is some indefinite kernel here upon which most people can agree, thereby making it possible to use the same umbrella term to cover all of these concepts, but as soon as one attempts to define and specify the expression, disagreements quickly arise. Freedom is what W. B. Gallie termed an 'essentially contested concept', an idea whose nature lends itself to controversy.[4] Gallie demonstrated that there are systematic similarities between such concepts. In the first place, they contain a kernel around which there is relatively broad consensus, and of which one can readily give a few uncontroversial examples. Second, these concepts are then used to make value judgements. Third, they are so complex that they allow for meaningful variations. And fourth, their components are so unspecified or vague that they can be expanded upon in more than one way. The freedom concept fulfils all of these characteristics to a greater extent than most other concepts. Therefore it would also be naive to think that a book such as this could settle the debate on what freedom 'actually' is. Providing the most coherent and consistent narrative for different aspects of human freedom, and hoping that it appears convincing, is the most that I can hope to accomplish. In the freedom debate, indisputable arguments – things that would sweep all doubt aside – simply do not exist. All we have are theories and observations that strike us as being more or less plausible.

Montesquieu opens his discussion of freedom in *Spirit of the Laws* by asserting that no word has so many different meanings as does the word 'freedom'.[5] And as Abraham Lincoln put it in his speech on liberty and slavery in 1864:

> The world has never had a good definition of the word liberty, and the American people, just now, are much in want of one. We all declare for liberty; but in using the same *word* we do not all mean the same *thing*. With some the word liberty may mean for each man to do as he pleases with himself, and the product of his labor; while with others the same word may

mean for some men to do as they please with other men, and the product of other men's labor. Here are two, not only different, but incompatible things, called by the same name – liberty.[6]

In his well-known essay 'Two Concepts of Liberty', Isaiah Berlin further pointed out that there are over 200 documented meanings of the word 'liberty', and he has simply undertaken to discuss two of them.[7] One consistent feature of the freedom concept, therefore, is its variety of meanings, which is possibly greater than for any other concept. As such, there is room for significant misunderstandings. When two people discuss 'freedom', they are not necessarily talking about the *same* phenomenon. And there is hardly a neutral principle that would enable us to determine what 'real' freedom entails. The formulation one gives to a particular concept of freedom ultimately depends upon the values one brings to the table.[8]

In this book, I will focus more on freedom's political aspects than on its metaphysical ones, simply because the former are the most important to our lives. Our desire for freedom stems from our experience of freedom's direct opposite – oppression. Oppression occurs in many forms, ranging from our nearest relations to an encounter with a powerful government machine. A common factor here is that one cannot avoid acting against one's will or cannot act according to one's will, at least without incurring sanctions that seem worse than the alternative. Therefore as John Dewey has observed, 'What men have esteemed and fought for in the name of liberty is varied and complex – but certainly it has never been a metaphysical free will.'[9] The metaphysical aspects of freedom are certainly not immaterial, because when it comes to freedom's political problematic, our viewpoint will in part be determined by metaphysical considerations about the sort of beings we humans are. At the same time, our ideas concerning political freedom can have consequences for our evaluation of those metaphysical questions. For example, Isaiah Berlin's renunciation of determinism seems to be partially motivated by his take on political freedom, since he considers it crucial for agents to have different action alternatives open to them.[10] We can further observe that our views on freedom of will seem to have consequences for our actions. Psychological experiments have shown that people whose belief in freedom of will has been weakened are more likely to cheat, to give themselves illegitimate advantages and so on, than people whose belief remains intact.[11] In the same way, a concept of metaphysical freedom of will can apparently affect our interpretation of existence as meaningful, because meaning here seems to be linked to the idea that we can help shape a certain future for ourselves and others, that we can actually make a *difference* and create *another* world.

'Freedom', however, is not the only expression with multiple meanings.[12] The same is also true of several terms that designate specific positions within the freedom debate. For example, 'libertarianism' is used for positions within both the ontological and the political arena. However, the ontological term and the political term are logically independent of one another. A person can be an ontological libertarian without being a political libertarian, and vice versa. As a result, it would probably be advantageous to use different terminology for the ontological and the political positions, though I believe there to be little danger of confusion here. In the first place, it will be obvious whether we are addressing the ontological or the political questions at any particular point. And, in the second place, not much attention will be paid to political libertarianism. Indeed, it should be mentioned that the actual scope of 'political libertarianism' is unclear. The concept principally occurs in American contexts, where its meaning is similar to what in a European context would be called 'classical liberalism'. However, it also extends beyond that to encompass certain anarchist positions.[13] In this book, I will approach liberalism as an ideology that desires a strong state, but at the same time emphasizes that the state's domains should be limited. That means that there are certain varieties of libertarianism, namely the anarchist ones, that do not fall under the category of liberalism.[14] The opposite is also true. Most people would place a philosopher like Rawls within a liberal framework, yet hardly anybody would call him a libertarian. In the relevant section, I will generally use the term 'liberalism' – and this in a European sense that is also quite complex and vague – while the idea of political libertarianism will be used only rarely.[15] In this book, namely, 'libertarianism' will mainly refer to an ontological position. All references to the political position will be clear from context. Ideologies such as liberalism and conservatism simply do not have clear boundaries, and neither of them is capable of supplying the necessary and sufficient conditions for rightfully labelling something 'liberalism' or 'conservatism'. That means that the boundaries between the different ideologies will always remain indefinite, and disagreement will persist regarding what the 'true' incarnation of a given ideology actually is. Despite this disagreement, however, certain concepts will emerge as more central than others.

I also want to point out that the expression 'freedom of will', which often occurs in this book, in no way implies that there is a separate entity inside of us that goes by the name of 'will' and that has the property of freedom. In this book, freedom of will coincides with freedom of action: it is a characteristic of our actions. Freedom of will means having the ability to make decisions, to act on the grounds of one's practical reason, to establish goals and evaluate different courses of action as being better or worse for reaching those goals. If one does not like the expression 'freedom of will', one can always replace it with 'freedom of action'.[16]

The book is divided into three main parts:

(1) *The Ontology of Freedom.* Here I tackle some of the funda-mental questions regarding freedom's existence, about how one can approach freedom's actuality in a world governed by laws, and why freedom is such an important part of being human. After discussing voluntariness in chapter One, which will take Aristotle as a spring-board, I will turn to the determinism problematic. Originally, I had planned to engage in a thorough examination of the debate between hard determinists, libertarians and compatibilists. Upon closer examin-ation, however, I decided to greatly curb this discussion. The reason for my decision here is that it is difficult to see that the debate has actually gone much of anywhere. Instead, it has yielded a wealth of extremely sophisticated philosophy, with a sometimes head-spinning degree of difficulty. And though the debate has surged back and forth with arguments and counterarguments, as all philosophy tends to do, it seems to be as far from any clarification as ever. I also believe that I do not have anything substantial to add to this debate; furthermore, most of it is tangential in terms of my actual purpose with the book. Nonetheless, I have elected to give the debate a short introduction in chapter Two, though I do not draw any firm conclusions here. Instead, I approach the problem by another route. I am actually inclined to think that the best strategy here would be to place a hefty set of paren-theses around the whole discussion concerning the extent to which free will is compatible with determinism – or indeterminism, for that matter – and instead progress in a more pragmatic fashion in order to examine how widespread conceptions of voluntariness, sanity and accountability can be illuminated by what we actually *know* about ourselves and the world, instead of getting mired in metaphysical

speculation. At the same time, I also recognize that it is necessary to outline some of the more controversial topics, if for no other reason than to demonstrate why and how we can make headway on the freedom problematic without the metaphysical issues having come to any satisfactory resolution. In chapter Three, I take up Peter F. Strawson's theory of reactive and objective attitudes and further develop my own viewpoint on the conditions for freedom and responsibility. Chapter Four concludes the book's first part with an account of autonomy.

(2) *The Politics of Freedom.* This section takes up the thread from the previous chapters and, keeping in mind the understanding of human nature outlined in chapters One to Four, it explores how a society ought to be constituted. The matter of a society's organization, of the frameworks that should be put in place for the individual's development, must be answered according to our perception of what kind of being we humans are. Chapter Five addresses the liberal democracy as a form of government. Chapter Six then discusses the difference between positive and negative freedom with Isaiah Berlin as its point of departure, and this discussion is followed by a foray into value pluralism and moral realism. After that, I explore the new republican critique of negative freedom in chapter Seven. Chapter Eight discusses the relationship between equality and freedom, and focuses on exactly what type of equality can be justified within the framework of the freedom concept as outlined in the previous chapters, as well as on what type of equality proves conditional for universal freedom. This is followed by an excursion detailing the way in which political utopias have proven recipes for political catastrophes. In chapter Nine, I focus on certain basic characteristics of the history of liberal rights, and thereafter I compose a list of the fundamental rights that every free society should embrace. Chapters Ten, Eleven and Twelve are devoted to the three rights on that list that I believe have particularly come under pressure in liberal democracies of late: the right not to be the object of paternalistic intervention, the right to informational privacy and the right to freedom of expression. In chapters Five to Twelve, the discussion largely centres around the formal characteristics of any society that wants to defend and promote its citizens' freedom. The discussion dwells only to a limited extent on the concrete, social conditions that are also unquestionably essential to the realization of freedom in people's lives. I consider the conversation surrounding these conditions to be a sociological rather than a philosophical undertaking.

(3) *The Ethics of Freedom*. This section further builds on the considerations taken up in the previous chapters and, having clarified freedom's ontological foundations and political frameworks, it attempts to address freedom's purpose. Chapter Thirteen is devoted to the implications that the freedom problematic has for moral choices and for meaning in life.

The book has a logical progression from one chapter to the next, but it was written so that each section might also be read individually. Readers who find the first part, 'The Ontology of Freedom', excessively challenging or who are simply more interested in political subjects can skip the first four chapters and begin with 'The Politics of Freedom'. It goes without saying, however, that every author hopes to have their book read in its entirety.

PART I

THE ONTOLOGY OF FREEDOM

I

To Act Voluntarily

We consider human beings to be the sole objects of moral praise or censure, at least if we are thinking rationally. It makes no sense to react to non-human phenomena in the same way. That is not to say, however, that we never respond like that. When the Icelandic volcano Eyjafjallajökull erupted on 14 April 2010, thereby interrupting air travel, it certainly seemed as though a number of stranded passengers blamed the volcano itself for their inconvenience. Yet these things do happen and a volcano cannot be blamed for its eruptions.

We also sometimes relate to animals as if they were moral agents, even though we know that to be illogical, considering that humans are essentially different from other animals. The matter, however, was not always viewed in this light. During the Middle Ages and the Renaissance, for instance, animal trials were sometimes conducted.[1] A famous example is the sow in French Savigny that was tried for the apparently shocking and allegedly premeditated murder of a five-year-old child.[2] And not only was the sow tried: her six piglets were also accused. As was customary, the sow and her piglets were assigned a defence lawyer to plead their case. Though he was unable to save the sow, he did manage to win the six piglets an acquittal. Sure, they had been found at the crime scene smeared with the boy's blood. However, their youth and their mother's undeniably bad influence were extenuating circumstances in their favour. Pigs in particular were often awarded severe sentences in these cases, because they grunted loudly and in general behaved poorly during the trial. The number of these animal trials reached its climax in the early 1600s, but the practice continued for quite a while thereafter, and a few examples even date from the twentieth century.

I hope that by now the reader is scratching his head. However, what is it that seems so unreasonable here? The relevant fact is that these trials overlook an essential difference between humans and animals – namely, that human beings are the only moral creatures on earth. Of course, we humans are a part of the natural world, but we differ from everything else on the planet in several crucial respects. We have social practices and norms, institutions and implements that no other animal possesses, not even the most highly developed primates. In this context, it is also worth mentioning that Darwin, the man who more than any other helped to establish the connection between humans and the rest of the animal kingdom, agrees that our moral conscience is the thing that most sets us apart. He writes that 'the moral sense or conscience' is the most important distinction between human beings and lower animals.[3] (By 'lower animals' here, Darwin means every animal but us.) For 'A moral being is one who is capable of comparing his past and future actions or motives, and of approving or disapproving of them.'[4] And, as Darwin further observes, 'we have no reason to suppose that any of the lower animals have this capacity.'

Human beings are unique – we are the only creatures capable of morality. This moral perspective, however, is meaningful only if the being that possesses it can *evaluate action alternatives* in terms of a *normative* perspective, and can then *choose* between these alternatives. As far as we know, humans are the only creatures that meet these criteria, each of which is a prerequisite for the moral sense. As such, human beings are the only moral creatures on earth. We are the only animal that can be held morally accountable.

As Aristotle writes in the first book of *Politics*:

It is thus clear that man is a political animal, in a higher degree than bees or any other gregarious animals. Nature, according to our theory, makes nothing in vain; and man alone of the animals is furnished with the faculty of language. The mere making of sounds serves to indicate pleasure and pain, and is thus a faculty that belongs to animals in general: their nature enables them to attain the point at which they have perceptions of pleasure and pain, and can signify those perceptions to one another. But language serves to declare what is advantageous and what is the reverse, and it is the peculiarity of man, in comparison with other animals, that he alone possesses a perception of good and evil, of the just and the unjust, and other similar qualities; and it is association in these things which makes a family and a city.[5]

For Aristotle, the fact that man is a 'political animal' – an animal who lives together in a society with others of the same species – is inextricably tied to our linguistic ability. This linguistic ability further enables a rational exchange of ideas to take place between individuals, and this is what gives us our sense of justice and injustice, good and evil.

The question of human freedom, which we will explore in this book, has its roots in mankind's particular normative abilities. Agents capable of accountability, among other things, must have some understanding of fundamental moral concepts, like justice, and fundamental moral responses, like praise and censure. This understanding does not need to be advanced, but without a general grasp on these things one will not be able to orient oneself in a normative universe and, accordingly, cannot be held responsible. Furthermore, agents must have a certain amount of control over their actions: they should be able to choose to do X instead of Y. Of course, there are any number of borderline cases and controversial examples, but for the most part we can readily identify who warrants a moral and juridical response and who falls into another category. That is to say, some people can be held morally and legally responsible for what they do and others cannot, and this responsibility is inextricably tied to human freedom. The fact of the matter is that freedom implies responsibility.

Aristotle seems to have been the first to develop a theory on moral responsibility. He writes:

> Now, things that come about as a result of force or on account of ignorance seem to be involuntary. That which is forced is something whose origin is external, since it is the sort of thing to which the person who is acting or undergoing something contributes nothing – for example, if a wind, or people who have control over someone, should carry him off somewhere.[6]

Aristotle establishes two criteria for voluntary action here: (1) *Knowledge*: an agent must be clear about what he or she is doing. (2) *Control*: an action must be agent-controlled, and not the result of force from natural causes or other agents. Aristotle further develops these ideas and draws even more distinctions – among other things, between what is involuntary and what is non-voluntary – in order to deal with the difficult borderline cases, but that is not a subject we will pursue in this context. Instead, it is easy enough to see why *both* of the above criteria are necessary conditions for voluntariness. An agent who physically controls his actions, but who lacks knowledge of the situation and about the possible consequences of his actions, cannot be said to have acted voluntarily. If someone slipped poison into my coffee, for example, and I passed the cup to someone else in order to be nice, I cannot be accused of voluntarily poisoning that other person. Similarly, I cannot be said to have acted voluntarily if I am fully informed about a situation, but have no control over my actions. Say that I know that someone will die if I push a button, and everything in me wants to avoid that action. However, I am also tied to a chair with a heavy lead weight attached to my arm. Ultimately, my arm will give out, and when it inevitably sinks down, I will be forced to push the button. In this case, my actions were clearly involuntary.

In terms of the knowledge criterion, we can explain it like this: an action can only be ascribed to an agent if that action can be explained in such a way that the agent is capable of recognizing his intention at the time of the action. Let us take the following example: I am standing barefoot in the bathroom, right where the floor is wet, trying to mount a new light fixture. In order to avoid a shock, I have switched off the main fuse to the apartment. My wife comes home to a dark house, sees that the main fuse is off, and flips it on again. As a result, I receive a powerful electrical shock and die. When the police question my wife about her actions, she will not say 'I was trying to kill my husband' but simply 'I was trying to turn on the light.' The extent of her knowledge at the time of the action was such that killing me was unintentional. Our knowledge, of course, is always limited and most of the things we do not know are irrelevant (like who manufactured the light fixture I was trying to mount). When it comes to the relevant knowledge that we lack, we can distinguish between those things we can be blamed for not knowing and those things for which we cannot be blamed. Let us return to our example. If a blown fuse was a usual occurrence and, furthermore, if I had not told my wife that I would be mounting the light, she could not be blamed. On the other hand, if I had told her that I would be mounting the light, and if it were unusual for the fuse to go out, she could be blamed for not checking to see if, indeed, I was in the bathroom working with electricity. It would not be enough for her simply to say 'I forgot.' In this case, she should have taken steps to ensure that she did not forget. Ignorance does not counter responsibility, because it is our responsibility to make sure we know certain things.

Of course, an agent who is subject to severe manipulation does not meet the knowledge criteria either. Agents must instead be evaluated according to the actual possibilities they have to gain adequate knowledge about an action's context and consequences. We often find extensive manipulation characterized as 'brainwashing'. However, brainwashing, at least as it appears in popular culture, in films such as *The Manchurian Candidate*, is by all accounts pure fiction.[7] We are incapable of 'reprogramming' people so that they become machines who act in direct contradiction to their values and desires so that they, for example, become 'robots' who assassinate heads of state and others. Such brainwashing would be next to impossible. That does not mean, however, that manipulation and other types of influence cannot significantly shape people. How extensive this manipulation must be in order for the agent to be considered incapable of meeting the knowledge criterion is a matter of judgement.

Agent control, on the other hand, implies the ability to choose to undertake an action, and that idea presupposes a certain lack of coercion. There are cases of coercion where an agent entirely lacks the ability to act otherwise: for example, if something prevents the agent from physically moving about as he wishes or there is a mental mechanism that impairs his ability to choose otherwise. What about situations in which the agent still retains the ability to choose between various action alternatives? Coercion is gradated, after all, and it is difficult to establish some clear, universal criterion for cases in which its use is so extensive that an agent can no longer be said to have acted voluntarily. At this point, we can perhaps distinguish between *pressure* and *coercion*, since pressure gives your choice unwanted guidance, while coercion deprives you of the ability to choose altogether. A thief who aims a gun at you and says, 'Your money or your life!' limits your freedom by imposing a choice on you that you otherwise would not have wished to make, but you are still free to choose in that situation. On the other hand, if the thief dosed you with a paralysing neurotoxin in order to snatch your wallet, your freedom of choice would not just be limited but eliminated. As such, we could say that the first thief applied pressure while the second used coercion. At the same time, the boundary between pressure and force is so vague that we might as well talk about *degrees* of coercion.

In general, voluntariness depends on the degree of force present, and an agent's responsibility is also gradated accordingly. Of course, one can certainly claim that most people who act under coercion – for example, because someone is threatening to harm their loved ones if they do not give up confidential secrets – are still acting voluntarily because they have different alternatives from which to choose. Though the agent is being forced to act, he can still select the action alternative that is most in keeping with his values and desires. If he chooses to give up confidential information for the sake of his loved ones' well-being, it is because he considers that well-being to be his top priority – though in principle he could have done otherwise. Nonetheless, most people will say that in this case the choice to give up confidential information was not entirely a free one. Even if the agent acted in accordance with his values and desires, after all, the action itself is not one he would normally approve of. Instead, the black-mailers are exploiting his values and desires in order to undermine his self-determinative ability, something most people would agree at least partially excuses the action. At the same time, we would not so readily forgive an agent who behaved in an identical way for the sake of personal gain, who accepted a large bribe, say, in exchange for confidential information. Yet what is the relevant distinction here? In this case, the agent also has a set of alternatives before him and has chosen to act according to those values and desires with which he identifies: namely, a desire for wealth. However, we would hold the second person accountable in a completely different way. Perhaps the answer is that although both agents act voluntarily and responsibly, the former can be excused on moral grounds, whereas the latter cannot. Concern for the well-being of another is a morally acceptable motive here, whereas personal gain is not. It must be observed, however, that coercion is an acceptable excuse only if there is some true danger of harm. The damage one does, furthermore, must be less than what is implicit in the threat. Needless to say, we would also accept that any situation in which one's loved ones were in danger could occasion a state of panic that would impair an agent's control: the ability, that is, to choose to undertake an action. In any case, it is clear that there will always be an evaluative question concerning the extent to which the criteria of knowledge and control have been met.

It goes without saying, however, that we can also question how much control we really exercise in our daily lives. Obviously, we do not go around making conscious decisions about everything we do on a daily basis, but instead do most things without subjecting them to explicit evaluation. Does this habitualness pose a threat to freedom?

John Stuart Mill explicitly warns us against the sway of habit, and writes: 'The human faculties of perception, judgment, discriminative feeling, mental activity, and even moral preference are exercised only in making a choice.'[8] Furthermore, 'The despotism of custom is everywhere the standing hindrance to human advancement.'[9] Kant, too, underscores that it is important to prevent habitualness, because it deprives us of freedom and independence.[10] For him, habits should be regarded as a kind of force: the force of habit. And though habits *can* be coercive, they usually play a *positive* role in our lives. Habits express a form of understanding, because they are rooted in the way one interacts with one's environment.[11] Indeed, without habits the world could not appear meaningful, since our habits bind the world into a whole against which backdrop individual things also can appear meaningful. Without habits, the world would simply fall apart. Hegel, for example, characterizes habit as a second nature.[12] Habits may be learned, but they are so strongly internalized that they approach the purely instinctive in terms of their immediacy and necessity; at the same time, they can always be altered. Nonetheless, without habit we could not do much beyond the purely instinctive. When I am on the tennis court, the less I must think about what I am doing, the less ostensibly self-conscious I am, the better I play. Does that mean that my actions on the court are not voluntary? No, because I know what I am doing and I am in control of my actions. Furthermore, I voluntarily chose, particularly as a teenager, to spend a lot of time in practice so that I could do what I do on the court. I agree with Jonathan Jacobs, therefore, that we should not regard habit formation as something that essentially limits our ability to act voluntarily, but rather as a crucial component in the *development* of voluntariness.[13] Some habits will obviously hinder freedom. Yet without a broad repertoire of habits, voluntary actions would not be possible. As a result, most habits do not impair freedom, but are a prerequisite for it. Since it is within your power to change your habits, moreover, the excuse of falling victim to habit does not gainsay responsibility.

Responsibility is inextricably tied to freedom of action. Being accountable accords one special status in the universe, because accountability brings with it a unique recognition. As Dostoevsky writes, responsibility is an acknowledgement of freedom:

> In making the individual responsible, Christianity thereby acknowledges [the individual's] freedom. In making the

individual dependent on every flaw in the social structure, however, the doctrine of the environment reduces him to an absolute nonentity, exempts him totally from every personal moral duty and from all independence, reduces him to the lowest form of slavery imaginable.[14]

In this case, the question becomes whether this interpretation of mankind's moral responsibility is consistent with what we otherwise think we know about the world in which we live. If freedom is a characteristic that cannot be reconciled with other beliefs that we regard as incontrovertibly true, we must also discard our views on moral responsibility, since that, too, presupposes freedom.

Up to this point, we have seen that an individual acts voluntarily if he or she fulfils the two Aristotelian criteria of knowledge and control. Furthermore, we have discussed the significance that different kinds of force, pressure and manipulation ought to possess in our evaluation of the extent to which these criteria have been met in various situations. In visiting these subjects, I have so far assumed that an agent *can* have the relevant control over his actions, but in the next chapter I will examine whether or not this assumption is defensible.

2

Freedom and Determinism

We all have a freedom consciousness. John Locke writes that nothing is more evident to him than the fact that he is free.[1] Samuel Johnson remarked that 'you are surer that you can lift up your finger or not as you please, than you are of any conclusion from a deduction of reasoning.'[2] However, this in itself is no guarantee that our freedom consciousness corresponds to the world's true character. For all we know, our freedom consciousness might be pure illusion. For instance, the biologist E. O. Wilson claims that free will is simply an illusion created by molecular processes.[3] Many theories point to the illusionary nature of free will. Indeed, Samuel Johnson goes so far as to suggest that 'all theory is against the freedom of the will; all experience for it.'[4] However, the matter is not so simple as that. Many theories also support free will and many experiences speak against it. And when it comes to Johnson's assertion about the lifting of a finger, the neuro-physiologist Benjamin Libet has developed a much debated experiment that, many argue, demonstrates that we can neither lift a finger nor refrain from doing so just as we please. Instead, finger lifting is an activity that begins in the brain *before* our consciousness gets involved.

Our consciousness of freedom, therefore, can act as no guarantee that we are actually free. As I sit and write these words, I think that it is entirely up to me to decide if I will write one sentence more or if I will leave off and play with my cats for a while. When I choose to write one more sentence, I think that it is entirely up to me to decide what will go into that sentence, that, for example, I can choose to write something I believe to be untrue if I so desire. That is how we all think. Still, it could be that we are the victims of a systematic self-deception and that we are not free at all. Our self-deception would have its roots in the fact that we are not conscious of the causes that determine our actions.

In his 'Prize Essay on Freedom of the Will', which was awarded the prestigious gold medal from the Royal Norwegian Society of Sciences and Letters in 1839, Arthur Schopenhauer argues that a freedom consciousness can in no way be considered proof of the fact that we actually *are* free. He describes a man who at the end of his workday thinks that it is completely up to him to decide what he will do, if he will take a walk, go to the club or the theatre – or, for that matter, simply abandon his normal existence and head out into the world, never to return. However, the man instead thinks that it is entirely of his own free will that he decides to go home to his wife like usual. Schopenhauer compares this man to the water in a pool:

> This is just as if water were to say: 'I can form high waves (as in a storm at sea); I can rush down a hill (as in the bed of a torrent); I can dash down foaming and splashing (as in the waterfall); I can rise freely as a jet into air (as in a fountain); finally, I can even boil away and disappear (as at 212 degrees Fahrenheit); however, I do none of these things now, but voluntarily remain calm and clear in the mirroring pond.' Just as water can do all those things only when the determining causes enter for one or the other, so is the condition just the same for that man with respect to what he imagines he can do. Until the causes enter, it is impossible for him to do anything; but then he *must* do it, just as water must act as soon as it is placed in the respective circumstances.[5]

Obviously, water can occur in all of these forms, but not just like that. The point of the comparison is that the water is not aware of all the elements that must be present for these events to occur. And yet, the causes that work on water are decisive for how it behaves. The water's lack of knowledge regarding these causes do not make them any less real. The same is true of we humans, Schopenhauer argues: my freedom consciousness is just a lack of awareness about those causes that in reality determine my behaviour. We can also express it like this: not being aware of determining causes is not the same as being aware of not being determined by causes.

It could well be that this is indeed the truth of the matter, that we simply lack knowledge and awareness of the causes that are fully determinate for what we do. It is entirely possible that something other than my will brings about those movements that we experience as voluntary.[6] An epiphenomenalist, for example, regards consciousness as a kind of by-product of the brain's operations. Of course, not too many epiphenomenalists are found among philosophers, but there are a few. And although the epiphenomenalist will admit that it does indeed seem as though consciousness is guiding our actions, he or she will maintain that in reality consciousness cannot affect anything at all. In this sense, we can say that there is a one-way causal relationship between the brain and consciousness, that the brain gives rise to the phenomena of consciousness, but that consciousness cannot affect the brain (or anything else for that matter). As Daniel M. Wegner writes:

> The experience of consciously willing action . . . serves as a kind of compass, alerting the conscious mind when actions occur . . . The experience of will is therefore an indicator, one of those gauges on the control panel to which we refer as we steer. Like a compass reading, the feeling of doing tells us something about the operation of the ship. But also like a compass reading, this information must be understood as a conscious experience, a candidate for the dreaded 'epiphenomenon' label . . . Just as compass readings do not steer the boat, conscious experiences of will do not cause human actions.[7]

We think we experience our decisions affecting the physical world – that is something the epiphenomenalist will also concede. However, the experience that it is 'I', in the sense of my will, that for example lifts my arm is no guarantee that this is actually the case. It may well be, as Colin Blakemore suggests, that the perception of will is an invention of the brain.[8] The fact that this idea is certainly possible, however, does not mean that it is true. Indeed, it can be objected that such assertions are not scientific, but simply have the appearance of it, since they can neither be scientifically proved nor disproved. We find correlations between mental processes and brain activity, but obviously that does not show that it is *the brain* that thinks. At most it shows that a certain part of the brain is active when a person thinks.

Of course, it is legitimate to search for those objective causalities that enter into actions, but that search will entirely miss the bar if a person simply presupposes that a given action does not also have subjective attributes like intentions or that these attributes can at most be regarded as illusionary. The objective look and the subjective look at our actions will each pick out different characteristics, and it appears difficult to avoid an epistemological dualism here.[9] Neither our knowledge of the physical world nor our experience of ourselves as willing and thinking beings can give us any conclusive answer to the question concerning the extent to which freedom of the will is possible. Therefore let us first take a closer glance at the theories of determinism and indeterminism before continuing our discussion about the extent to which free will exists in a deterministic and an indeterministic universe respectively.

Determinism and Indeterminism

Determinism is a metaphysical theory according to which everything in the world is connected by absolute causal relations. According to determinism, the state of all things in the universe at moment t is – taken together with natural laws – a product of the state of the universe preceding t. It further follows that the state of all things in the universe after t is a product of its state at t. If we assume that we have complete knowledge of the universe's state at t, as well as of all natural laws, then we can in principle predict every future event, every movement from the smallest elementary particle to the largest astronomical body. And we will also be able to predict all human action. That is to say, there is an absolute symmetry between past and future in the sense that the future is as immutable as the past. There is only one possible future. As William James has formulated it: 'Possibilities that fail to get realised are for determinism pure illusions; they never were possibilities at all.'[10]

Determinism expresses a kind of conditional necessity: 'If . . ., then . . .'. It assumes that the second link in the chain necessarily follows from the first, and that this necessity is of causal character.[11] Modal-logically formulated, we can say that in every logically possible world the determined event will occur when the determining conditions (causes and natural laws) are also present. According to determinism, every event has *sufficient* causes that can completely explain it. If event X has sufficient causes, then X and only X can happen. Succinctly put, determinism argues that every event has sufficient causes. It is a principle that we presuppose in both our everyday lives and in our scientific investigations. When we have knowledge of the causes that are sufficient to explain a phenomenon, we think we have an adequate explanation of that phenomenon. However, the question becomes whether or not we can prove that this type of necessity is actually present in the world: whether a certain set of causes always *are* a sufficient condition for X to happen.

Obviously, in scientific investigation one must be able to posit determinism as a methodological strategy and this means assuming that X has sufficient causal conditions because then and only then can one give a complete explanation of X. In the meantime, one cannot make the jump from this type of methodological presupposition to ontology, to the idea that the world really *is* what one has presupposed. To say that for scientific purposes we attempt to explain every phenomenon in this way does not mean that every phenomenon actually *lets* itself be explained like that. After all, there is an awful lot that we are in no position to explain today; and what of it we will be able to explain in the future we just cannot know today.

In *Lectures on Freedom of the Will*, Ludwig Wittgenstein argues that our concept of necessity stems from the fact that we regard descriptions of nature as if they manifested natural laws that are themselves 'train tracks' that everything must follow.[12] The necessity of these laws appears to be contained in our very concept of 'law', since a systematic deviation from the law prompts us to reformulate it so that the law also covers all deviations. We believe, furthermore, that this new formulation describes a necessity, and even though we might not have a law that covers the phenomena, we nonetheless assume that there must be such a law – as yet unknown – that is capable of covering them. Otherwise, there would be no law for these phenomena and we are unwilling to allow for such a contingency. As a result, Wittgenstein argues that there seems to be an element of fatalism in our concept of natural laws – as if those laws had been written down in a book by a god. This book, moreover, 'would really contain an authoritative description of those rails on which all these events run'.[13] However, Wittgenstein rejects the metaphor of a divine book, arguing that there is no empirical evidence that supports our faith in necessity – and still we maintain that belief. At the same time, what we in fact observe are regularities. But even though you observe a regularity, you can still say of the object in question: 'It is free, but now it chooses to go regularly.'[14] The deterministic viewpoint is seductive, because it leads us to believe that something must happen in exactly *that* way, whereas Wittgenstein argues that the correct idea would be to say: 'it may have happened *like that* – and also in many other ways.'[15] An observed regularity cannot tell us that a single outcome was indeed the only one possible.

We must distinguish between epistemology and ontology, between what we can *know* about the world and what the world *is*. If determinism is true, then we can in principle predict every future happening, but that is quite different from suggesting that we are capable of making such predictions in praxis. As it so happens, experiments ostensibly conducted in the same manner under supposedly identical conditions seldom yield exactly the same results. Even in a strictly controlled laboratory setting, variations usually do occur. As Nancy Cartwright has pointed out, for example, Newton's Laws are only true under extremely strict *ceteris paribus* conditions – that is, under otherwise equal circumstances – but such conditions are hardly to be found out in the world.[16] This implies that in reality it is only under very limited circumstances that we can make absolutely precise predictions; and it is worth noting here that it is only on a macrophysical level, where Newton's Laws are applicable, that our power of prediction is nonetheless at its greatest. On a microphysical level, our predictive ability is considerably lower, and that is also true for mental and social phenomena.

The fact that we are incapable of predicting every event with full certainty is uncontroversial. In particular, quantum physical objects are characterized by such a high degree of uncertainty that we can only speak of probabilities. Among most of the other sciences as well, we can only predict events with a certain degree of probability, but there will always be variations in accuracy. And there are also large variations within physics, where quantum phenomena do not seem to act deterministically, whereas those physical objects that we can directly observe with our senses predominantly seem to do so. In short, it seems that we have determinism on some levels, but not on others. According to what we know today, a general determinism lacks scientific basis. Indeed, present-day science supports instead the concept of a universal indeterminism with individual sub-systems that exhibit so strong a regularity that they appear deterministic.

The question surrounding the extent to which physics supports determinism has been given too much weight, at least in the sense that many assume that the matter can be settled in the physical arena alone – implying that one overlooks the relevance of this question to higher ontological levels. The point here is that higher ontological levels do not allow themselves to be entirely reduced to lower; that new causal characteristics occur at higher levels; and that it is not simply higher levels that are affected by lower, but also lower levels that are affected by higher. Though we may have all the relevant information about a lower level, furthermore, that does not allow us to explain all the characteristics of a higher level. There are many levels of analysis. Each of these levels has its own objects, laws and concepts. And although the different levels are not completely independent of each other, they also cannot be completely reduced to one another. Studies conducted on lower levels doubtlessly illuminate higher levels, but only to a limited extent. New causal characteristics occur at each new level, and a particular level cannot be explained by simply dividing it into its individual components and then describing the characteristics of each one. Instead, the interaction between the totality of the parts at a higher level is precisely what shapes these characteristics. When Denis Noble wanted to develop a mathematical model for pacemaker rhythm in the heart, for example, it proved to be impossible to carry out the task simply by looking at how the individual molecules behaved – it was only by looking at the system as a whole and considering how the whole determined the rhythm of the parts that the project could be executed.[17] Naturally, the characteristics of the whole are to some extent a product of the characteristics of the parts, but the characteristics of the whole also provide frameworks for how the parts will function. Events at lower levels lead to changes in higher ones; conversely, changes at higher levels also lead to changes in lower ones. Not just in the realm of human action, therefore, but also when it comes to many other animals' behaviour does it prove logical to operate with a causality that does not just proceed from down below to the top, but also from the top and downwards. This will present a major problem for those who want to base a deterministic theory on physics alone.[18] The relevant difference between humans and other animals is not the fact that a human alone is capable of top-down causality, because that is also plausible of a number of other animals, but instead that a human has certain cognitive skills – among them a normative desire, which gives a human certain causal characteristics that other animals do not possess.

Meanwhile, this difference between humans and other animals has a tendency to be omitted as soon as *genetic* determinism enters the discussion. Indeed, it initially may seem strange that the question of genetic determinism has been the subject of so much debate, since genetic determinism is presumably no different from any other form of determinism. If one believes that elementary particles determine behaviour, it is to these elementary particles that one will look in order to explain behaviour; and whatever intentions the actor believes he or she had are in a certain sense irrelevant. In the same way, a genetic determinist will start with genes, and whatever intentions the actor believes he or she had will at most be regarded as a genetic product. There is in principle no real difference between these two forms of determinism. In my opinion, the reason genetic determinism strikes so many people as particularly disquieting is that other forms of determinism refer in a certain sense to things outside of us, to external causes, while genetic determinism seems to reach into our very being and appears to annihilate every shred of autonomy we might feel we have in the face of external causes, leaving no logical room for an independent, free will.

It is an indisputable fact that parts of my being are genetically determined, like the fact that I was born a human and not a panda. After all, my parents' genes were only compatible with creating a human child and not a panda cub. On the other hand, in the face of this obvious assertion, we must also add that my parents' genetic material was simply a necessary and in no way sufficient condition for the fact that this particular human child could come into the world. The relationship between genes, organisms and their environment is of such a nature that it is impossible to privilege the one over the other. A piece of DNA is certainly a key part of the causal basis for a given characteristic, but it is only that – a *part*. From a model where the causal arrow simply points from DNA on up to the organism, we now have a model where the causal relationships go in all possible directions. Of course, one can ask here what all of this has to do with freedom. Obviously, a system with causality extending in all directions can be exactly as deterministic as a system that exclusively operates with a down-top causality. All the same, there is a decisive difference here, because one must start with the organism as a whole. There is no room for the concept of genes that obstinately control the whole organism. In my opinion, a fairly sober interpretation of recent biology does not shed any significant light on the metaphysical aspects of determinism. In much the same way that we are in no position to predict human behaviour by focusing on the elementary particles of which a person consists, we are in absolutely no position to do the same by focusing on our knowledge of that person's genetic material.

If we were actually capable of predicting every single event with great precision, that would certainly give us grounds to assume that determinism is valid. Since we are in no position to make predictions of this kind, however, the argument for determinism falls away. In the meantime, we cannot categorically assert that determinism is wrong, for it is entirely probable that one day we will develop theories with far more predictive ability than today's. Still, the empirical evidence we have today yields very little support for universal determinism.

At this point, it might be tempting to turn to indeterminism, which can briefly be described as the concept that an event *does not* have sufficient causes. Indeterminism does not necessarily imply that whatever happens in a given causal relationship is completely up to chance – it is entirely compatible with the notion that we can indeed say what *usually* will happen. From an *epistemic* perspective, however, we are now in a situation where one and the same set of causes do not necessarily lead to X, but can just as well lead to Y or Z. It is here that many have attempted to find an opening for human freedom and the first person who turned to an indeterministic position in order to salvage the concept of freedom is Lucretius. In *On the Nature of Things*, which was written around the middle of the first century BCE, he postulates that atoms can deviate somewhat from their course and that this creates room for freedom.[19]

At the same time, there is no scientific evidence for universal indeterminism. The only thing that could disprove determinism might be a case where an actor does X and then does Y under exactly the same conditions. But that is of course impossible, because an actor could never do X and Y under exactly the same conditions. An even greater problem is that indeterminism does not necessarily contribute much to a defence of freedom and responsibility. If one wants to defend the idea of freedom from the threat determinism can present, it is because one assumes that determinism robs the actor of control over their actions. However, indeterminism does not supply the actor with control, but basically with just an element of chance – and chance is no more free than a strict causal relationship. Why should the fact that an action is *not* determined by a causal chain give us reason to equip an actor with freedom and responsibility? If you actually lived in a universe where external objects, as well as your own body, did not follow the laws of physics, and where everything that happened was utterly random, you would be anything but free: you would be imprisoned in an incomprehensible universe where you had no control over anything. Essentially, the absence of determinism yields nothing but chance, and chance definitively does not imply freedom and responsibility. Anyone who wants to use indeterminism as part of a defence of freedom must accordingly demonstrate how the absence of determinism is compatible with the idea that an actor can have *control* – that is, an ability to initiate actions by choice.

Many, or presumably most present-day physicists reject determinism and give indeterminism their support. The same is true of philosophers who specifically work with the philosophy of physics. Among philosophers who do not specifically work with the philosophy of physics, it is more common to argue for determinism. In the meantime, the fact that so and so many physicists and/or philosophers throw their support one way or the other is of little importance. Philosophical and scientific questions are not usually decided by a show of hands.

Most philosophers will grant that the truth or falsehood of determinism is a contingent question: determinism is neither necessarily true nor necessarily false. This implies that its truth or falsehood cannot be settled through philosophical arguments, but rather through an empirical investigation of the world. In the meantime, no empirical investigation could answer the question once and for all. It is principally impossible to give a scientific proof of who is correct. Still, this does not mean that scientific theories and discoveries are irrelevant for the determinism problematic. On the contrary, they can provide us with much that is material to an understanding of how humans behave and why we do what we do. However, they cannot solve the question once and for all. As Patrick Suppes puts it, the deterministic metaphysician can safely cling to his viewpoint in the certainty that it can never be refuted empirically, but the same is also true of the metaphysical indeterminist.[20]

In general, these brief remarks on determinism and indeterminism have got us no closer to an understanding of freedom, so we must now go further and see what kind of picture emerges when we add human actors to the mix. First, though, we will take a small detour and consider the extent to which recent neurological research supports determinism.

Excursion: The Brain and Free Will

No one has shown that determinism is true, much less that free will is an impossibility. In the meantime, a number of scientific studies have produced results that some people have interpreted as offering this proof, and I will briefly touch on some of the most well-known and more recent.

Benjamin Libet conducted a number of experiments in the 1980s that many have taken as proving that free will is nothing but an illusion.[21] The most common interpretation of these experiments is that they offer proof that the human brain chooses to act before we ourselves are conscious of that decision. In other words, it is the brain, not consciousness, that determines action. The experiments typically involved a subject being asked to make a certain movement, like bending a wrist or a finger, whenever he or she was ready. At the same time, an EEG (electroencephalogram) was used to measure the activity in the brain that would show that the subject had decided to make a movement. This so-called 'readiness potential' was then observed in a part of the brain that is especially connected with voluntary actions. As it turns out, an increase in readiness potential can be observed about half a second before one observes changes in the wrist or hand muscles. This is to be expected, of course, because it takes that amount of time for the impulses to travel from the brain to the muscles. However, Libet introduced an additional element into his experiment by having the subject watch a clock, so that they could observe exactly when they became conscious of their intention to bend the wrist or the finger. The results were startling to say the least, since they showed that the readiness potential could be glimpsed a third of a second *before* the subject was conscious of deciding to act. Libet concluded that the brain itself determined to act, or at the very least to commence the action, before the subject undertook any conscious decision. In short: the brain initiates actions before consciousness enters the picture.

A complicating factor here is that one can observe an increase in readiness potential without any action resulting, and that implies that one cannot use readiness potential to predict actions with any great precision. Libet's explanation for this fact was that consciousness has a kind of 'veto right'. Because conscious will enters the scene before the muscles contract, but after the increase in readiness potential, Libet hypothesized that consciousness can stop any brain-initiated action.

Indeed, it might be tempting to chalk Libet's results up to observational error, to the idea that the experimental situation generated the results, that the time lags associated with consciousness caused the subjects to mistake the point at which they actually became aware of making a decision, and so on, but for the most part Libet's data has proven robust. There are a number of methodological objections one could also direct at his experiments, but I will concentrate on the philosophical implications that can be drawn from them, if we simply assume that Libet's data is valid.

New studies have also followed Libet's, where the use of FMRI (functional magnetic resonance imaging) has yielded even more dramatic results.[22] In these studies, the subjects were asked to relax while they watched a screen with letters streaming across it. They were supposed to decide whether they would push a button with their left or right index finger and were asked to remember what letter was on the screen at that point in time. Relevant parts of the brain showed activity an entire five to seven seconds before the subjects were conscious of deciding to act, and if one takes into account delays caused by the measuring apparatus, the number can be as high as ten seconds. That lapse is too long here to be termed an inconsistency in subject reporting time, which was the explanation one could be tempted to level at Libet's results. The researchers could even predict, though with relatively low precision (60 per cent) – enough, anyway, to demonstrate that it was more than mere chance – whether the subjects would push the right or the left button. This prediction could be made a full seven seconds before the subjects themselves were conscious of deciding one way or the other.

What conclusions can we draw here? One thing we *cannot* conclude is that free will is an illusion or that these experiments support a deterministic view of mankind. The experiments do give us reason to think that unconscious processes in the brain pave the way for action, but they do not enlighten us as to when we make a decision to act in one way or another. The low predictive ability also weakens any deterministic implications one wishes to draw, since it appears that consciousness has the capacity to make a choice other than what brain activity might suggest. The most that Libet's experiments demonstrate is that readiness potential is a necessary but not a sufficient condition for action, since an increase in readiness potential can be observed without any action resulting from it. It should also be mentioned here that Libet himself considers a non-deterministic theory of human behaviour to be a *scientifically* more attractive hypothesis than a deterministic one, and he argues that his experiments do not support a deterministic viewpoint.[23] He also concludes that there is better evidence for the idea that conscious, mental processes can in fact control certain brain functions than that they cannot.[24] Finally, Libet believes that there is better support for a causality that goes both ways, from the brain to consciousness and from consciousness to the brain, than for a one-way causality that simply travels from the brain to consciousness.

An amusing example of the influence consciousness can have on the brain is that readiness potential is actually influenced by people's ideas concerning freedom of will: readiness potential is reduced in subjects whose faith in free will has somehow diminished![25] If we now assume that readiness potential is a necessary condition for voluntary action, it seems that those who do not believe in freedom of will have worse neurophysiological conditions for voluntary action than those who believe that freedom of will is a reality.

Second, one can question whether or not these experiments provide an accurate picture of human choice as it typically happens. Libet focuses on something that, in a certain sense, is rather removed from what is normally addressed in discussions surrounding the issue of free will, where it is taken for granted that agents act for *reasons*, particularly reasons that the agents find reasonable after some consideration. In general, the only reason Libet's subjects acted as they did is that they were complying with his request to bend a wrist or a finger. They were not confronted with a choice about *how* they should act, but only *when* they should act, and it is unclear the transfer value this would have to normal agency.

So when do the actions observed in the experiments actually begin? We can argue that, in one sense, they began long before any increase in readiness potential was observed, since the agents had already formulated their intention to bend a wrist or a finger at some point in the future. Viewed in this light, we can say that activity of consciousness precedes activity in the brain. And the idea can be extended even further. As Raymond Tallis points out, the real context of Libet's experiment is much broader, since the decision to bend a wrist or a finger is set in motion days or weeks in advance when the subject makes the time to participate, travel to Libet's laboratory, familiarizes himself with the experiment and so on, before finally arriving at the moment of finger-bending. This idea involves a very complex set of intentions and actions that unfold over a large period of time, and it is not clear how much one limited window into it all – when the relationship between readiness potential and finger-bending is measured – might tell us about the conditions for human action in general.[26]

There is no good reason to conclude from Libet's experiments that consciousness is helplessly pursuing the brain here. In view of all the practical reasoning, considerations and decisions that must take place over time, there is no reason not to regard consciousness as being actively involved throughout, rather than simply as a 'straggler' along the way.[27]

We know that changes in the brain accompany changes in consciousness, and vice versa. The causal chain seems to extend both ways. However, we actually understand very little about the *relationship* that exists between neural states and states of consciousness. Going by what we know today, however, we can say that it is unwarranted simply to claim an identity between the brain and consciousness.[28] There is no reason to suppose that your consciousness is simply a by-product of your brain. A brain is not aware, *you* are. No doubt the brain is a central factor in your being conscious, but that is all. Consciousness presupposes the interplay between the brain, the whole body and that body's environment.

The neurosciences have certainly made great strides, but we also have a tendency to overestimate how much they can tell us. For example, many people seem to think that a more scientific explanation for a particular aspect of human action or thought requires some reference to brain activity. Michael S. Gazzaniga, who founded the discipline of cognitive neuroscience, has remarked that there is a widespread 'superstition' about what a brain scan can tell us.[29] Among other things, he points to studies that show that people consider explanations of psychological phenomena to be more trustworthy if they are accompanied by a brain scan, even though the image in question has no relevance to the explanation. They even consider explanations that are scientifically inferior but accompanied by pictures to be more trustworthy than explanations that are scientifically solid but have no pictures attached.

There is what we might call a 'brain fetish' going around. Yet if you look exclusively to the brain, you will not find any freedom, because freedom is not to be found there. Nonetheless, Francis Crick writes: '"You", your joys and your sorrows, your memories and your ambition, your sense of personal identity and free will, are in fact no more than the behaviour of a vast assembly of nerve cells and their associated molecules.'[30] What Crick does here is proceed from an observed correlation between neural activity and consciousness phenomena to an assumption that a one-way causality exists between the two, where neural activity generates consciousness phenomena, but not the reverse. Furthermore, he assumes a radical reduction can be made, such that there is an identity between the two and consciousness *is* nothing but a neural activity. The most tempting thing to do in this case is to label such ideas speculative metaphysics in scientific garb. Be that as it may, what we have is a reductionism driven to the positively absurd. Reductionism assumes that properties can be explained in a purely additive manner: that is, that an object's properties are the sum total of the properties belonging to that object's individual parts. The problem is, even if we possess all of the relevant information about a lower level, we cannot use that to fully explain the characteristics of a higher level. Each level has its own objects, laws and concepts. The different levels are not completely independent of each other, but they certainly cannot be reduced to each other. Furthermore, there is every reason to suppose that causality does not only go bottom-up, but also top-down.[31] Assumptions like Crick's that something 'really' is no different from some other (presumably more basic) thing generally explains away rather than explains the phenomenon in question. And to explain a phenomenon is to do something other than to explain it away.[32] Studies of properties at lower levels can undoubtedly shed light on properties at higher levels, but only to a limited extent. New properties present themselves at each new level, and that new level cannot be fully explained by simply dividing it up into its component parts and describing the properties of those parts. In terms of freedom, reductionism is a recipe for never finding it. If you only think in terms of particles, molecules and cells, you will never find free will. On a particle physical or neurophysiological level, there is no point in distinguishing between actions that are products of thorough consideration and those that come about through reflex. There is no freedom, intentions or norms on such levels of analysis, and it would be a mistake to look for them there. Free will occurs on an entirely different ontological level.

It is a mistake to look for freedom in the brain. As a matter of fact, it is a mistake to look for the self in the brain. The self is the centre of my body and my world. We cannot locate it just by pointing to it, but if we nonetheless want to situate it, we might say that the self is simply found in the body. Kant underscores this idea in his early work *Dreams of a Spirit Seer*, where he observes that if we try to find *where* the soul is, we might as well say: 'where I feel, it is there that *I am*. I am as immediately in my finger-tip as I am in my head . . . *My soul is wholly in my whole body, and wholly in each of its parts.*'[33] Being conscious means being present in the world with a body that acts, which entails a normative dimension for us humans. If a friend breaks a promise, one can in principle regard that as an objective causal occurrence, but in that case one loses the morally relevant aspects of that action. We inhabit not just a physical universe, but also a normative one. And in this universe, we do not just relate to each other as physical objects, but as moral subjects.

Incompatibilism and Compatibilism

In terms of human freedom, we might imagine that the following possible positions exist:

1. Humans are determined, not free.
2. Humans are not determined, but free.
3. Humans are determined and free.
4. Humans are neither determined nor free.

(1) and (2) are incompatibilistic theories, which suggest that freedom and determinism are irreconcilable. Position (1) is often called 'hard determinism', while (2) is known as 'libertarianism'. Position (3), which is termed 'compatibilism', argues that freedom and determinism are reconcilable. Position (4), which rejects both freedom and determinism, has no established name, but is often called 'scepticism'. We can represent them in the following table:[34]

	DETERMINISM	FREEDOM	TERM
1.	Yes	No	Hard determinism
2.	No	Yes	Libertarianism
3.	Yes	Yes	Compatibilism
4.	No	No	Scepticism

Compatibilism is often characterized as 'soft determinism'. The terms 'hard' and 'soft' determinism can be misleading, of course, because they can give the impression that 'soft' determinism is less deterministic, that it operates with a less strict causality or the like. However, the two positions are equally deterministic; they differ not in their views on determinism, but rather in their views on freedom. The distinction between them consists in one thing: a hard determinist will argue that determinism and freedom are incompatible, while the weak determinist will argue that they are compatible.[35]

Most contemporary philosophers are compatibilists, but a number are also libertarians. Hard determinists are less common, but that position is also well represented.[36] Scepticism is the least widespread position, but it too has its strong advocates.[37] Some theorists combine positions and will, for example, attempt to unite hard determinism and compatibilism.[38] Generally speaking, however, most people, irrespective of culture, seem to think that the universe is indeterministic and that determinism is incompatible with moral responsibility.[39] In other words, our 'natural metaphysics' seems to be libertarian. Meanwhile, that alone does not settle the question, since it also happens that 'most people' have been wrong about a number of things over the course of history. However, it at least indicates that hard determinists and compatibilists essentially have a greater burden of proof than the libertarian does.

Incompatibilism

Incompatibilism is the most 'intuitive' approach to the relationship between freedom and determinism. For the most part, it is how non-philosophers interpret the problem. Yet a number of philosophers will also argue that determinism undermines the possibility of freedom and responsibility. Peter van Inwagen, for example, has formulated the so-called 'consequence argument', which says that if determinism is true, all of our actions will necessarily be the product of natural laws and distant past events. However, since we cannot alter natural laws or events that took place before we were born, the consequences of those things, including our actions, are not our responsibility.[40]

The issue here is that free actions cannot be rooted in causes. From a practical standpoint, everyone would readily admit that actions must have causes. The problem arises when one suggests that actions must have *sufficient* causes, so that a given set of causes will result in X and only X. If an action has sufficient causes, then an agent could not have acted otherwise, and it is only if an agent could have acted otherwise he can be said to have acted freely. If freedom of will exists, causal explanations cannot provide *the complete* truth regarding our conduct. At the same time, causal explanations must be a *part* of the truth if we are to place ourselves within the natural order.

There are two varieties of incompatibilism: hard determinism and libertarianism. Let us first look briefly at hard determinism, which suggests that determinism is true and that freedom cannot exist because it is not compatible with determinism. The hard determinist will argue that in order for freedom to be possible, a number of alternatives must be open to the agent, that is, an agent could have acted otherwise than he or she actually did in a given situation. Choice implies being able to do *X* or *Y*; even if I choose *X*, I *could* have chosen *Y*. A determinist will insist that my choice to do *X* instead of *Y* is causally determined. If I had chosen *Y*, it would be due to an entirely different set of causes than those that led up to *X*, because the set of causes preceding an action can only result in that one single action. When it comes to determinism, then, I obviously have no *choice*; deterministic necessity renders freedom impossible. Necessity in this context, furthermore, is distinct from a choice made under pressure. For example, if someone threatens to harm my family if I do not do *X*, there is clearly a compelling reason to choose *X*, but I could also choose *Y*. Pressure must be distinguished from determinism's absolute necessity. Indeed, if the determinist is correct, we have no more possibility of controlling what happens to us than a gear in a clock, a tumbling stone or a salmon returning to a river to spawn. However, this directly conflicts with the experience of ourselves as agents: we all have a freedom consciousness. For his part, the hard determinist will admit that this is true, but will also argue that our freedom consciousness is not the consciousness of true freedom – rather, it is an illusion.

One major problem with hard determinism is that it so strongly conflicts with our moral intuitions. Responsibility and guilt are absent from a hard deterministic universe. In this respect, one can say that all agents are morally equal, since they have no capacity for guilt nor any responsibility for their actions. Let us then imagine a person whose personality undergoes a gradual change, a man who steadily becomes more aggressive and violent after having been peaceful and friendly all of his life. Finally, a trifle causes him to lose control and he takes another person's life. As it turns out, he has a large brain tumour in the area associated with aggression and there is a real possibility that both his personality changes and the murder were caused by that tumour. After having had the tumour surgically removed, he returns to his former peaceful and friendly self. Most people will think that this man should not be held morally and legally responsible for his action, since it was seemingly occasioned by a pathological condition rather than by a free choice. Let us now take another example: a man grows up in a good environment and has no obvious mental defects, but is extremely vain and always demands the best. In order to obtain an expensive watch, a Patek Philippe Nautilus chronograph in gold worth u.s.$90,000, he murders an acquaintance who has just bought one for himself and takes the watch. Most people will intuitively conclude that this man must certainly be held accountable for his action and punished. The problem the hard determinist faces is that he cannot distinguish between the two people's guilt and responsibility, since they have both been determined to act as they do. The determining causes may vary in each case, but that has no relevance for an evaluation of guilt and responsibility. Neither person is free, and neither can be rationally held accountable for their action. Of course, such counterintuitive consequences ensure that few people come out in favour of hard determinism.

Let us now turn to libertarianism, which argues that human beings are not determined, but free. The variety of libertarian positions is so broad there are not many common denominators aside from a general agreement that determinism is incompatible with freedom, that determinism is unsustainable and that human beings are free. I will not take the time to review all the different libertarian positions, but will limit myself to sketching a few of the most widespread ideas and arguments.[41]

A libertarian and a compatibilist will agree on many things, such as the fact that human beings are free and that freedom presupposes a lack of force. However, if a person is to be considered free, the libertarian requires more than the compatibilist. Most libertarians admit that actions have causes, but they argue that agents can only act freely if their actions are not determined by pre-existing conditions. We might imagine that my decision to give $5 to a beggar stems, among other sundry causes, from my conviction that we should help others in need. In the meantime, the libertarian will argue that in exactly the same situation, with identical convictions and other sundry causes, I could have walked right by that beggar without giving him a penny. In other words, I could have acted otherwise from how I actually did. Many people will object that a different choice requires a different causal history, but is that objection convincing? *Must* a different causal history exist in order for one to choose X instead of Y? If I am going to take a piece of chocolate from a box, there is no obvious reason that choosing one with marzipan must be occasioned by an entirely different causal history than choosing one with dark chocolate. Or what if I decide to holiday in Barcelona rather than Rome? I have no problem accepting that an agent can choose one *or* the other alternative under identical conditions. A determinist, on the other hand, will assume that every action has sufficient causes, and that it therefore follows that a different causal history must precede the choice of X or Y respectively. That is a problematic assumption, however, and one that requires justification.

Others will object that the choice of X or Y is irrational if there is not some preceding difference that could explain why one was selected above the other, but I do not find this objection convincing. Both X and Y are rational choices even if I do not have a compelling reason – or any reason at all – for preferring one alternative over the other. There are situations in which we seem to have equally good reasons for choosing one alternative over the other, where there are no apparent causes that could explain the choice of one alternative over the other, and where we nonetheless pick one. Such choices appear to be completely up in the air until the time of decision, and if they really *are* unsettled, that is tantamount to libertarian choice.[42] At the same time, a libertarian has not accomplished much if he has merely demonstrated that this particular type of choice is free, because despite everything this is a relatively marginal phenomenon. Nonetheless, he has demonstrated that the general *possibility* of libertarian choice exists, and will argue from there that the same libertarian freedom also applies to all other types of choice. In short, the libertarian will maintain that libertarian freedom can easily be glimpsed when the choice is between equal alternatives, but that it is also present in choices where the agent has a rational reason to choose one alternative over another.

Still, any relevant theory on free will must contain something more than mere indeterminism. In order for libertarianism to get anywhere, it needs an element that can put a stopper in pure chance. The most common libertarian response to this challenge is that the agent must have some form of rational control over his actions. As a result, a number of libertarians support so-called agent causality, which means that actions are caused by the agent in a way that is not neatly attributable to prior circumstances. We can consider Aristotle to be an early representative of this viewpoint. According to him, if an action originates with the agent, it is therefore up to the agent to decide to carry out that action.[43] If we can choose to act, we can also choose *not* to act.[44] In his *Physics*, Aristotle further remarks that human beings are distinct from everything else that exists, because a person has the ability to move things without being himself moved by something else.[45] In other words, people can initiate events in a different way than anything else, and that also implies that people have the ability to prevent something from happening. The most well-known representative of this viewpoint in contemporary philosophy is Roderick M. Chisholm, who argues that the issue surrounding the source of libertarian actions is solved by not regarding actions as completely attributable to natural causal conditions, nor as random, nor as lacking in cause, but simply as being occasioned by the agent himself.[46] This solution is fully compatible with the idea that actions are partially determined by natural causal conditions, and it also allows us to retain a perspective on the agent as being part of a natural order without having to posit substance dualism or the like. It is also compatible with regarding the ability as a product of natural and cultural evolution.

Many critics of agent causality, however, have pointed out that the theory is not all that illuminating until one has explained how such causality is empirically possible. For example, Gary Watson argues that 'agent causality' is simply a label for what libertarians actually require, and not itself an enlightening explanation.[47] What should we then require of such an explanation? Instead of X causing Y, where X is an ordinary natural causal factor, Y originates in A, where A is the agent. Many will agree with this idea, but a libertarian proponent of agent causality will now claim that A must function as a cause in a way not fully explainable by any preceding causes. A initiates actions for *reasons*, and these reasons cannot be reduced to natural causal factors.

Let us imagine, then, that agent A intends to do X at point in time t, but right before t agent B gives A a variety of reasons that he should not do X (because it is immoral or simply inappropriate), and A finds B's reasons to be convincing. Accordingly, A will do Y instead of X. The question then becomes whether we gain an adequate understanding of why A does Y instead of X by simply saying that the causal relations preceding t were different in both cases. We might also imagine that an icicle hits A on the head and this causes him to do Y instead of X. Is there not a significant difference in being convinced by an argument and getting hit on the head by an icicle? Would we not underestimate this difference if we simply regarded both cases as a change in the causal relationship preceding t? In the first case, namely, we can say that there is a *reason* that prompts A to do Y instead of X, while in the second case there is only a *cause*. There is a substantial difference between *reasons* and *causes*.

This is an important distinction, because the very freedom that endows us with responsibility for our actions is also a freedom that entails being able to follow *reasons*. We must always begin with the *reasons* an agent provides for acting in a certain way, because it is here that we discover the nature of the action and why it took place. Indeed, a crucial difference between human beings and other animals is that human beings *act* for *reasons* and not because their *behaviour* has been determined by *causes*. To a rational agent, to a person, reasons will always be just that: reasons. Furthermore, reasons have a normative character to their logic that causes do not, and this includes the idea of being able to act otherwise. It is undoubtedly the case that Raskolnikov could have changed his mind in Dostoevsky's *Crime and Punishment*. Even if the causal chain leading up to the pawnbroker's murder had been exactly the same, Raskolnikov could have chosen not to commit the murder because there were good reasons to do so, and he could have followed those reason instead. Before the murder happens, therefore, Raskolnikov's action is undetermined – never mind that he planned the deed a month in advance and has walked the path to the pawnbroker's house so many times that he knows it takes exactly 730 steps to get there. Despite those things, Raskolnikov still wavers right up until the actual deed; extensive reflection and a thorough evaluation of different action alternatives precedes the actual murder.

Human freedom is made possible not because our actions are uncaused, but because we have the ability – which other animals lack – to do what Raskolnikov does and imagine and reflect upon different alternatives. Naturally, we act according to our desires and preferences, right along with all the other animals, but we can also *choose* how we act, given these desires and preferences. As a result, freedom does not mean the capacity to alter the causal chain leading up to an action and certainly not the ability to break with natural laws, but simply this: to be able to envision and reflect on different alternatives, and to choose which one to bring about.

The mental phenomena that guide my body also see my decisions translated into actions. Yet freedom is the ability to decide how I will act, and this means determining, or even occasioning, the question: will I do *X* or *Y* in a given situation? One can perhaps claim that it is rather misleading to use the term 'cause' in this context, because as a cause I function differently from other causes. A billiard ball that hits another billiard ball and causes it to roll cannot decide if the second ball will go right or left, but I can pick up a billiard cue and determine which way the second ball will head. Many people will argue that reasons are in fact causes and that explanations rooted in reasons are, in reality, causal explanations, while others claim that the relationship between a reason and an action must be understood conceptually, and not causally. Personally, I am part of the latter camp, because reasons have a normative character not preserved by a causal vocabulary. Therefore one can even suggest that a discussion of agent causality is simply an unsuccessful attempt to apply causal terms to action explanations.

What, then, is an action explanation? If someone asks: 'Why did John lift his arm?', one can always say that electrical impulses followed the neural pathways from his brain to his shoulder and arm, at which point they caused the muscles to contract. However, not many people will consider that to be a particularly enlightening explanation of *why* John lifted his arm, in part because it entirely lacks context and in part because it says nothing about John's intentions. For an explanation of John's action to provide us with an *understanding* of the action *as* an action, and not merely as a behaviour, it must contain a discussion of John's intentions, and these intentions must further be interpreted according to context. As a result, a more satisfying explanation would be: 'He lifted his arm to stop a taxi, and he did it because he was running late and needed to pick up his daughter from her kindergarten before four o'clock.' This explanation focuses on John's *goal* at the time of action. It is purpose-driven. And when it comes to mental phenomena such as intending, desiring and deciding, purposefulness proves integral to explaining exactly what was intended, desired and decided. On the other hand, a purely causal explanation describes a world where such purposefulness has no place. Of course, it is not wrong to try and causally explain a certain behaviour, but it is also important to remember that such explanations will always make incomplete action explanations, because by definition they exclude precisely that which makes an action an action.

In terms of our example, we can imagine that John's practical reasoning occurred in the following way:

1. I want to pick up my daughter from the kindergarten before it closes.
2. I can make it if I take a taxi.
3. I can stop a taxi by lifting my arm and signalling the driver.
4. I am lifting my arm.

Practical reasoning does not represent my decision to act as necessary, neither logically nor causally speaking. Instead, it provides a *teleological* explanation with a *goal*, which was my *reason* to act in a certain way. We can also say that it explains the action, not in terms of mental states that stand in a causal relation to other events, but rather in terms of what these mental states actually contain: reasons.

Obviously, the above is not a causal explanation, and some people will think it is no explanation at all, because they assume that the only adequate explanations are causal ones. A. J. Ayer argues that any choice without a causal explanation is completely random in character, and therefore I could not be held accountable for it.[48] This viewpoint presupposes that causal explanations are the only alternative, and that assumption is more than dubious. For those who want to adopt a purely causal analysis of our conduct, all the considerations and choices preceding an action will be something that *happen* to us, whereas we should consider them instead something that we are *doing*, something for which we are responsible. Your views on the world form the basis of your actions, and these conceptions are normally ones for which you – so long as you have not been seriously manipulated – can be held accountable.[49] As mentioned above, our explanation of John's action is teleological, and I will argue that this is sufficient to understand the action. Of course, sometimes we are unable to completely explain an action in this way – unable, that is, to regard it as a product of practical reasoning with logical premises and an agreement between premises and conclusion – and at this point there is usually a need for a causal explanation.

A deterministic universe contains no such explanation gap, since everything by necessity has a causal connection to everything else. An indeterministic universe is another matter entirely: decisions can swing one way, but they could have gone the other way as well, and therefore it is obvious we cannot explain an action in terms of its sufficient conditions. That does not mean that no explanation is possible, of course, and certainly not that an indeterministic universe is by its nature chaotic. On the contrary, there is no reason why such a universe cannot be relatively stable, and we can often predict human actions with comparatively high precision based on our knowledge of intentions and desires – and without having mapped out a set of causes and physical laws. As John Dupré has pointed out, we humans are not sources of chaos in an otherwise well-ordered world, but are rather well-ordered and reliable entities in a world that often seems chaotic.[50] If you agree to meet a colleague at a certain café next Wednesday at 1 pm, you can usually be certain that he or she will be there at the appointed time, but you will not be able to predict with equal certainty next Wednesday's location of the paper that blew by while you were fixing that appointment. Our causal characteristics, including the ability to establish and follow plans far into the future, are unique on the earth.

One could also argue, however, that such predictability, that such regularity of conduct, supports determinism. Science itself is based on the observation of regularities, though we must say that there is quite a chasm between observing regularities and arguing that certain established patterns are *necessary*. Nonetheless, we draw these conclusions not just about lifeless objects, but also about human actions. The idea that human actions are guided by natural laws is based on our observation of regularities in nature, and we expect to find corresponding regularities in human behaviour that would allow us to jump from regularity to necessity. In *Lectures on Freedom of the Will*, however, Wittgenstein argues that, in the first place, we do not find such regularities in human behaviour, at least not to the same extent; but even if we did, it still would not follow that we were determined. As he puts it: 'There is nothing about regularity which makes anything free or not free.'[51] Wittgenstein further compares a falling stone to a thief who steals a banana, or more precisely, he questions this comparison. The argument runs that it is just as inevitable for the thief to steal the banana as it is for the stone to fall. Yet what is meant here by 'inevitable'? 'Inevitability' must arise from the observation of regularity, but in the thief's case there is no such regularity – or rather, any regularity we might discover in the thief's case (for example, that he already showed crooked tendencies in childhood, and has followed that course later in life) is hardly reminiscent of stone-related regularities. Indeed, one thing that characterizes human beings is *discontinuity*. Of course, the argument could be made that at some future date we will find a regularity that puts the thief on the same level as the falling stone. Still, do we have any real *reason* to assume this will happen or is this assertion simply rooted in the seductive, deterministic picture? No logically compelling reason speaks for one or the other alternative. It may be that such a regularity is out there, but we have no reason to suppose it. And even if it does exist, we have no reason to leap from regularity to necessity or unfreedom. The thief who steals a banana has entirely different characteristics than a falling stone, and we must understand these characteristics if we are to understand the thief.

In this context, libertarians will argue that if every aspect of our behaviour has prior conditions that are causally sufficient to determine it, then moral responsibility does not exist because freedom cannot exist. Still, what no one has ever proven – or will ever prove – is that my essential self, that which should fully determine my actions, is itself determined by causes beyond my control. That such causes are coincident, and can be so to a greater or lesser extent, should be relatively unproblematic for most libertarians to concede. Here they would also argue that such coincidence leaves more than enough room for freedom. And though freedom can be said to occur in degrees, depending on how great a role these other causes play, a degree of freedom is freedom nonetheless.

At the same time, humans beings are creatures with limited room for action. It is not just a matter of will to determine which spaces are accessible to us and which are not, but is also a result of our physical properties. Never mind how much I might desire it, my legs will never be able to launch me ten metres up into the air. On the other hand, it should be underscored that our physical properties are not set in stone, but instead have comparative flexibility. They are partially modifiable by our will, for example, if we choose to train up specific skills. However, will is not some intangible substance capable of directly influencing the world, but is integrated into a body that will always be susceptible to limitations.

Actions must take place within a framework set by natural laws; natural laws, however, are something that we can *utilize* to accomplish what we desire.[52] For example, I cannot simply will away gravity in order to fly. What I can do, say, is build a hang glider and use the laws of aerodynamics to accomplish just that. I am an acting being, which means I can adapt the laws of nature to my own purposes.

How strong are libertarianism's claims? It can certainly be argued that indeterminism is just as plausible as determinism and that this, therefore, creates a logical space for libertarian freedom. As mentioned above, however, the situation requires something more than mere indeterminism – it also requires an explanation of how we can *control* our actions in an indeterministic universe. And it is difficult to say that, in this respect, libertarians have given a completely satisfying explanation, if one also assumes that this explanation must be causal. For their part, libertarians could argue that it is a misconception to demand a causal explanation here, since our understanding of human action must be based on reasons rather than causes and, furthermore, these reasons do not let themselves be reduced to causes. However, libertarians cannot claim to have definitively demonstrated that determinism is false, so let us take a closer look at compatibilism, which provides an account of freedom that is consistent with determinism.

Compatibilism

As the name implies, a compatibilist will claim that determinism and freedom are compatible entities. That does not mean, however, that compatibilists necessarily believe that determinism is true. They will seldom argue for determinism's validity, but will simply suppose it for the sake of argument, and will further maintain that even if we posit that determinism is true, free will is still possible.

Aristotle writes that, among other things, freedom assumes that actions originate with agents. Origination in this context, however, can be understood in a variety of different ways. If I am free in a libertarian sense and choose to perform an action independent of external causation, it is clear that I am the source of that action. But say that I am a person who loves to dance and that I always start dancing when I listen to a certain type of music. Let us also imagine that there is a set of causes sufficient to explain my fondness for dancing, so that I am causally determined to do it. Dancing would still originate with me because I enjoy it. Since dancing originates with me, furthermore, it must be regarded as an expression of my freedom, even though I am also strictly determined to dance. Therefore I am both determined *and* free. To the compatibilist, determinism is what makes it possible for you to perform the actions you desire.

A compatibilistic interpretation of free actions is based on a distinction between behaviour that is determined by external forces and behaviour that is determined by individual choice and desire. An action is free as long as nothing is preventing an agent from acting as he or she wishes or is forcing the individual in question to act contrary to his or her wishes. The action, moreover, is completely determined by the situation in which the agent finds himself, and that situation is itself fully determined by preceding causes, but the action is just as determined by *the agent's* condition. The action, however, would not be free if something were forcing him or her to carry it out.

A compatibilist will therefore argue that it is mistaken to assume that freedom presupposes the absence of causal necessity. Freedom only requires the absence of force, where force here implies an action is being carried out contrary to an agent's desires. Force means that one is going against one's desires because one is being threatened, has been imprisoned and so on. As a result, freedom consists in not being physically or psychologically *compelled* to do what one is doing. Your personality may be completely determined by things beyond your control (upbringing, genetic disposition and so on), and that in turn are completely determinative for how you act, but nonetheless compatibilists will argue that your actions are free. Freedom is basically nothing more than being able to act as one desires – given one's individual make-up. Your every action might be determined from the moment you were born, but you are nonetheless free to the extent that you are able to act as you wish. From this perspective, freedom and determinism are entirely compatible. The only thing that can hamper freedom is the presence of force.

People often try to deny responsibility for a certain action or a general behaviour by saying: 'That's just how I am.' The idea seems to be that if an action or behaviour directly springs from how one *is,* that action has, in fact, not been chosen and therefore entails no responsibility. However, as Bernard Williams has remarked: 'If one acknowledges responsibility for anything, one must acknowledge responsibility for decisions and actions which are expressions of character – to be an expression of character is perhaps the most substantial way in which an action can be one's own.'[53] Hume develops the same viewpoint:

> Actions are by their very nature temporary and perishing; and where they proceed not from some cause in the characters and disposition of the person, who performed them, they infix not themselves upon him, and can neither redound to his honour, if good, nor infamy, if evil. The action itself may be blameable; it may be contrary to all the rules of morality and religion: But the person is not responsible for it; and as it proceeded from nothing in him, that is durable or constant, and leaves nothing of that nature behind it, it is impossible he can, upon its account, become the object of punishment or vengeance. According to the hypothesis of liberty, therefore, a man is as pure and untainted, after having committed the most horrid crimes, as at the first moment of his birth, nor is his character any way concerned in his actions; since they are not derived from it, and the wickedness of the one can never be used as a proof of the depravity of the other. It is only upon the principles of necessity, that a person acquires any merit or demerit from his actions, however the common opinion may incline to the contrary.[54]

Hume's point here is that free actions are brought about by an agent's acts of will and basic desires. For Hume, human will is a *cause* of actions. In this regard, he is in line with many libertarian theorists. He sharply distinguishes himself from them, however, because he also regards will as exclusively the *effect* of prior causes. As a result, will is just one of many elements leading up to an action. He further rejects the idea of coincidence. To believe in coincidence is simply to lack knowledge of contributing factors. Within certain frameworks, it is therefore possible to predict human actions. Such predictions must necessarily take an agent's motives as a point of departure, because they determine the actions the agent will choose to perform. And although we will not always be able to predict how a person will act, this is only because we lack an overview of all the complex causal relations. Indeterminism is accordingly excluded, and if one makes indeterminism a condition of freedom, freedom will also be excluded. For Hume, freedom is only possible if it is the ability to act or not to act according to decisions of will. Viewed in this way, freedom is simply the absence of any force that contradicts one's desires. In this context, Hume further underscores that it is only because actions are tied to *the agent* through causal relations that we have any basis for holding the agent morally responsible for their actions.

From a compatibilistic standpoint, a free and responsible agent is one who can be influenced by incentives and sanctions, rewards and punishment. A dog whose set of desires has been completely determined by genes and training, and that then behaves accordingly, seems to fulfil the compatibilistic criteria for a free agent. Nonetheless, we do not hold an animal morally responsible in the same way that we do humans, and an explanation is required for this difference. We can posit here that agents can be influenced in the 'right' way, and this right way must include the ability to be swayed by *reasons*.[55] If an action springs from an agent's own desires and preferences, and the individual can further be influenced by incentives and sanctions (and can also relate to reasons), then the agent can be regarded as free and responsible.

In our discussion of libertarianism, I used the following example: we can imagine that my decision to give $5 to a beggar indeterministically stems, among other sundry causes, from my conviction that we should help others in need. In the meantime, the libertarian will argue that in exactly the same situation, with identical convictions and other sundry causes, I could have walked right by that beggar without giving him a penny. In other words, I could have acted other than I actually did. The compatibilist will say that this is impossible, and if I chose to act otherwise, some difference in my desires or other causes must have preceded that choice. To the compatibilist, the statement 'could have acted otherwise' must be conditionally understood as 'could have acted otherwise if the causes and so on that preceded the choice had been different'.

One problem with a conditional analysis of 'could have acted otherwise' is that it is not difficult to end up regarding actions that are intuitively free as unfree. Let us imagine that I suffer from a severe case of claustrophobia and that you do not know that. We are scheduled to meet on the sixth floor of a building, and you ask if we should take the lift or the stairs. I will, of course, take the stairs on account of my claustrophobia. Could I have acted otherwise and taken the lift? Due to my claustrophobia, that alternative was not open to me. Nonetheless, proponents of a conditional analysis might now say that I could have taken the lift if I had wanted to, and therefore my choice of stairs rather than lift was free. Meanwhile, they will have assumed a causal history in which I did not have claustrophobia. That means we are left with the peculiar conclusion that I could have acted otherwise despite the fact that I could not have acted otherwise. We can take another example. A severely psychotic person, who has no use of his practical reason, will satisfy a conditional analysis – after all, if he were not psychotic and had wanted to act otherwise, he would have done so – and must therefore be considered free. It is for such reasons that a conditional solution to the requirement of 'could have acted otherwise' has not garnered much acceptance.

Another compatibilistic approach is to challenge the assertion that freedom and responsibility entail the idea that one could have acted otherwise. Harry Frankfurt has provided some much debated counter-examples designed to show that the latter argument is not tenable.[56] He asks us to imagine two people, Jones and Black, where Black wants Jones to act in a certain way, X. We should further assume that Black can manipulate Jones – for example, through brain control – and that he has the ability to predict whether Jones will choose X or Y right before Jones decides. However, Black wants to adopt a passive role, and so he lets the situation unfold until just before Jones decides. If Black sees that Jones will choose X, he will remain passive. If he sees Jones will choose Y, he will use his power to make Jones choose X instead. The only possible outcome here is for Jones to do X, either by his own choice or due to Black's manipulation. In other words, Jones is in a situation where he cannot act otherwise. Let us further imagine that Jones indeed chooses X of his own free will. In this case, Jones can be held accountable for his choice, despite the fact that he could not have acted otherwise. Is the example Frankfurt gives us convincing? The first thing to say is that this type of philosophical example – which relies on assumptions that have logical, but not actual possibilities, since they could not happen in the world in which we live – do not strike me as very persuasive. Even setting that objection aside, the example is still not very convincing. A libertarian could object that the example presumes that determinism is valid – because only in a deterministic universe could Black predict Jones's action – while that presumption is rejected outright by the libertarian. For argument's sake, a libertarian might indeed postulate that Black has the ability to control Jones, but he would also say that Black – who on principle basis cannot predict Jones's action – must choose to intervene anyway, which would exempt Jones from all responsibility, or neglect to intervene, which means Jones could have acted differently. In either case, Frankfurt's example does not demonstrate that one can be held responsible *and* lack the ability to act otherwise. However, it is altogether possible that Frankfurt's argument does not hold water, even if we assume that Black really does have the ability to predict Jones's actions. The reason for this is that it is not obvious that an action originated by Jones would be *the same* as an action originated by Black. If Jones chooses X of his own free will, he is clearly responsible for X since he is the action's source. This same idea could also have produced Y, of course, which would have forced Black to intervene. In this case, Jones would no longer be the source of X, and as a result Black instead of Jones would be responsible for the action. I will now contend that an action's identity cannot be separated from its origin, because in order to understand an action we must also understand its origin. And because we have two essentially different origins, one involving Black's intervention and one without, it is misleading to say that the two actions, Xj (origin: Jones) and Xb (origin: Black), are identical. Even if it Jones's body performs both actions, Xj and Xb are still non-identical, and if they are non-identical, Frankfurt's argument fails. As it turns out, Jones was never in a situation where he could not have acted otherwise, because he could have done Xj or Xb (or for that matter Y, if Black had fallen asleep at the brain controls). In other words, Frankfurt has not given us a convincing example of how Jones

could not have acted otherwise and also have been held fully accountable. Of course, my objection to Frankfurt's example will give rise to
new counterarguments, but I will not pursue those here.[57]

As far as I can see, compatibilists have yet to provide a convincing
solution to the problem of reconciling determinism with the ability to
act otherwise. The conditional analysis is not sufficient and Frankfurt's
counterexamples do not demonstrate that the requirement for being
able to act otherwise should be discarded.

However, compatibilists also have trouble explaining a number of
actions that we usually regard as free. Say that I like to drive fast, but
that I comply with the speed limit because I do not want to get caught
in a speed trap. In this case, something has impaired my ability to act
according to my desires, namely, the fear of getting caught. Viewed in
this light, my choice is unfree when it comes to speed limits.[58] How is
that action any different from surrendering a wallet to a thief armed
with a knife because one is afraid of getting stabbed? Are both actions
unfree because there is an element of external pressure or force? Are
they equally unfree? All our actions take place within an established
set of causes and desires, where we often choose to refrain from fully
realizing those desires, because otherwise we would be met with external sanctions of one type or another. As a result, the weak determinist
would conclude that in praxis we are generally unfree, despite the fact
that we can essentially be considered both free *and* determined.

Essentially, the complex set of problems that face compatibilistic
positions are not connected to whether compatibilistic freedom concepts are consistent with determinism, for clearly they are. First and
foremost, these problems are tied to whether these freedom concepts
are correct, whether they give a valid analysis of freedom of will. In
this sense, all that the compatibilist requires is some form of *voluntariness*, namely, that an agent can act in accordance with his or her desires
and is not subject to an external force that conflicts with those desires.
The incompatibilist requires something more than that: in addition to
voluntariness, an agent cannot be completely determined, but rather
must possess some form of independence with respect to the chain of
causes that precede an action. For my part, I cannot see that the compatibilistic viewpoint provides a convincing account for the idea that
freedom and responsibility do not entail an ability to act otherwise or
that determinism is consistent with the idea that an agent could have
acted otherwise. In the absence of such arguments, I find it difficult to
support a compatibilistic analysis.

Conclusion?

In my estimation, it remains open as to whether determinism or indeterminism provides a true description of the world. For all we know,
some ontological levels may be deterministic and others indeterministic. This means that the extent to which human beings are or are not
determined is also an open question. As a result, it is problematic to try
and embrace either a compatibilistic or an incompatibilistic theory of
freedom. After having gone through a substantial portion of the more
recent philosophical literature on incompatibilism and compatibilism,
the only conclusion I can draw is that there really is no basis for
concluding with respect to this question. Truly convincing arguments
for or against determinism or for or against libertarianism just do not
appear to exist.[59] Intuitively speaking, I personally incline towards
some form of libertarianism, but my arguments for this position are no
better than those already put forth by others. Therefore I choose to
basically let the problem stand unresolved. Most of my arguments
later in the book do not depend on any resolution here, though certain
points I make regarding autonomy do seem difficult to unite with a
compatibilistic position. Indeed, I will argue for what certain forms of
compatibilism outright reject, namely, that freedom means having the
ability to act otherwise than one actually did. For any compatibilistic
theory to gain my acceptance, however, it must give a satisfactory
account of this ability within its theoretical framework. As far as I can
see, such an explanation has yet to be provided.

On a practical level, everything I write from this point on is irreconcilable with hard determinism. Given that fact, should I not try and
refute this position before moving on? The problem here is that hard
determinism, like libertarianism and compatibilism, *cannot* be definitively disproven. In terms of this question, there just is no ultimate
refutation, and there probably never will be. Therefore I will take a
different approach to the issue and underscore that the idea of specifically human moral responsibility is crucial to our entire worldview.[60]
We praise, condemn, reward and punish people for their actions, and
these social practices rest on the belief that people are responsible for
their actions. This kind of responsibility is completely irreconcilable
with hard determinism, something the hard determinist will also
readily admit. A world without responsibility, though, is hardly recognizable. The question then becomes whether the hard determinist's
arguments for his position are so convincing that we would be willing

to renounce such an essential component of our worldview. For me the answer is obviously negative, but I must also accept that the hard determinist sees it otherwise. The aforementioned social practices, moreover, certainly do not offer incontrovertible proof that hard determinism is false, but it is reasonable to say that they do impose a heavy burden of proof on the hard determinist. In this respect, compatibilists also have their work cut out for them, because they must show that determinism is reconcilable with such practices.

My take on the issue of determinism/indeterminism and compatibilism/incompatibilism is ultimately 'agnostic', because I do not see that we have sufficiently good grounds to choose some alternatives over others.[61] Like most people, my intuition inclines me in the direction of an indeterministic and libertarian position, but I also recognize that such a position poses significant problems. At the same time, I will argue that the hard determinist and the compatibilist bear a greater burden of proof than the libertarian on account of the central role played by the concepts of freedom and responsibility in our everyday psychology, in our relationship to ourselves and others, to social institutions and to the law. Both must substantiate – not prove, for no definitive proof exists – that determinism can provide a correct description of the conditions necessary for human action. Furthermore, the hard determinist must demonstrate that determinism cannot be reconciled with freedom, while the compatibilist must show that it is actually consistent. Of course, the libertarian also has a burden of proof and a responsibility, for he must provide a plausible explanation for how freedom, as he interprets it, is possible. He has a certain starting advantage, however, on account of the greater burden of proof imposed on his opponents.

As it turns out, this chapter has essentially brought us no closer to answering the question surrounding the extent to which freedom of will is even possible. In the next chapter, we will see if approaching the issue from a more practical and psychological perspective does not better serve us.

3
Reactive and Objective Attitudes

One starting point for evaluating free will is concretely examining how we relate to each other as acting individuals. This approach is particularly associated with Peter F. Strawson and his article 'Freedom and Resentment'.[1] Normally, when one person is injured by another, the injured party casts blame. Strawson refers to the sense of having been wronged as a *reactive attitude*. Reactive attitudes are a decisive component of interpersonal relationships. Try to imagine a world where humans beings lacked moral, emotional responses, where there was no moral praise or censure and so on. That world would be entirely unrecognizable. This fact says something about how basic these human responses are, so basic that we can scarcely liberate ourselves from them. Reactive attitudes are, therefore, the norm, but occasionally we also make exceptions to them, for example, if an individual seems to be acting under compulsion, clearly does not understand what he is doing, or the like. If someone steps on my hand while trying to help me, the physical pain would be just the same as if that person had done it deliberately, but my reaction would be different in each case. I would attach moral blame to the second, not the first instance.[2] That is to say, under certain conditions we suspend our reactive attitudes and evaluate the acting individual otherwise than we normally would have done. The agent is excused in our eyes.

Strawson distinguishes between two types of excuse.[3] The first type involves showing that the agent did not have malicious intent or was simply being careless, and that whatever happened was just an accident. The agent, who normally would warrant a blame reaction, was the victim of *circumstances* and, in this case, should be exempted from blame. The second type involves showing that the agent cannot be blamed under any circumstances, because he lacks the relevant faculties for autonomy. He is not a valid object for a reactive attitude, but only for an *objective* one.[4] Instead of being held morally and legally accountable, the agent is seen as requiring treatment or control. Of course, the foregoing is not true just for blame, but also for praise reactions. We can take an example from the TV show *House MD*. On one episode, a person who appears to be extremely altruistic is shown to be mentally ill; his behaviour has been caused by a metabolic disturbance. When it becomes clear that the agent's altruism is not due to practical reasoning, but instead to a dysfunction, there is no more point in morally praising him. If we take an example involving blame, we could say that I would certainly feel insulted if someone were throwing obscenities at me out on the street and that I would blame that individual. If I happened to hear that the individual in question was a Tourette's sufferer, however, which means his behaviour is attributable to the disorder, my evaluation and reaction would change. The situation would still make me uncomfortable, but I would not blame the person for my discomfort. In short, I would shift from a reactive attitude to an objective one.

The distinction between reactive and objective attitudes is nothing less than a part of the everyday metaphysics we all bear around. As Rousseau points out: 'In all the evils which befall us, we look more to the intention than to the effect. A shingle falling off a roof can injure us more, but does not grieve us as much as a stone thrown on purpose by a malevolent hand. The blow sometimes goes astray, but the intention never misses its mark.'[5] We will normally adopt a reactive attitude to a person who throws a rock at us, but if we determine that a reactive attitude has no basis, we can shift to an objective one. Taking an object attitude toward the rock thrower, however, means that in some sense we consider that individual to be on a level with the shingle that did not intend to fall on someone: simply a link in a causal chain. Such perspectival shifts are part of our daily lives, where first we blame someone, but then find that circumstances dictate that we change our attitude. If John and Paul are standing around talking while John eats a hot dog with ketchup, and suddenly John tosses the hot dog onto Paul's white shirt, Paul will normally take a reactive attitude to John and blame him for the action. The situation will change, however, if John exclaims that he did not mean to do it, and that George actually pushed him. At that point, Paul, if he is reasonable and John is trustworthy, will shift to an objective attitude because he realizes that John was a link in a causal chain beyond his control. If it additionally becomes evident that George is standing behind John and smirking, and Paul further knows that George is no stranger to this type of mischief, Paul will normally take a reactive attitude to John and hold George liable for his ruined shirt.

We can further illustrate this idea with a literary example in direct conflict with such intuitions. In Samuel Butler's novel *Erewhon* from 1872 – where Erewhon is the name of a country the narrator visits and is also an anagram for 'nowhere' – we find a peculiar system of punishment. The sick and disabled are hauled into court and severely punished, while frauds, thieves, pyromaniacs and the like are regarded as individuals requiring care and assistance. As the narrator remarks:

> This is what I gathered. That in that country if a man falls into ill health, or catches any disorder, or fails bodily in any way before he is seventy years old, he is tried before a jury of his countrymen, and if convicted is held up to public scorn and sentenced more or less severely as the case may be. There are subdivisions of illnesses into crimes and misdemeanours as with offences among ourselves – a man being punished very heavily for serious illness, while failure of eyes or hearing in one over sixty-five, who has had good health hitherto, is dealt with by fine only, or imprisonment in default of payment. But if a man forges a cheque, or sets his house on fire, or robs with violence from the person, or does any other such things as are criminal in our own country, he is either taken to a hospital and most carefully tended at the public expense, or if he is in good circumstances, he lets it be known to all his friends that he is suffering from a severe fit of immorality, just as we do when we are ill, and they come and visit him with great solicitude, and inquire with interest how it all came about, what symptoms first showed themselves, and so forth, – questions which he will answer with perfect unreserve; for bad conduct, though considered no less deplorable than illness with ourselves, and unquestionably indicating something seriously wrong with the individual who misbehaves, is nevertheless held to be the result of either pre-natal or post-natal misfortune.

> The strange part of the story, however, is that though they ascribe moral defects to the effect of misfortune either in character or surroundings, they will not listen to the plea of

misfortune in cases that in England meet with sympathy and commiseration only. Ill luck of any kind, or even ill treatment at the hands of others, is considered an offence against society, inasmuch as it makes people uncomfortable to hear of it. Loss of fortune, therefore, or loss of some dear friend on whom another was much dependent, is punished hardly less severely than physical delinquency.[6]

Erewhon is interesting because it provides a glimpse of an inverted human morality, where people are held accountable for things we typically think of as being beyond the individual's control and not held accountable for moral defects we would normally regard as being blameworthy. Interestingly enough, we can argue that our society is becoming more like Erewhon, since people are increasingly held responsible for their health, while the opposite is true of traditional moral defects, which are regarded as causally determined more often than they once were. Though reactive and objective attitudes can certainly change with time and place, however, the attitudes in *Erewhon* are so absurd that they would never become a reality.

In the meantime, objective attitudes are the exception and reactive attitudes are the rule. Our relationships to each other, our moral standards and our judicial culture all presume that we tend to regard each other as beings capable of choice, beings who know what they are about, who have reasons for their actions and who can be held accountable for them. If the opposite were true, if objective attitudes were the rule and reactive attitudes only the exception, we would hardly regard each other as *people*, but merely as things caught up in a causal chain beyond our control. When we take an *objective* attitude, we interpret a given action as being unintended by the agent in such a way that he or she cannot be considered culpable. Instead, the agent is primarily regarded as a link in a causal sequence.

Yet, in contrast to what Strawson seems to think, an objective attitude does not require that one be a determinist. For example, a libertarian can accept that an agent's action is caused by a neuro-physiological defect and still consider a system to be indeterministic. An objective attitude simply implies that the subject did not play a controlling role. And this is where a problem for Strawson's theory arises – namely, that our philosophical ideas conceivably influence our reactive attitudes. While Peter F. Strawson argues that determinism cannot influence reactive attitudes, his son, Galen Strawson, points out that, contrary to his father's beliefs, reactive attitudes are not so easily distinguishable from incompatibilistic intuitions.[7] If people's libertarian intuitions are weakened, it is not unreasonable to assume that their reactive attitudes will also give way to objective attitudes, and they will accordingly be less inclined to hold themselves and others accountable for their actions. Peter F. Strawson, in contrast, argues that the theory of reactive attitudes supports compatibilism. However, reactive attitudes can also give us reason to embrace a more libertarian position.[8] Despite my initial description of the theory as being not metaphysically, but more practically and psychologically based, we nonetheless see that weighty, metaphysical issues have again taken the stage.

One objection that can be made to the theory of reactive attitudes, of course, is that just because we hold one another accountable does not mean that we have legitimate grounds for doing so. It is entirely conceivable that we might ascribe responsibility to each other for no good reason, for example, because responsibility itself is an illusion. And that may well be the case. At the same time, the burden of proof will be on those who make this argument, because the viewpoint contrasts so strongly with our social practices and common intuitions. However, as Strawson underscores, these attitudes are so deeply ingrained that we cannot ever be rid of them – no matter how strong the arguments against them may be. Besides, we humans are not capable of adopting a thoroughly objective attitude in any case.[9]

A weaker objection would be that, though reactive attitudes are not themselves illegitimate, we do mistake their legitimate objects. This objection is more plausible, because we have already seen that reactive attitudes vary with historical and geographical context. The case of the animal trials, for example, shows there was once a much larger framework for such attitudes. A less bizarre example would be the existent variations in the age of criminal responsibility: fifteen years in the Nordic countries; ten years in England; and seven years in India. A general trend here is that the class of people considered to be appropriate objects for reactive attitudes is steadily decreasing. For all we know, many of those who today are held responsible for their actions should not have been. Or perhaps the exact opposite is true: many who are not held accountable today actually should have been. The only solution to the problem is to attempt to establish criteria for when an agent rationally can and should be held responsible, and then apply these criteria as a corrective to reactive attitudes. This idea, for example, must function as a central component in any theory on autonomy.

In concrete cases, for instance, in a courtroom setting, significant uncertainty will attend these evaluations, such as when a violent offender has suffered damage to the brain's frontal lobe. We know that a person with damage to this region can undergo changes in behaviour and can become more violent. As a result, we might more readily accept that the act in question was occasioned by the injury, and that the requirements of voluntariness – and therefore of moral and legal responsibility – have not been met. However, that conclusion would be hastily drawn. If we consider the group of people with a frontal lobe lesion, we find they have a violence rate of 11 to 13 per cent, whereas the violence rate for the general population is 3 per cent.[10] That implies that 87–9 per cent of people with a lesion on their frontal lobe are *non-violent*. As a result, the extent to which a person in this group is morally and legally responsible for their actions must be decided on an individual basis. The fact that such brain damage is present certainly gives us reason to take a closer look at whether an objective attitude is more appropriate than a reactive one, since we have reason to doubt that the voluntariness requirements, which we normally would accept as given, have been met. At the same time, a frontal lobe lesion cannot itself be considered sufficient reason to absolve a person of culpability. The line between voluntary actions and involuntary behaviour is not sharply drawn, after all, and we have little reason to think that more extensive use of brain scans, say, will make the matter any clearer. In principle, this idea can be extended to all actions. Complete certainty will always elude us. Instead, there will consistently be an element of doubt concerning whether a given action is truly voluntary – both when it comes to people with lesions on their frontal lobe and those who are healthy. All we can do is follow the best evidence there is.[11]

A decisive point regarding the extent to which a reactive or an objective attitude is appropriate in a given situation is the question of whether the agent could have acted otherwise. In order for freedom to be possible, a number of alternatives must seemingly be open to the agent; that is, the agent must have been capable of acting otherwise than he or she actually did. The phrase 'capable of acting otherwise' implies the absence of a *strict* necessity. As a result, we are talking about more than just the overwhelming desire for something, as in the Lutheran formulation: 'Here I stand, I can do no other.' If an agent could not have acted otherwise, we will suspend our reactive attitude and will not hold them accountable for their action.

An agent is an appropriate object for a reactive attitude only if he can be said to be in charge of who he is. Galen Strawson clearly formulates this problem. As he writes, it is only if you are responsible for the way that you *are* – at least when it comes to variety of important mental aspects – that you can be held morally accountable.[12] And yet, since we cannot determine the way we are in these respects, moral responsibility is itself illusionary. This argument may seem convincing, but in reality it is quite problematic. Strawson bases his claim on exceptional cases, like the fact that small children and mentally ill individuals are not responsible for their actions because they lack the adequate control. At the same time, he maintains that these cases are not actually exceptional, but are rather the rule: the pertinent lack of control, and therefore of moral responsibility, is a universal human phenomenon. This implies that control entails the ability to determine what one *is*, and that what one *does* follows from what one is. Control is understood to be purely causal in nature. However, one logical objection is that our means of distinguishing between typical agents and exceptional cases is *not* a purely causal principle. When we differentiate between small children and adults in terms of responsibility, it is not because we believe that the causal sequence that lies at the root of the child's self-formation is essentially different from the causal sequence that preceded the adult's self-formation. The crucial distinction here is instead the ability to develop a more or less adequate understanding of the world, of the self, of causal relations and of normative demands. The causal history underlying the child's understanding does not exempt the child from moral responsibility. The exemption was justified by the fact that the child's understanding is inadequate. The same is true of a person with a severe mental illness.

Causal history alone does not absolve an agent of responsibility for her actions. Yet this assertion seems to directly conflict with a normal reaction we have when we read about people who grew up in circumstances so terrible we assume that they are so damaged that they are not blameworthy, or that at the very least their capacity for blame has been substantially diminished. In short, their upbringing becomes a mitigating circumstance. Nonetheless, I will argue that it is not causal history that is crucial, but rather the agent's actual faculties, as long as his actions occur under conditions where his faculties are not seriously impaired, for example, because the person was acting under duress.

Let us imagine two agents, *A* and *B,* who grew up under very different circumstances, where *A* was subjected to serious abuse and neglect, while *B* had a safe and warm upbringing. As a result, their causal histories are very different. Yet *A* and *B* have both committed crime *X*. In this case, we will often see *A* in a milder light than *B*. One possibility here is that we have committed an error in judgement, that there is no reason to be more lenient toward *A* than *B* because both are the product of their biological heritage and social environment – that is, both can only be viewed as products of a causal chain. However, why should one causal sequence be any more mitigating than another? The decisive factor here is not the causal chain, but rather the agents' capacities. If, despite her terrible childhood, *A* is a person with a good grasp of normative demands, and furthermore does not suffer from any emotional or cognitive disturbances that undermine her practical reason, there is no grounds for her causal history to prove mitigating. And if, despite his favourable childhood, *B* shows a lack of comprehension for basic normative demands, and furthermore suffers from the relevant cognitive or emotional disturbances, there is no reason his causal history should prove aggravating. That does not mean that causal history is irrelevant to our evaluation of an agent, because a particular causal history can give us good grounds to assume that an agent suffers from certain defects – we might have observed this connection in other agents, for example – but the causal history itself does not gainsay or lessen the agent's responsibility. Instead, his or her actual capacities decide the case.

I will make one exception to the rule that capacities should be the relevant criteria, rather than a causal history, and that is when an agent deliberately places himself in a state where his capacities are seriously reduced or eliminated. A typical example is when a person under the influence of drugs causes serious harm to another. In my opinion, the same applies to a mentally ill person who, while in a 'normal' period, chooses not to take his medication because it has unpleasant side effects, and then has a psychotic episode where he takes another person's life. Since the person is aware that psychosis can result from his unmedicated state, and since he still deliberately chooses not to take medication, he is also responsible for the results of that decision. The same is true of a person who over time cultivates certain traits that incapacitate normal moral responses. Aristotle writes that if a person is to be held responsible for the base actions springing from his character, he must also be held responsible for the formation of that base character.[13] This formulation, however, leaves it open as to whether or not we can actually have such responsibility: either we are responsible for our character and, accordingly, for the actions that arise from it or we are not responsible for our character and certainly not for our actions. Aristotle chooses the first alternative: we are responsible for who we *are*, for who we have become. From this viewpoint, agents can be held responsible for actions resulting from a character so fixed that it severely limits their ability to act otherwise.[14]

Nevertheless, this position is threatened by a regress problem: if I am responsible for the formation of the character from which my actions arise, I must also be responsible for the character that formed that character and, furthermore, for the character that formed the character that formed that character. At some point, we must halt the regress if this position is to be defended. We must assume that a previous character exists that does not have some sufficient cause in an even more previous character. The agent, furthermore, must have the ability to determine what type of character will be formed, and to make what Charles Taylor calls a 'strong evaluation' that does not have sufficient causes. However, we shall return to 'strong evaluations' in chapter Thirteen, and will not pursue the idea further here. Suffice it to say, the agent does not need to undertake any character formation from the ground up, something that is difficult to imagine in any case, since this must necessarily always occur on the basis of some prior character. At the same time, the character already in existence cannot limit any future character to one single possibility. A strong evaluation requires a *reason* rather than a natural cause to determine if your future self will be X or Y. The reason, in this context, further acts like a cause that cannot be neatly attributed to a prior cause. Your actions stem from your decisions, and these decisions are rooted in who you are. But you are also a being with the ability to reflect upon and change who you are. You are *autonomous*. That is what makes you responsible. You are responsible for who you are, for your character. It is *your* character. And that is what makes you the proper object of a reactive attitude.

In our discussion of reactive and objective attitudes, we have again encountered the weighty, metaphysical issues from chapter Two, since a reactive attitude's legitimacy hinges on the agent's capacity to have acted otherwise than he actually did. We have also seen that the agent's causal history is essentially irrelevant for an evaluation of the agent's responsibility, since that must be determined with regards to an agent's characteristics. It is to these characteristics I will now turn in my discussion of the concept of autonomy.

4

Autonomy

Freedom implies having personal responsibility, it *gives* you responsibility, and this responsibility is made possible based on the sole
assumption that you are free.[1] What does it mean to be *personally*
responsible? In general, it implies that the subject and object of
responsibility are one and the same person. *I* am responsible for *me*, for
what I choose to do, for what I choose to believe and for the type of
person I want to become. Being responsible for oneself also extends to
one's emotions. We hold each other accountable not only for what we do,
but also to a certain extent for what we feel and believe. The idea here
is that feelings and perceptions can be either adequate or inadequate
in terms of their objects, and furthermore that it is in the subject's
power to modify them. In terms of such everyday metaphysics,
emomotion and perceptions are not merely taken as given, but rather
as something the individual can affect in his work with himself.

Autonomy poses a contrast to a life dominated by coercion, as well
as to a life where the capacity to choose lies dormant, where one simply
lets circumstances dictate where one ends up. Accordingly, the autonomous life is the self-defined life which regards the capacity of choice as
central.[2] Though other people can play a supporting role, they cannot
make me autonomous – at most they can help to ensure that the necessary conditions for the development and utilization of my autonomy are
present. The conditions for autonomy are located both internally and
externally, both in our cognitive abilities and in the existence of a sufficient number of real action alternatives. In this chapter I will mainly
concentrate on the internal conditions, while the external ones will be
discussed more extensively later, particularly when I address Amartya
Sen's and Martha Nussbaum's so-called 'capability approach'.

The Greek word *autonomia* is a combination of *auto* and *nomos*, which mean 'self' and 'law'. To be autonomous is the capacity to give oneself laws or to decide for oneself. The expression was first used in a political context with reference to the Greek city-state; an autonomous city was one whose citizens, instead of being subject to a foreign power, made their own laws.[3] The expression was later extended to include individuals.

Like 'freedom', 'autonomy' has acquired several different meanings, from being considered synonymous with political freedom in a negative and/or positive sense to the idea that an agent is self-governing in a compatibilistic or a libertarian sense. Autonomy is often tied to concepts such as dignity, independence and authenticity and is also used to indicate that an agent has special status. As a result, 'autonomy' denotes both a faculty and a status level that entails certain rights. These two meanings are intertwined: the status is awarded to someone on the basis of the faculty. That also implies that a significant impairment of that faculty can have consequences for the status. This matter is not so simple, however, since the autonomy faculty must be interpreted as variable, whereas the status – and the rights it implies – is absolute. The autonomy faculty, moreover, always indicates a *degree* of autonomy, from minimal autonomy to ideal autonomy. No one fulfils the conditions for ideal autonomy, while some individuals fall short of the limits for minimal autonomy. This is true of small children, for example, who have not yet developed the skills necessary here, particularly in the cognitive arena. Coma patients will also fall short for obvious reasons. Additionally, there are a number of difficult cases: for instance, people with certain mental illnesses who, depending on what day it is, register above or below the limits. The point is that all people over a certain age are presumed to have the faculty of autonomy, and this idea entails certain rights.

To have autonomous status means having authority over one's own life, and it is illegitimate of others to forcibly intervene in this sphere without the agent's authorization. Autonomous status is awarded to the individual because of his ability to execute and control actions based on *reasons*. To be autonomous is to be self-governing. It is inextricably tied to our human dignity, to that which separates us from all other animals. Being autonomous means being responsible for one's own life, both when things are working out and when things are going to hell. We could say autonomy implies being one with yourself, in the sense that you act according to reasons that in a definitive – albeit difficult to explain – way are your *own*. Being an autonomous subject means relating to oneself in such a way that one can be considered responsible for the thoughts and actions the self occasions, so they all can be said to be one's *own*. However, autonomy requires more than an agent's being able to follow his every impulse unchecked. In this case, anything capable of self-transport must be considered autonomous. No, the agent must be self-governing in a more robust sense.

The distinction is often made between moral autonomy and personal autonomy. Whereas moral autonomy is the ability to impose moral principles upon oneself, personal autonomy is a presumably morally neutral characteristic that an agent can develop in all aspects of his life, and not simply a moral question. This distinction can be misleading, however, since it can give the impression that an agent is limited to having only moral or only personal autonomy, whereas a fully autonomous agent must have both. The autonomous agent must be able to impose moral principles on themselves, while also being able to govern their actions without reference to the relevant moral aspects.[4]

Roughly speaking, there are three types of theories regarding the faculty aspect of autonomy: (1) hierarchical, (2) authenticity-based and (3) Kantian. Hierarchical models more or less consider the agent to possess a higher-order positive identification with his lower-order desires: that is, to have a second-order ability to critically reflect over his first-order desires, as well as the ability to accept or transform these desires.[5] Broadly speaking, authenticity theories argue that a person is autonomous if his or her beliefs and desires have come about in certain ways; if they are based on rational reflection and are not the product of force, deception, manipulation and so on. Being autonomous means acting according to reasons, considerations, attributes and so on that are not imposed externally, but are instead part of what we might call the agent's authentic self.[6] The third type, the Kantian, can be regarded as a more radical version of authenticity-based theories, and will argue that only an action motivated by such moral laws as an agent gives himself can be considered completely autonomous.[7] I will not dwell on the Kantian theory here. Instead, I will concentrate on hierarchical theories, and will also draw in moments from the authenticity-based theories. It should be underscored, however, that the distinction between authenticity theories and hierarchical ones is not always clearcut, because the authenticity requirement can also be said to entail an agent's ability to reflect upon and identify himself with his own particular values and desires.

Harry Frankfurt, for his part, interprets autonomy as involving an agent's higher-order positive identification with his lower-order desires. I might have a first-order desire to drink wine, and if it is a desire I want to have and, furthermore, one with which I identify, then wine drinking is an autonomous action. However, if I do not want to have that desire, and am nonetheless moved to action by it, my wine drinking will not be autonomous. The same will be true of all my other desires. Frankfurt argues that who you are and what you do will always have sufficient causes, and that means that, causal sequences being what they are, you could not have been different or acted otherwise. According to Frankfurt, freedom is therefore found in *wholeheartedness*, in performing an action because one desires to do so, and because it is a desire that one wishes to have. When you are wholehearted, when your will is undivided, when you are fully and completely devoted to something, then you enjoy a special kind of liberty.[8] Frankfurt claims that more freedom than this is not humanly possible.[9]

The question now becomes whether this explanation is *sufficient* to account for autonomy. Frankfurt argues that freedom of action requires that there be an accordance between what one does and what one desires to do.[10] However, there is a problem with this idea, namely, that it is entirely compatible with, for example, a slave in chains who, realizing he will never escape his situation, achieves freedom of action by transforming his will and desires to accord with a wish to now be in chains. We can further imagine that this slave wholeheartedly embraces his imprisoned state, for instance, by contextualizing it within a religious framework, where all that he suffers while in chains endows his life with largely religious purpose. Yet it would be extremely counterintuitive to claim that this slave can in any way be considered to be a paradigmatic example of a free individual – he is instead the polar opposite of it.

In addition, we can ask if wholeheartedness is *necessary* for the condition of autonomy. Frankfurt argues that a person is free to the extent that he also wills what he desires, that is, that he desires the particular will that he has.[11] Another way of expressing this idea is that there is a concordance between first- and second-order desires. In order to illustrate this concept, Frankfurt distinguishes between a voluntary and an involuntary drug user, where the involuntary user states that he is moved to abuse drugs against his will.[12] In contrast, the voluntary addict desires to act as he does and is therefore free. According to Frankfurt, a second-order identification with a first-order desire is also sufficient for moral responsibility.[13] Yet people also perform actions with which they do not identify and about which they are not wholehearted, and we still hold them accountable. A paedophile may wish he did not sexually desire children, but if he nonetheless acts on this desire, he is just as responsible as the paedophile who actually identifies himself with his paedophilic tendencies. According to Frankfurt's model, however, it seems we would be forced to conclude that the first individual did not act freely because he did not have a second-order positive identification with his first-order desire. And if the action was not free, he cannot be blamed for it. However, very few people would be willing to exempt a paedophilic offender from moral censure. In other words, Frankfurt's model has implications that strongly contrast with our deeply held moral intuitions. Furthermore, Frankfurt's theory seems unable to account for either the necessary or the sufficient conditions for autonomy.

Frankfurt contends that being responsible for one's character – and for the actions that arise from it – is not a matter of originating or creating that character, but of 'taking responsibility for it'.[14] As we have seen, Frankfurt defines freedom as an agreement between first- and second-order desires. In principle, such harmony can be established by bringing one's first-order desires into accordance with one's second-order desires or by bringing one's second-order desires into accordance with one's first-order desires. Frankfurt consistently favours the second alternative, because he maintains that there is actually very little we can do to change our first-order desires. In this context, he places great emphasis on 'volitional necessities', which means that a person cannot help but will certain things, and also means there are certain things a person cannot avoid doing or refrain from doing.[15]

The problem here is that autonomy also seems to require that we have the ability to reflect upon and change ourselves, which means altering our first-order desires in light of our higher-order evaluations. Autonomy implies a particular responsibility for one's self, not only for what one does, but also for who one *is*. The objection, of course, can be raised that most of what goes into making us who we are is not something that we have *chosen*. The issue then becomes whether it is meaningful to say that all of us are responsible for who we are. John Stuart Mill takes up this idea, criticizing what he calls 'fatalism', even as he defends determinism or 'necessitarianism':

Now, a necessitarian, believing that our actions follow from our characters, and that our characters follow from our organization, our education, and our circumstances, is apt to be, with more or less of consciousness on his part, a fatalist as to his own actions, and to believe that his nature is such, or that his education and circumstances have so moulded his character, that nothing can now prevent him from feeling and acting in a particular way, or at least that no effort of his own can hinder it. In the words of the sect which in our own day has most perseveringly inculcated and most perversely misunderstood this great doctrine, his character is formed *for* him, and not *by* him; therefore his wishing that it had been formed differently is of no use; he has no power to alter it. But this is a grand error. He has, to a certain extent, a power to alter his character. Its being, in the ultimate resort, formed for him, is not inconsistent with its being, in part, formed *by* him as one of the intermediate agents. His character is formed by his circumstances (including among these his particular organization); but his own desire to mould it in a particular way, is one of those circumstances, and by no means of the least influential. We can not, indeed, directly will to be different from what we are. But neither did those who are supposed to have formed our characters directly will that we should be what we are. Their will had no direct power except over their own actions. They made us what they did make us, by willing, not the end, but the requisite means; and we, when our habits are not too inveterate, can, by similarly willing the requisite means, make ourselves different. If they could place us under the influence of certain circumstances, we, in like manner, can place ourselves under the influence of other circumstances. We are exactly as capable of making our own character, *if we will*, as others are of making it for us.[16]

Mill is an avowed determinist, but at the same time he rejects what he calls fatalism, according to which the agent is a helpless victim of external causes. Mill interprets freedom of will not as the absence of causes, but rather as the absence of force. In other words, he adopts a standard compatibilistic viewpoint. Causes always determine our actions. And though causes likewise shape our characteristics and motives, these do not make up a uniform group; among those causes the individual can inherit, for example, is the impetus to better and change ourselves. As Mill sees it, certain motives are compelling, and for these we cannot be held responsible – a point that anticipates Frankfurt's theory of volitional necessities. We can resist other motives, however, and the fact that we can alter them makes us responsible. Mill's viewpoint is also related to Aristotle, who argues that no person can avoid acting in keeping with his character, but since we partially originate our character – that is, we partially create or shape ourselves – our actions are, in a certain sense, nonetheless voluntary.[17]

According to Mill, a person is free if he could have acted otherwise than he did, given that he had sufficiently good reason for doing so.[18] Mill explicitly rejects the idea that our actions could ever vary from the desire or aversion that is strongest at the moment, or that we would even be conscious of such an ability.[19] As a result, he concludes that the difference between a good and a bad person is not that the good person is capable of keeping desire in check, but rather that the good person's impetus to do right is stronger than his impetus to do wrong. Here is the goal of a moral education: to promote a desire for the good and to weaken any desire that tends in the opposite direction, as well as to establish a clear intellectual standard for right and wrong.

The question here is whether Mill's determinism is reconcilable with the perfectionistic individualism – and the stress this places on the individual's responsibility for self-formation – that is so central to his political philosophy. In general, Mill's position can be described as a form of compatibilism that is closely related to Hume's, where the presumptive fact that human actions are determined by causes is not regarded as irreconcilable with the idea that human beings also possess a self-determinative capability. In the meantime, Mill's position is problematic because he does not seem clear on how the reflexive knowledge of self can lay the groundwork for genuine self-determination, where we choose to transform ourselves in keeping with the understanding and the ideals of what we *should* be. If Mill's deterministic suppositions are correct, it seems to follow that the agent's very wish to fashion his character in one way rather than another is not something over which the agent has authority. In other words, Mill just appears to have shifted the problem a notch over from first-order to second-order desires without having given us reason to believe that our second-order desires are any freer than our first. Of course, we can introduce third-order desires for our choice of second-order desires, but that simply shifts the problem another notch over. In order to stop an endless regress here, it appears that we must posit an ability to shape higher-order desires, where the higher-order desires cannot simply be attributed to external causes and can also be used to modify lower-order desires.

One objection that can be levelled at hierarchical theories of autonomy, however, is that, as agents, we hardly ever ask ourselves which exact urges and desires we actually want to have move us to action.[20] Instead, we question the goals we should have and the means we might use to attain those goals. Nonetheless, I will argue that this objection is not exactly to the point. Even if we do indeed tend to reason like that, the hierarchical model is not therefore irrelevant to an understanding of human conduct. We are, after all, beings capable of self-reflection. In particular, we find that we are moved to act in ways that are not always entirely compatible with each other. Our motives often conflict, and this compels us to reflect on these motives. We find some motives undesirable and others such that we want them to play a larger role in our lives. Naturally, we reflect over what goals and values we ought to embrace, but we also consider how we might work with ourselves in order to better realize these goals and values in our lives. And that entails making a second-order evaluation of our first-order desires. To take an example from my own life: I had an explosive temper up until I was around fifteen to sixteen years of age. We can say that, when provoked, I had a first-order desire to lash out at the world. However, I also realized that this reaction was inappropriate. Acting out of anger to such an extent was something I no longer wished to do. Since my second-order desires did not agree with my first-order desires, I began to work on myself, so that I would no longer function in that way.

In principle, however, autonomy does not require that I make any deliberate modifications to my first-order desires. It is crucial, though, that I *can* do that. We can imagine, for example, a child who is born into a family of ringmasters will decide to follow in his family's footsteps. When his father dies, he becomes a ringmaster and conducts himself accordingly. His whole upbringing, after all, was geared towards this end, and other alternatives, such as selling the circus or changing occupations, do tempt him. As long as he knows that, theoretically speaking, he could have chosen another alternative, but prefers instead to carry on the family tradition, he must be considered autonomous.

As Gerald Dworkin points out, there are other major problems with regarding autonomy as exclusively a second-order identification with first-order desires.[21] In the first place, it seems reasonable to suggest that autonomy must affect large swathes of a person's life, whereas the kind of identification in question can change from one day to the next. Say that yesterday I identified with an overwhelming desire to drink alcohol, while today I do not; instead, I want to remain sober, even if the urgent desire to drink persists. Have I therefore lost the autonomy that I had only yesterday? This does not appear to be very plausible. In the second place, the lack of such identification does not seem to be the central issue at stake when a person's autonomy is violated. If agent A puts sleeping pills into agent B's drink, and A then abuses B, it is obvious that A has violated B's autonomy, but that is hardly just because the sleeping pills have made it impossible for B to make a second-order identification with his first-order desires. Instead, it is because B's entire ability to reflect – and to offer resistance – has been impaired. In the third place, it seems that, when it comes to autonomy, merely being able to change one's second-order desires is insufficient. Autonomy appears to require something much more significant: namely, that a person not just be capable of reflecting on and identifying himself with his first-order desires, but that he also have the ability to modify these desires and actuate his new desires in his conduct. Incidentally, we can also observe that the inhabitants of Walden Two, and for that matter of Walden Three, which I discussed in the Introduction, will meet the autonomy requirements set forth by the hierarchical model, and that does not speak well for the theory itself.

John Christman has argued that the crucial point for autonomy is not whether a person can identify himself with his urges and desires, but instead whether a person accepts *the process* that occasioned their formation.[22] In order for agent A to be autonomous with regard to desire X, A cannot have opposed the process that preceded X's formation. This lack of opposition further presupposes that A meets the basic rationality requirements and that his ability to self-reflect has not been undermined by severe self-deception or the like. In my opinion, Christman's theory is untenable. The fact that it cannot provide a necessary condition for autonomy can be shown by the following example: as a child, Paul did not want to learn to read. There was nothing standing in his way, but for some reason he strongly resisted learning. This so angered Paul's father that he hit Paul repeatedly to force him to learn. His father had the best of intentions, of course, and believed that not only would Paul use the ability in his education and professional life, but that Paul would receive intense pleasure from participating in the world of great literature. In order to avoid a beating, Paul sat down and became an avid reader. Though his father had the best of intentions, however, it is clear that the method he employed to reach his goal was unacceptable. When Paul grew up, he discovered that his father had, in fact, been right, that reading great literature was one of his favourite pleasures in life. Still, he cannot accept the process that got him there, namely, the physical abuse inflicted by his father that helped shape his desire for reading great literary works. Provided that Paul meets other autonomy requirements, it appears illogical to suggest that, when it comes to reading, he is not autonomous because he cannot accept the process that got him there. That is to say, the question of Paul's autonomy at a given point in time depends on the attributes he has at that point in time, not on what might have occurred prior to that. Paul has his own reasons for continuing to read, and he can always set books aside if he come to evaluate his life otherwise.

As previously mentioned, in order to be autonomous one must act according to *reasons*. It would seem, therefore, that we can largely identify autonomous actions with rational actions – and also the reverse, where actions that are less rational become less autonomous. At the same time, an autonomous agent should be able to reject rationality as a norm for his actions without losing his autonomy as a result. We can, for example, picture an agent who decides to generally act on impulse without thinking too much about his choices. Or we can also take Luke Rhinehart's protagonist 'the Dice Man', who leaves his next action to a toss of the die.[23] At this point, we appear to have reached a paradox surrounding the possibility for autonomous choice and actions that are less than rational. The paradox vanishes, however, if we say that reason is still involved in choices where an agent elects to do something other than his reason night dictate, or makes it a matter of impulses or dice. Whatever the case, reason is still involved. A point from Kant's theory of action, which Henry Allison has termed the 'incorporation thesis', becomes relevant here: namely, that an impulse or inclination can determine an agent's ability to choose only if that agent has agreed to incorporate it into his maxim of conduct.[24] Furthermore, an agent must freely have chosen to let desire lead him if an action results. The agent in question *chooses* to follow his impulses or whatever the die might say, and that choice is autonomous. We would not, for instance, consider the agent any less responsible for the action just because he let dice decide his action alternative. While it is not unreasonable to suggest that the agent loses *some* autonomy by letting a die toss determine what will happen next, the agent still made an autonomous choice to let the die decide the case.

Being autonomous means acting according to reasons, considerations, attributes and so on that are not externally imposed, but are instead a part of what we might call the agent's authentic self. The authenticity requirement implies the ability to reflect over, modify and identify oneself with one's values and desires. Ideal autonomy implies that a person is completely authentic and free of every external influence that could interfere with the self, and obviously there is no person who conforms to that ideal. Let us, then, concentrate on the other end of the scale. Every plausible account of minimal autonomy must be compatible with the idea that every adult who does not suffer from some serious, obviously debilitating pathology must be considered autonomous. Clearly, the reason for this is that such evaluations have consequences for the individual's moral and political status. In particular, autonomy imposes limits on paternalism.

It is important that we do not establish too ambitious an autonomy concept, therefore, because it has such far-reaching implications for personal status and rights. When we talk about acting according to one's very own reasons, we presume that the person has certain key abilities to think rationally, that he lacks emotional disturbances that could undermine his rationality, and that he has a more or less adequate grasp on his own faculties. In order to fully or partially deny people the autonomy faculty, it is not enough to just demonstrate that they have made some exceptionally bad choices. In that case, we would all be out of luck, since rational choice is not our strongest suit.[25] A person cannot be denied autonomy solely because he lacks any knowledge of what is in his best interest. The fact of the matter is that very few of us know what is in our best interest. When people insist on making what we interpret as bad choices, we obviously have the right to advise them otherwise, but if they will not be swayed, they must be allowed to maintain what we consider to be mistaken ideas or delusions. In order to be regarded as autonomous, a person must be able to critically reflect on his ideas, and to choose to uphold or reject them; however, we should never require that the person have *certain* ideas or desires. I might think that a person has a number of mistaken conceptions about the world or has desires that I – and most others – would consider to be extremely detrimental, but that is not enough for me to deny that person the autonomy faculty. The boundary, however, must be drawn at what we might term *bizarre delusions*, but we could scarcely formulate any clear boundary here. Nonetheless, even if I do not want to deny a person autonomy, despite whatever delusions he or she may have, there is still a vague boundary concerning how tenuous a person's grasp on reality must be before that person indeed falls below the limits for minimal autonomy.

A more adequate grasp on reality, in contrast, will help to increase a person's autonomy. As Stuart Hampshire puts it: 'A man becomes more and more a free and responsible agent the more he at all times knows what he is doing, in every sense of this phrase, and the more he acts with a definite and clearly formed intention.'[26] This implies something other than the Stoic belief that only the wise are free, and that freedom itself does not come in degrees.[27] As the Stoics saw it, one's every desire and conception formed a tightly woven net, such that the least misconception would corrupt the whole, and freedom must accordingly be lost. On the contrary, I will emphasize that freedom is something that is indeed gradated, and that the work we undertake with ourselves must be interpreted as a liberating process that can result in a higher degree of freedom and self-determination – though we will never reach what we might term absolute freedom.

However, an autonomous life requires more than just conditions internal to the agent. It also involves conditions that are institutional and material in nature, and it is to these that we will now turn.

PART II

THE POLITICS OF
FREEDOM

5
The Liberal Democracy

We now move from the fundamental questions concerning the ontological conditions for human action to the matter of which society best suits a being with these characteristics. As we will see, an autonomous existence requires people to have a significant number of alternatives and lifestyles open to them and the liberal democracy is the governmental form that best safeguards pluralism.

Of course, the liberal democracy is under no illusions that a paradise on earth can ever be realized. Instead, it assumes that every society must contain individuals and groups whose values and interests are in conflict and that each of these will try to define and direct the society in keeping with their own particular values and interests. As a result, the liberal democracy attempts to formulate a set of laws designed to ensure that these conflicts can peacefully unfold. It also establishes an inviolable freedom space for all its citizens. Naturally enough, other forms of government and ideologies, each with an associated freedom concept, do exist, but they appear both unconvincing and outdated in comparison with the liberal democracy. In this respect, one might suspect me of adopting a position similar to that found in Francis Fukuyama's essay on history's end.[1] In keeping with most others, I tend to regard Fukuyama's concept of history following Communism's collapse as exaggeratedly optimistic. Indeed, one can say that his central point was anticipated and accurately summed up by the Pet Shop Boys' song 'West End Girls' (1984):

> We've got no future, we've got no past
> Here today, built to last
> In every city, in every nation
> From Lake Geneva to the Finland station

There is no historical past or future because history is over – it has reached its final destination, and there we all will exist, everyone in the world, from Lake Geneva, the centre of European capitalism, to Finland Station in St Petersburg, where Lenin arrived by train from Swiss exile on 3 April 1917. As it happened, however, history started up again.

Fukuyama borrowed the philosophical basis for his history concept from Alexandre Kojève's interpretation of Hegel, which maintained that history had reached its culmination with the completion of Hegel's work *The Phenomenology of Spirit* (1807).[2] That is to say, history had reached a point where mankind now interpreted the ideal state to be a liberal republic where everyone would acknowledge each other as equals. Obviously, Hegel was aware that no state on earth actually *was* like that. That was an empirical fact of little significance, however, because *the idea* of the liberal state had been planted in the world and would of necessity spread itself. Fukuyama revitalized this idea again after the two contenders to the liberal state, communism and fascism, seemed to be historically shelved phenomena, and he concluded that we must therefore witness the spread of liberal democracy to the entire globe.

Fukuyama's later book, *The Origins of Political Order*, begins with an admission that what the 2000s actually brought us was the retreat of liberal democracy, and a situation marked with several authoritarian regimes instead, among them in the former Soviet states, Iran, Venezuela and China.[3] Despite the fact that one-third of the earth's population lives under dictatorships or authoritarian governments, however, he by and large stands by his earlier analysis because, to his mind, no recognized *philosophical* alternatives to liberal democracy yet exist.

However, Fukuyama's argumentative strategy does shift from his earlier to his later work. In both works, he regards the liberal democracy, with its three pillars – a strong state, a law-governed state and a state accountable to its citizens – as the best governmental form. Whereas earlier he saw liberal democracy's spread as a matter of historical necessity, however, he now glimpses an entirely different contingency regarding the extent to which liberal democracy will be realized in various countries across the globe. He appears to have replaced a Hegelian historical metaphysics with a Darwinistic alternative, and the Darwinistic universe is a product of chance in a wholly different way – not to mention that it lacks a *telos*, an end goal.[4] One question that presents itself here is how Fukuyama can sustain his *normative* idea of liberal democracy's superiority within this Darwinistic framework, but that question will not be pursued here.

In Fukuyama's most recent article to date on the subject, 'The Future of History', he writes that the liberal democracy is, in part, the standard ideology for most of the world because it provides an answer to and is foundational for certain socioeconomic structures.[5] There are exceptions to this rule, such as Iran and Saudia Arabia, which instead embrace theocracy, but the Arab Spring demonstrated a shift toward liberal democracy in that part of the world as well. The only true challenger to liberal democracy is China, which has combined an authoritarian government with a market economy, though the state does interfere here substantially more than in most other market economies. For various reasons, however, Fukuyama does not believe that the Chinese model will prove a serious alternative to liberal democracy in countries beyond East Asia, and he also assumes that a growing middle class must prompt changes in the Chinese model as well, because the political will of the Chinese middle class will not differ much from that of the middle class in other nations. According to Fukuyama, the greatest threat to liberal democracy is actually that technologically driven economic development will lead to growing inequality and a shrinking middle class. This is a crucial point, because the middle class has formed the political basis for liberal democracy all along. This development can well result in a mobilization against liberal democracy, and lead to the formation of a new ideology, 'an ideology of the future', but that ideological alternative has yet to be developed. As a result, Fukuyama's position here is substantially different from what it was in *The End of History*, because now that history is so absolutely on the move again, liberal democracy can no longer be regarded as history's high point – and endpoint.

Nonetheless, Fukuyama is correct in pointing out that liberal democracy has spread itself with surprising haste. In 1892 there was, strictly speaking, not one genuine liberal democracy on the face of the earth, since it was only the following year that New Zealand became the first nation to grant women suffrage. According to *Freedom in the World*, an annual index published by Freedom House, in 1950 there were only 22 liberal democracies, whereas in 2012, despite a decrease from 2005, there were 87 liberal democracies containing 45 per cent of the world's population.[6] But though there has been rapid development here, there is still a long way to go until liberal democracy can be said to have gained an actual hegemony on the earth. At the same time, it can largely be considered to have a philosophical hegemony. In essence, no philosophically acceptable alternatives to liberal democracy exist today.

So what is a liberal democracy? If we look at the term's components, we can say that 'liberal' indicates that a state's power over its citizens should be limited and 'democracy' that the citizens should have power over the state.[7] Such a brief description, however, glosses over the tension inherent in the expression itself. A liberal state is not necessarily democratic and a democratic state is not necessarily liberal. A state where a democratic majority overrides its minorities and fails to grant them the right to freedom of expression and freedom of religion, and that confiscates their property on top of that, will in principle remain democratic, but it is certainly not liberal. We might also imagine a regime that respects most liberal rights and does not interfere too much in how its citizens live their lives, and is thus relatively liberal. At the same time, this liberal society denies its citizens the right to vote and so by definition cannot be considered genuinely democratic. It must be mentioned that the two are deeply intertwined: a democracy without such liberal rights as freedom of expression and freedom of the press will be a democracy only in name, and a liberal state where the citizens do not have the right to influence the state's government through voter participation is not genuinely liberal.

Liberalism establishes principles for limiting the legitimate exercise of power, and essentially argues that the state's power shall be restricted to what its citizens can recognize while still regarding themselves as autonomous and equal. Furthermore, certain mechanisms exist to help keep the use of power in check, such as the separation of powers. As Wilhelm Röpke formulates it: 'The liberal therefore views every concentration of power with suspicion, because he knows that every power that is not kept in check by an opposing power will be abused sooner or later. He sees only one effective means to preserving human liberty: the distribution of power and the establishment of opposing powers.'[8] He further advises against confusing power of the people with freedom of the people, since it might appear that giving people unlimited power would also maximize their freedom. Yet the power of the people must also be kept in check by fundamental rights that serve to protect the individual citizen against whatever the democratic majority might decide.

Historically speaking, the liberal state is the result of a long process which eventually saw the absolute power of heads of state eliminated, partly through minor reforms and partly through violent upheavals. Instead of a head of state with absolute sovereignty, then, the idea was that a political power's legitimacy actually rested on the consent of the governed. This idea was clearly formulated by John Locke in his *Second Treatise of Civil Government*, but was also anticipated by Thomas Hobbes and other thinkers.[9] Furthermore, there are certain rights that heads of state cannot just overlook and that the people must agree that the head of state will protect. Of course, the head of state, given citizens' consent, can also have other tasks, but he can never legitimately violate these rights. In a democracy, it is the people who are sovereign.

When we addressed freedom on a fundamental level, we saw that community is intrinsic to the idea of freedom as a phenomenon, since reactive attitudes are social occurrences that play out in interpersonal relationships. In the political sphere, however, there is potentially an antagonism between freedom and community. The relationship between them is not unambiguous, because freedom can only be realized within a community, but a community can pose a threat to freedom. Within the liberal tradition, the central idea – whose goal, moreover, is to limit this threat – is *rights*. Rights are absolutes that no community, for example, no democratic majority, can overlook. Indeed, majority will is only one conception of the good, and since liberalism prioritizes the right over the good, it therefore follows that majority will cannot legitimately place itself above individual rights. From a liberal perspective, protecting individual rights against violation from other individuals, groups and, for that matter, the state itself is the central justification for the state's existence.

Some liberal thinkers, such as Wilhelm von Humboldt, have argued that this is the state's *only* legitimate task: 'The State is to abstain from all solicitude for the positive welfare of the citizens, and not to proceed a step further than is necessary for their mutual security against foreign enemies; for with no other object shall it impose restrictions on freedom.'[10] Within the liberal tradition, there is indeed broad consensus that herein lies the state's most fundamental task, but most people will grant the state more forms of authority and responsibility than Humboldt does. For example, most people believe that the state is also responsible for ensuring that all its people, by virtue of their status as citizens, have access to education and a certain level of material goods. If we take a brief foray into liberalism's history, we find that Locke, for instance, insists that every individual has the right of ownership to – and therefore the right to determine – his own life and the fruit of his labours, and that the state's most important task is protecting these rights. However, he also believes there is a universal imperative to help mankind, including helping those who are unable to help themselves. The right to accumulate goods is also limited by the idea that sufficient – and acceptable – resources are also available to others.[11] In addition, Locke explicitly states that no one has the right to let his fellow man starve.[12] For his part, Montesquieu insists that the state has duties of welfare, like ensuring that every citizen has a basic level of food, clothing and healthcare.[13] We will return in detail to Adam Smith's and Thomas Paine's views on welfare duties later. We can further remark, however, that Kant claims the state is responsible for caring for its most disadvantaged citizens. Richard Cobden – the ringleader of so-called Manchester liberalism, perhaps the most pure form of economic liberalism – supported state-financed obligatory schooling for the least well-off. And so we arrive at more contemporary liberalism. From its inception up until the present day, the idea that the state has duties of welfare has proven an important element in liberalism.

The liberal tradition is not anti-statist. For example, an important chapter in Adam Smith's *Wealth of Nations* is devoted to the way in which individual freedom's growth is inextricably bound with state formation and the strengthening of central institutions.[14] Smith explicitly states that freedom only exists if institutions are there to uphold laws. Liberalism, furthermore, considers political freedom to be rights-based, and rights can only exist if they are protected. However, it is also clear that the state must be limited so as to ensure that it will not eventually threaten the very rights it was meant to protect. If someone within the liberal tradition explicitly focuses on rights violations by the state, it is not because the state is the only entity capable of violating rights, but first and foremost because the state is more powerful than individuals and groups and therefore presents a greater danger. At the same time, a liberal will emphasize that in some parts of the world the state poses no such danger, because it is impotent. In no way can this 'stateless' situation be considered an ideal, however, because people are usually then subjected to extensive abuse from political and criminal groups, and their freedom wants protection. A strong state is a necessary condition for political freedom.

Indeed, quite a bit of empirical evidence suggests that increased amounts of political freedom ensure people increased amounts of material prosperity. Nonetheless, this is not the foremost justification for political freedom. As Tocqueville put it:

> I do not think that a genuine love of liberty ever arises out of the sole prospect of material rewards, for that prospect is often barely perceptible. It is indeed true that in the long run liberty always brings comfort and well-being and often wealth to those who are able to preserve it. At times, however, it temporarily hinders the use of such goods. At other times despotism alone can ensure their fleeting enjoyment. Those who prize liberty only for the material benefits it offers have never kept it for long.[15]

Freedom has a more than mere instrumental worth. I will not argue that freedom is the highest value, much less the sole one, but I will contend that it is a good of higher order than most other goods. The fact that the burden of proof is upon those who seek to limit people's freedom also reflects this idea. Essentially, the basic liberal premise is that every person has a right to do as she desires, as long as there is no good justification for why the person should not be able to act in that way. Furthermore, the individual does not need to explain his conduct — it is more than enough for her to say, for example, that she just wanted to do something. In contrast, those who want to prevent that person's action, by laying down a prohibition or something similar, have the burden of proof on their side; if that is not met, it cannot be considered legitimate to stop the person from doing what she wants. This justification must further be given in a way that is comprehensible to the average citizen, who then has the opportunity to speak for or against it. As a result, liberalism's fundamental ideal is that individuals and groups should generally be allowed to live their lives in keeping with their beliefs about what gives life value and meaning. John Stuart Mill describes 'a circle around every individual human being' — and the individual must be allowed to determine who has permission to tread there.[16] External interference in the individual's life must be limited as much as possible.

Liberalism is not a theory of the good, but rather of the right.[17] A liberal theory does not provide a recipe for the good life, but simply observes that the good life can take many forms and attempts to set forth the conditions necessary for the realization of these. Liberalism also attempts to define how we can ensure individuals a space in which to live their lives as they see fit, well knowing that sometimes they will do things that will have disastrous consequences for themselves and others. Hobbes gives us the principle of 'silence of the laws': that is, everything not expressly forbidden is allowed.[18] And though Hobbes's theory will strike us as illiberal today – considering his idea that every single member of society surrenders the right to self-determination to a single individual, the sovereign, whose power is almost unlimited – he was nonetheless crucial to the further development of the universal rights concept, as well as to ideas of the liberal subject and the constitutional state.[19] Be that as it may, all limits to freedom are exceptions that must be explicitly grounded because they imply the diminishment of a higher-order good. At the same time, it is clear that freedom is not an absolute good, because reasons can be found to limit freedom in certain situations where other goods outweigh it. However, a presumption *for* freedom exists. As Edmund Burke expresses it, 'liberty is a good to be improved, and not an evil to be lessened.'[20]

Liberalism is not a complete theory of freedom, but only a theory of freedom's political aspects. The liberal concept of freedom defines limits on politics and on the law, not on ethics itself. At the same time, liberalism insists that it is necessary to distinguish between these limits. Law should have broader boundaries than morality. That means we can legally carry out a number of immoral actions, but the actions are still immoral in character. One might have good reason to morally condemn a number of actions without simultaneously thinking these actions should be banned. A Kantian argument against legislating morality is also fitting here: making morality a matter of law deprives people of the opportunity genuinely to act morally!

Here it would also be appropriate to venture some brief comments on economic liberalism. The argument is often made for a strict distinction between political and economic liberalism. On a purely conceptual basis, is is perhaps not out of the question to allow economic freedom to stand as its own point. In praxis, however, it is difficult to imagine a state that preserves political freedom without also allowing economic freedom. For this very reason, the liberal tradition from Locke to Montesquieu and beyond has considered economic freedom a crucial component of political freedom. Liberalism typically argues that economic freedom promotes political freedom, but that the connection is not strictly necessary. For example, China currently serves as an example of a country where an increase in economic freedom has not seen a corresponding increase in political freedom.[21] However, if we consider history and the world in general, it is a general fact that regimes with minimal economic freedom are, so to speak, without exception regimes with minimal political freedom, and usually regimes with extensive economic freedom are also regimes with extensive political freedom. Indra de Soysa and Hanne Fjelde have documented that states with less economic freedom for private individuals tend to be characterized by greater political oppression.[22] It can be tempting to say that economic freedom is a necessary but not sufficient condition for political freedom. This argument was put forth, for example, by Milton Friedman, who explicitly rejected the idea that capitalism is a sufficient condition for political freedom, though he believed it to be a necessary condition.[23] He made that argument in 1962, long before modern China proved a counterexample to those who might argue that capitalism is a sufficient condition. Amartya Sen contends the same thing in a number of his works.

Regardless, we can say that a wealth of empirical evidence shows that, in praxis, political and economic liberalism are closely linked. Those who wish to separate them must do more than simply eliminate the economic aspects from classical liberalism and then argue that what remains is a political liberalism with no ties to the economic. At the very least, they must sketch out a societal model that shows in some detail how the most central non-economic values in the liberal trad-ition can be safeguarded despite the fact that all economic ones have been eliminated. That task would be a demanding one, to put it mildly: a liberal society is an economic democracy. My interpretation here is in keeping with Stein Ringen, who writes: 'economic democracy [is not] a matter of collectivizing economic power but of redistributing it between persons . . . Democracy rests on an individualistic philosophy, it is about power to *persons*.'[24]

If we compare different rankings of countries with the greatest economic freedom to the UN's Human Development Index,[25] we find a clear coincidence. Countries whose inhabitants enjoy extensive eco-nomic freedom generally have the highest living standard, the highest education level and the best health. Even more surprising is the co-incidence between economic freedom and the Gini-coefficient.[26] Countries with the greatest economic freedom are also countries with the *least* economic inequality. Conversely, countries with the least economic freedom are also countries with the greatest economic inequality. It should be noted, however, that a number of important exceptions to this general correlation exist. For example, the USA,

Great Britain, Singapore, Australia and New Zealand are countries that score highly in terms of economic freedom and yet have considerable economic inequality. Nonetheless, the general correlation is astonishingly robust. The different arguments for and against economic liberalism, however, shall not be pursued further in this context.

The most fundamental characteristic of a liberal democracy is ultimately that every citizen has an inviolable freedom space. In essence, the following chapters will be devoted to examining different aspects of that space.

6
Positive and Negative Freedom

The distinction between positive and negative liberty is particularly associated with Isaiah Berlin, though Berlin gives Benjamin Constant credit for authoring this distinction. However, one can also find a similar idea in Kant's practical philosophy. At the same time, it is worth remarking that Berlin did not consider the distinction between negative and positive freedom to be exhaustive. In his well-known essay on the subject, he observes quite early on that there are over 200 documented meanings of the word 'liberty', and that he has simply undertaken to discuss two of them.[1] Of course, the two that he chose are of the utmost importance. Berlin emphasizes that the distinction between negative and positive liberty is also the distinction between two fully legitimate questions with attached – but often irreconcilable – answers.

Thomas Hobbes is usually considered the author of the negative liberty concept, though it is worth remarking that Hobbes's negative liberty concept differs from that put forth by most later thinkers in the liberal tradition. Hobbes writes: 'By liberty is understood, according to the proper signification of the word, the absence of external impediments.'[2] Hobbes's concept of liberty is purely negative and physical. He writes, for example, that being locked out of a tennis court is no impediment to freedom, so long as you did not desire to go onto the court and play.[3] The only relevant issue here is whether your desired alternative is open to you. Hobbes formulates it like this: 'A free-man, is he, that in those things, which by his strength and wit he is able to do, is not hindered to what he has a will to.'[4] Being free means not being prevented from doing something that one physically wills with one's body to do.[5] The reason *why* one wants to do it is beside the point. Someone acting out of terror, for example, would be just as free as someone acting out of a positive desire. To be free is synonymous with acting according to one's wishes, in keeping with one's volitions, and to avoid something out of fear is a desire like any other, not something that undermines freedom. As mentioned earlier, Hobbes adopts the basic principle of 'silence of the laws': that is, everything not explicitly forbidden is allowed.[6] Where the law is not silent, however, it thunders. The law should instil fear, and Hobbes emphasizes that no emotion makes people less inclined to break the law than fear.[7] State-threatened punishment outweighs any possible benefits of assaulting others, and therefore the fear of punishment assures that citizens can enjoy a peaceful coexistence. For Hobbes, the fear regimen is fundamentally free.[8]

It should be added, however, that Hobbes does not support maximizing negative liberty. His thought lacks the anti-paternalism that is so pervasive in the liberal tradition. Indeed, he writes: 'For the use of laws (which are but rules authorized) is not to bind people from all voluntary actions, but to direct and keep them in such a motion as not to hurt themselves by their own impetuous desires, rashness, or indiscretion; as hedges are set not to stop travellers, but to keep them in the way.'[9]

Hobbes's definition of freedom is meant to be taken literally. For him, freedom is nothing more than the absence of obstacles for setting a body in motion.[10] It thereby follows, he remarks, that a prisoner in a large cell has greater freedom than one in a small cell. However, it also follows that if a prisoner succeeds in convincing himself that he actually wants to be shut up in a tiny cell, then he will be just as free as someone not impeded by locked doors. After all, Hobbesian freedom is, by definition, not being prevented from moving about as you like, and according to this definition, the willing prisoner in the tiny cell would enjoy complete freedom. It goes without saying that this is more than a little counterintuitive, and therefore the Hobbesian version of negative freedom does not have many supporters.

Let us now turn to Berlin. It is customary to regard negative liberty here as the *freedom from* something. In this context, freedom consists of *not* being enjoined with or subject to something. Unfreedom, then, is when something in any way hinders us in our life's development – or is perceived as doing so – and freedom must, therefore, be understood as being free of that which hinders us. Positive liberty, on the other hand, is often described as the freedom *to* do something. As I will show, however, this idea is misleading when it comes to how Berlin distinguishes between negative and positive liberty – and how we ought to distinguish between them ourselves. Instead, negative freedom is a question of which possibilities are open to me, while positive freedom is a matter of who or what is controlling me.

Negative liberty is first described by Berlin as follows:

> I am normally said to be free to the degree to which no man or body of men interferes with my activity. Political liberty in this sense is simply the area within which a man can act un- obstructed by others. If I am prevented by others from doing what I could otherwise do, I am to that degree unfree; and if this area is contracted by other men beyond a certain mini- mum, I can be described as being coerced, or, it may be enslaved.[11]

In short, negative liberty is characterized by the absence of external impediments, and these impediments must furthermore be products of 'alterable human practices'.[12] This last condition is important, because we therefore avoid having to consider natural phenomena, such as gravity, which, for example, thwarts my desire to levitate, as limitations to my freedom.

Distinguishing between manmade and natural impediments has direct plausibility. Say that I am fond of sunning myself on the grass in a public park. Heading there to lie in the sun is a part of my freedom. However, if lying on the grass in that park now becomes prohibited, and violations are punished with discouragingly large fines, I have lost my freedom to lie in the grass. In another case, we might imagine that lying in the grass was still allowed, but that a fire has wiped all the grass out, and so for obvious reasons I cannot lie there and sun myself. In a third case, we might imagine that it is perfectly fine to lie in the grass, and that the grass is green and lush, but it turns out that I have developed a severe grass allergy, and therefore I choose to avoid lying in the grass, even if it is both legally and physically possible, because I wish to avoid swollen, itchy and runny eyes. In all three cases, I can no longer do what I like to do – namely, sun myself on the grass in the park – though the reasons or causes for my being unable to do so are essentially different. In a politically relevant context, it only makes sense to regard the first example as a restriction of my freedom, because it is only here that another *agent* has limited my action space.

The reasons for prohibiting my action may be completely legitimate, but my freedom has nonetheless been restricted.

In the meantime, the distinction between manmade and non-manmade impediments also has a significant grey zone. What about obstacles brought on by economic and structural conditions that are not personal in character, that cannot be traced back to single individuals' actions? They are distinguishable from natural impediments, which cannot be regarded as violating a person's political freedom, but they are also distinguishable from obstacles directly occasioned by another person or institution. Does the mass unemployment currently found in the southern European countries pose a limit to the jobless individual's negative liberty? If one considers it the result of failed economic policies, something that could have been avoided, than yes, indeed it can. A clearer example is the famine that occurred during China's Great Leap Forward, which claimed an estimated 45 million lives and was a politically engineered catastrophe.[13] In Berlin's sense, the famine falls rather unproblematically into the category of something that imposes limits on negative liberty, while a famine due exclusively to natural causes would not do that. Amartya Sen, for example, has demonstrated that widespread famines can occur without anyone's negative liberty having been violated.[14] At the same time, the fact should be indisputable that starving to death poses a serious restriction to one's freedom: to the possibility of leading one kind of life rather than another.

What about poverty? Berlin has difficulty tackling the issue of whether poverty poses a limitation to one's negative liberty. Certainly, he does concede that those who insist that poverty is a negative unfreedom have a convincing argument, particularly if it is the result of deliberate human action.[15] However, it instead seems to follow from his negative liberty analysis that unfreedom and poverty must remain distinct entities, because otherwise one leaves the door open to burdening the negative liberty concept with other positive determinations, thereby diluting the concept itself. Furthermore, it is certainly not the case that all poverty is caused by deliberate human action. On the contrary, poverty has been the basic starting point for every human society, and different societies have worked to overcome it with varying degrees of success. Poverty caused by other agents does exist, but that is the exception rather than the rule. On the whole, poverty should not be regarded as a *negative* unfreedom from a Berlinian perspective. That does not mean that Berlin would consider the issue of poverty irrelevant to an individual's freedom. On the one hand, he argues here that the importance of the war on poverty justifies a certain sacrifice of freedom, and on the other he writes that even though positive resources are not identical with freedom, they are among the most important requirements for the exercise of it.[16] Nonetheless, we must concede that this particular problematic is seriously underdeveloped in Berlin's thought. If poverty cannot be essentially regarded as a limitation of one's negative liberty, that implies nothing less than that negative freedom cannot adequately account for freedom, since poverty obviously *is* an impediment.

However, the fact that grey zones exist and that some freedom restrictions are not *negative* liberty restrictions does not signify that Berlin's negative liberty concept is not a significant improvement over the Hobbesian theory. We should further note that Berlin's definition of impediments is significantly broader than Hobbes's, and that he also regards threats, deception and manipulation as hindrances to free choice. In addition, Berlin advises against regarding negative liberty as solely the ability to do what one wants, because in that case all we have to do is eliminate desire in order to be free: 'If I find that I am able to do little or nothing of what I wish, I need only contract or extinguish my wishes, and I am free.'[17] In this case, a person who is chained to a bench, and who cannot move one millimetre in any direction, must be regarded as free so long as they can convince themselves that they do not actually want to move that millimetre. To label this counter-intuitive would be putting it mildly. Negative liberty is determined by the number of doors that are open, not just by the fact that the door I desire to walk through is open. On the most fundamental level, freedom simply means having a variety of action alternatives. In other words, I have free choice if I can elect to do X or *not* X. If X is forbidden, but *not* X is allowed, I lack free choice, because not only is it permitted but actually mandated that one do *not* X. Freedom requires both X and *not* X to stand open; it does not matter if I am only interested in one alternative. On this point, Berlin differs substantially from Hobbes, who believed that the only relevant question was whether my desired alternative was open to me. In contrast, Berlin argues that freedom presupposes that other alternatives also be accessible.

One prevalent idea in the liberal tradition is that having more freedom, and this includes freedom of choice, is preferable to having less. John Rawls is therefore typical when he suggests that freedom must be considered a primary good of which people would rather have more than less. He argues that people 'are not compelled to accept more [liberty] if they do not wish to, nor does a person suffer from a greater liberty'.[18] The thought here is that, all things being equal, you will always prefer $n + 1$ alternatives over n, and will see $n + 1$ as a freedom increase.[19] Agents generally prefer to have more alternatives than fewer.[20] Negative liberty, as it is interpreted by Berlin, is a freedom that maximizes the number of agent alternatives. This kind of freedom is also consistent with the idea that agents might actually choose to ignore many of the alternatives open to them, because the agent might wish to have fewer alternatives in a given situation. At the same time, the agent's desire for fewer alternatives cannot be used to legitimize limiting alternatives for other people.

In this context, we might imagine that I only wear one brand of white T-shirt and that it must be of a certain size and fit. When I shop for T-shirts, I accordingly regard all the other brands, colours and sizes as a 'racket' that makes it more difficult for me to identify what I want. Nonetheless, that gives me no reason to limit other people's T-shirt alternatives to match my preferences. Indeed, it should be observed that people might not only like different T-shirts from me. Many of them might also obtain satisfaction from the act of selecting from a variety. In this example, T-shirts could be replaced with electricity and telephone providers or whatever else one might wish. The point is that my specific desires are irrelevant when it comes to how many alternatives should be out there. It may well be that a specific alternative should be excluded, for example, because it somehow represents a rights violation, but every exception from the rule of non-interference must be justified.

Why is it important to have more than one's desired alternatives open? In this context, it would be useful to employ Amartya Sen's observation that we must stress both the opportunity aspect and the process aspect of freedom.[21] The opportunity aspect emphasizes that more freedom gives us greater opportunity to pursue our life's goals, and the process aspect emphasizes the importance to be had in the act of choosing. For example, one Saturday I find that I would rather sleep in than participate in my housing cooperative's group volunteer project. In the first scenario, nobody interferes with me and I get my way. In a second scenario, the other members are so irritated that I am shirking yet again that they forcibly retrieve me from the apartment. In the third scenario, those same members are so irate that I caused such an uproar last time that they threaten to thrash me if I dare to show my face again, so for my own safety I choose to stay inside. It is easy to say that the second example is a violation of my freedom, because I am forced to do something I do not want to do. In the first and third scenarios, I get to do what I want, namely, to be lazy and sleep late. Nonetheless, when it comes to my freedom there is an essential difference between the two cases, because in the first I have free choice and in the third the threat of violence forces me to choose a particular alternative. In other words, the process aspect varies substantially in the two scenarios, because it is a violation of my freedom if I am forced to do what I would have done anyway. Often, the opportunity and process aspects of freedom will tend in the same direction, but they can also be in conflict. If a person has a greater number of alternatives, the process aspect is amplified. However, dealing with more alternatives can be so demanding that a person ends up with a worse result than fewer alternatives would have given him, accordingly decreasing the opportunity aspect. In order to achieve a better result, he could, conversely, let another person, such as a professional advisor, decide, which would mean an increase of the opportunity aspect and a decrease of the process aspect. Each individual will weigh the two aspects differently. Some people will be more concerned with the end result and others with making their own decision. According to Sen, it is therefore critical to ensure that people have access to the process aspect and not just to the opportunity aspect of freedom, because being able to choose is an essential part of a person's well-being.[22]

Berlin concurs that people need more than negative liberty. As he writes: 'Freedom is not the mere absence of frustration of whatever kind; this would inflate the meaning of the word until it meant too much or too little.'[23] Berlin's negative liberty concept can largely be interpreted as purely descriptive, since it only specifies those action alternatives that stand open to the agent, and not the agent's attitude to and knowledge of these alternatives,[24] whereas a positive liberty concept is necessarily normative. Positive liberty consists in a person's ability to live his life in keeping with his *own* values. It is not about the absence of interference, but about having control over the life one leads. Berlin connects positive liberty to the question of who it is that will govern me. This question is rhetorical, because obviously the agent wants to govern himself. As Berlin writes:

> The 'positive' sense of the word 'liberty' derives from the wish
> on the part of the individual to be his own master. I wish my

life and decisions to depend on myself, not on external forces of whatever kind. I wish to be the instrument of my own, not of other men's, acts of will. I wish to be a subject, not an object; to be moved by reasons, by conscious purposes, which are my own, not by causes which affect me, as it were, from the outside. I wish to be somebody, not nobody; a doer – deciding, not being decided for, self-directed and not acted upon by other men as if I were a thing, or an animal, or a slave incapable of playing a human role, that is, of conceiving goals and policies of my own and realizing them. This is at least part of what I mean when I say that I am rational, and that it is my reason that distinguishes me as a human being from the rest of the world. I wish, above all, to be conscious of myself as a thinking, willing, active being, bearing responsibility for my choices and able to explain them by reference to my own ideas and purposes. I feel free to the degree that I believe this to be true, and enslaved to the degree that I am made to realize that it is not.[25]

In short, I want to be a valid subject, not an object. Subjects desire autonomy and autonomy requires more than simply the absence of coercion or interference. As such, autonomy cannot be reduced to negative liberty.

Berlin regards the desire for autonomy as completely legitimate, and explicitly states that positive liberty is a 'valid, universal goal'.[26] At the same time, he also believes that the pursuit of autonomy can develop into a threat to freedom. The threat arises if, in the first place, one distinguishes between authentic and inauthentic or true and false self-realization; in the second place, one believes that the distinction can be drawn by an entity outside the agent's self; and in the third place, one is willing to employ power to force the agent to realize himself in a way that one has identified as authentic or true.

Berlin's critique is not directed at positive liberty in general, but against a perverted version in which it has actually been transformed into its opposite. Rousseau, among others, is representative of this kind of perversion when he observes: 'Hence for the social compact not to be an empty formula, it tacitly includes the engagement which alone can give force to the rest, that whoever refuses to obey the general will shall be compelled to do so by the whole body: which means nothing other than that *he will be forced to be free.*'[27] When a community determines the way a person is to be free and gives itself the right to enforce that freedom by employing power, there is no autonomy. Pluralism also has no room in Rousseau's thought. As he puts it, I am simply mistaken if a vote count shows I have voted otherwise than the majority.[28] What I 'actually' will is to be decided by majority will; by its very definition, being free means locking step with the majority will. Accordingly, Rousseau argues, unfreedom would be synonymous with acting in keeping with my own personal will.[29] Obviously, this is the recipe for a totalitarian society in which the majority has assumed the role of tyrant. As Berlin underscores:

> Once I take this view, I am in a position to ignore the actual wishes of men or societies, to bully, oppress, torture them in the name, and on behalf, of their 'real' selves, in the secure knowledge that whatever is the true goal of man (happiness, performance of duty, wisdom, a just society, self-fulfillment) must be identical with his freedom – the free choice of his 'true', albeit often submerged and inarticulate, self.[30]

Positive liberty can easily become the thought that *this* is genuine freedom, and that if anyone else differs in opinion, they are simply mistaken and must be forced to find true freedom, according to how I interpret it.[31]

Conceptions of positive liberty are moralized, or at least normative, since they contain some idea of what an agent *ought* to choose. Opponents of a positive liberty concept often characterize positive liberty as maintaining that one, and only one, ideal should fill people's ears, but there is nothing preventing a positive liberty concept from being pluralistic. However, a truly pluralistic concept of positive liberty would be rather unproblematic from Berlin's viewpoint. A pluralistic, positive liberty concept does not particularly conflict with a negative liberty concept, and that weakens Berlin's assertion that positive and negative freedom are *irreconcilable*. Still, this is no great drawback to his theory.

In a controversial article, Gerald MacCallum has rejected Berlin's distinction between positive and negative liberty.[32] He argues that freedom must always be understood as an agent's freedom *from* something *to* perform or not to perform an action. However, that objection is based on a misinterpretation of Berlin's position; and Berlin actually paves the way for this objection when, among other things, he writes that liberty in the negative sense means 'liberty *from*, the absence of interference beyond the shifting, but always recognisable, frontier', and further suggests that the positive liberty concept is: 'not freedom *from,* but freedom *to* – to lead one prescribed form of life'.[33] Distinguishing between positive and negative liberty as freedom *from* and *to* can be pedagogically effective; when the distinction becomes the *definition* of these forms, however, one is unfortunately led astray. Berlin acknowledges that, as a general rule, positive and negative liberty must be freedom *from* and freedom *to*. However, he also stresses that a slave who fights for his liberty does not need to have a more specific concept of freedom than the fact that he wants to escape slavery.[34] The distinction he wants to make can more precisely be pinned down by saying that negative liberty is open, while positive liberty is closed; or that negative liberty is general, while positive liberty is more specific.[35] Negative liberty, on could say, is about pure *possibility*: it concerns possible actions, not real ones.[36] It is pertinent, therefore, that Berlin describes this freedom as 'the absence of obstacles to possible choices and activities – absence of obstructions on roads along which a man can decide to walk. Such freedom ultimately depends not on whether I wish to walk at all, or how far, but on how many doors are open, how open they are, upon their relative importance in my life.'[37] Yet where these roads and open doors might lead you is entirely undetermined, and it could just as easily be the freedom to read philosophy as to watch reality television, to fill one's nose with cocaine or embrace total abstinence, to help old ladies cross the street or to poke fun at them. In essence, negative liberty concept gives no direction as to which of these possibilities should be realized. Of course, we would be right to consider some of these alternatives as being more worthwhile or valuable, and others as more immoral or trivial, but such evaluations are not comprised by and certainly do not follow from the negative liberty concept. The negative liberty concept champions no specific form of self-realization above any other, but simply defines the outermost framework in which self-realization can take place. Limits must be placed on negative liberty, mainly because other people's rights will preclude certain action alternatives. Kant clearly articulates this idea:

> Man's *freedom* as a human being, as a principle for the constitution of a commonwealth, can be expressed in the following formula. No-one can compel me to be happy in accordance

with his conception of the welfare of others, for each may see his happiness in whatever way he sees fit, so long as he does not infringe upon the freedom of others to pursue a similar end which can be reconciled with the freedom of everyone else within a workable general law – i.e. he must accord others the same right as he enjoys himself.[38]

We can also put it like this: because happiness is undetermined, negative liberty must also remain open and undetermined.

Freedom must be interpreted as the opportunity to have control over one's life, to shape that life as one sees fit. In this respect, the scope of one's freedom is not just a question of existent negative limitations, but also of what positive alternatives are available – and not just potential alternatives, but real ones. One can have negative liberty per se without having positive, since lack of interference does not necessarily imply autonomy – for example, because a mental illness is undermining one's autonomy. However, one cannot have positive liberty without negative, because autonomy implies having alternatives, and that means there must be some room for choice that is not precluded by other agents. At any rate, any satisfactory account of freedom will contain both parts.

Charles Taylor criticizes the liberal tradition for basing itself too one-sidedly on a negative liberty concept, which is interpreted as the absence of external obstacles. A pure negative liberty concept has absurd implications, he argues, and it cannot safeguard many of the most important aspects of a liberal society. In the first place, a negative liberty makes no distinction between greater and less significant freedoms.[39] He insists that freedom must be understood as the absence of obstacles that keep us from doing what is *important* to us. When we think of freedom, Taylor argues, we normally distinguish between what is essential and what is inessential, which means that the loss of irrelevant or worthless possibilities does not strike us as any real loss of freedom. On the one hand, the objection can be raised that the loss of less significant freedoms is still a loss of freedom, and on the other, that it is not up to the negative liberty concept to distinguish between what is important and what is not. A proponent of the negative liberty concept would have no problem in acknowledging that some possibilities are more significant than others, and accordingly that some restrictions on freedom are of more weight than others. The crucial point for these proponents is that what is regarded as important or unimportant does not stem from the freedom concept itself, but is instead an evaluative question. And that evaluation must be left to the individual to make. Indeed, one can say that a considerable strength of the concept is the very fact that it does not make such distinctions, but rather leaves the question open.

At its heart, freedom is the ability to make choices, and all other aspects of freedom are premises and follow from this one fundamental phenomenon. It also follows that freedom increases when our room to make choices grows. Such a purely quantitative understanding does not take much account of qualitative differences, but that does not mean that these are irrelevant. Some choices are more important than others. Having the choice to criticize a nation's government is more important than having the choice of salted or unsalted peanuts. However, not everyone would see the matter as I do, and some people might consider peanuts to be more important to their lives than freedom of expression. People must have the opportunity to make such evaluations, and there is no objective matrix into which each and every choice could be placed according to their respective significance. Nonetheless, certain rights concepts can be used to make a rough distinction: the ability to express oneself is a universal right, whereas access to unsalted peanuts is not. Proponents of a negative liberty concept will argue that individuals must always have the ability to express themselves, and will also think people should also be able to eat salted peanuts if they so choose, but that no one is obligated to provide them with nuts. It is therefore difficult to consider Taylor's objection to the negative liberty concept as entirely hitting the mark.

Second, Taylor stresses that it is not only external, but also internal obstacles to freedom that are significant. Genuine autonomy not only means being able to act in accordance with one's desires – these desires must also be *authentic*. They will not be authentic if they are based on delusion, irrational fear or the like. As Taylor notes: 'You are not free if you are motivated, through fear, inauthentically internalized standards, or false consciousness, to thwart your self-realization.'[40] He further underscores that 'the subject himself cannot be the final authority in the question whether he is free; for he cannot be the final authority on the question whether his desires are authentic, whether they do or do not frustrate his purposes.'[41] By depriving the individual of the authority to evaluate whether his desires are authentic – because these desires might be based on the individual's inadequate understanding of self and environment – Taylor seems directly to facilitate widespread paternalism and to progress towards the very form of positive freedom against which Berlin warns. Yet that is not the case here, because Taylor does not believe there is a higher authority, such as a civil government or a system of experts, here. Taylor would further agree that far too many conceptions of the self and the good life exist for any one of them to be considered definitive in terms of what the authentic life and self actually are. Accordingly, Taylor's positive liberty concept will be pluralistic as well and, as mentioned above, this fits relatively unproblematically into Berlin's theoretical framework.

Berlin is not nearly so unequivocal a champion of a purely negative liberty concept as he is commonly perceived to be. In fact, he explicitly discards the idea that he is out to give an unqualified defence of negative liberty and to reject the notion of positive liberty, since that would constitute the very intolerant monism against which his whole argument is directed.[42] He also denies that negative liberty is the only value out there, or indeed the highest, and that implies it should not necessarily be maximized. For example, Berlin writes: 'The case for intervention, by the state or other effective agencies, to secure conditions for both positive, and at least a minimum degree of negative, liberty is overwhelmingly strong.'[43] And he outright rejects unrestricted *laissez-faire*.[44] In one significant passage, he writes that: 'The extent of a man's, or a people's, liberty to chose to live as he or they desire must be weighed against the claims of many other values, of which equality, or justice, or happiness, or security, or public order are perhaps the most obvious examples. For this reason, it cannot be unlimited.'[45] Indeed, he is so clear on this point that it is difficult to understand why so many see him as negative liberty's standard-bearer. He stresses that it is not just about negative liberty as an absolute value versus other inferior values, but that the matter is instead much more complicated.[46]

Berlin realized that the two conceptions of liberty can result in irreconcilable interpretations of the same ideal, namely political freedom. For example, the positive liberty concept can imply a state intervention that exceeds what is acceptable in terms of a negative liberty concept. That means that one cannot maximize negative and positive liberty simultaneously. The issue of political freedom, therefore, concerns the individual scope that positive and negative liberty should have, and the extent of each one will vary with society and historical context. Berlin is also open to the idea of restricting negative liberty, but he insists that this action must be characterized as reducing individual freedom, irrespective of the good that may result from it.[47] Every such restriction, furthermore, must be justified by the existence of some value that outweighs it in a given case. Even if there is no general rule for striking a balance between negative and positive liberty,[48] there are still certain minimum standards for negative liberty that *every* society must respect. Berlin will also insist that the more one deviates from negative liberty, the stronger the requirement for such justification becomes.

For the most part, I agree with Berlin's interpretation of negative and positive liberty, and I hope I have cleared up certain misunderstandings surrounding his theory. Nonetheless, there are still problems concerning the relationship between his concept of pluralism and his liberal theory – whether one actually follows from the other or, for that matter, if they are at all compatible. Furthermore, his negative liberty concept has been the object of sharp critique from new republican theorists. Berlin's account of the positive conditions for freedom is also unsatisfactory.

Excursion: Value Pluralism and Moral Realism

How does one balance negative and positive liberty against one another? Is there some objective norm that can tell us where boundaries should be drawn, and is this norm valid everywhere and at all times? Because of Berlin's value pluralism, his answer to these questions is basically negative.

> Pluralism, with the measure of 'negative' liberty that it entails, seems to me a truer and more humane ideal than the goals of those who seek in the great disciplined, authoritarian structures the idea of 'positive' self-mastery by classes, or peoples, or the whole of mankind. It is truer, because it does, at least, recognise the fact that human goals are many, not all of them commensurable, and in perpetual rivalry with one another. To assume that all values can be graded on one scale, so that it is a mere matter of inspection to determine the highest, seems to me to falsify our knowledge that men are free agents, to represent moral decision as an operation which a slide-rule could, in principle, perform. To say that in some ultimate, all-reconciling, yet realisable synthesis duty *is* interest, or individual freedom *is* pure democracy or an authoritarian State, is to

throw a metaphysical blanket over either self-deceit or deliberate hypocrisy. It is more humane because it does not (as the
system-builders do) deprive men, in the name of some remote,
or incoherent, ideal, of much that they have found to be indispensable to their life as unpredictably self-transforming
human beings. In the end, men choose between ultimate
values; they choose as they do because their life and thought
are determined by fundamental moral categories and concepts
that are, at any rate over large stretches of time and space, a part
of their being and thought and sense of their own identity;
part of what makes them human.[49]

This kind of value pluralism is not something that simply plays out in
the tension between different individuals and groups, but also within
the individual himself. It is obvious that value conflicts can unfold
between the members of a religious and a secular group, but one and
the same individual can also have a complex, social identity with
values that tend in different directions. Even if I describe myself as a
'liberal democrat', that identity can still contain substantial conflicts of
value. From this position, I would argue that freedom, equality and
welfare are all central ideas, though it is not clear how these values
should be weighed against each other.

However, value pluralism in no way needs to be regarded as
something negative. By opening the door to a variety of lifestyles, it
can just as easily be perceived as something that enriches our lives.
When different values and lifestyles do collide, however, the problem
cannot be solved by the majority of the population, for example,
imposing their preferred values and lifestyles on others in order to
'resolve' the conflict. As John Gray points out, peaceful coexistence
does not require common values, but rather common institutions that
allow for a variety of lifestyles to exist together.[50] In this case, coexistence also seems to require negative liberty. However, a problem arises
here: if there is no value-neutral scale that can be used to rank such
value plurality, it seems to follow that negative liberty is simply one
value among others. Berlin formulates it like that in a few places.[51] On
the other hand, the observation that pluralism requires a certain scope
of negative liberty becomes a prominent theme in texts like 'Two
Concepts of Liberty'. Yet these arguments are not immediately irreconcilable, because if a certain minimum amount of negative liberty
follows from value pluralism, negative liberty cannot be 'just' one

value among others, but must instead be a necessary component of every society that wants to respect that pluralism.

Value pluralism is the cornerstone of Berlin's thought: the fact that we humans pursue goals that are not merely dissimilar, but that are also at times incompatible. In my opinion, value pluralism is more foundational to Berlin than liberalism: that is to say, value pluralism justifies liberalism and not the reverse.[52] At one point, Berlin argues that liberalism and pluralism are logically independent, and observes that he can imagine a dogmatic and despotic liberalism that would outright reject pluralism.[53] Viewed in this way, the relationship between the two entities seems to be entirely contingent. Nonetheless, he also argues that liberalism *follows* from pluralism.[54] As Berlin sees it, value pluralism is a strong argument against people having a particular way of life forced upon them. It is also the reason why every decent society must grant its citizens a certain measure of negative liberty. Meanwhile, the extent to which Berlin is correct in asserting that value pluralism supports liberalism is a matter of debate. In particular, John Gray has argued that the opposite is the case, and that Berlin's value pluralism actually undermines his liberalism.[55] In order to determine to what extent this is true, we must take a closer look at Berlin's value pluralism.

It must be underscored at the outset that, no matter whether we are talking about an empirical or a normative approach, Berlin is not a relativist. Descriptive or normative ideas must prove their worth in a confrontation with reality; it is here that certain concepts will emerge as more adequate than others. And the common philosophical anxiety that value pluralism precludes rational evaluation is little in keeping with actual practice. The fact is that we constantly make such judgements, and either our evaluations are irrational or the philosophical requirement of some neutral scale is pointless.[56] Indeed, when philosophy is so out of touch with actual practices, it is philosophy that must give way. In any case, we cannot simply argue whatever we wish without allowing the real world to correct us. Of course, many mutually incompatible ideas will also stand the reality test.

It is thus far clear that Berlin is a pluralist. Nonetheless, he believes that people's ideas tend to overlap quite a bit, and that our ability to rationally defend them is tied to this fact:

> What rationality means here is that my choices are not arbi-
> trary, incapable of rational defence, but can be explained in

terms of my scale of values – my plan or way of life, an entire outlook which cannot but be to a high degree connected with that of others who form the society, nation, Party, Church, class, species to which I belong . . . Men, because they are men, have enough in common biologically, psychologically, socially, however this comes about, to make social life and social morality possible.[57]

Indeed, he goes even further and argues that universal values do exist: 'There are universal values. This is an empirical fact about mankind . . . There are values that a great many human beings in the vast majority of places and situations, at almost all times, do in fact hold in common, whether consciously and explicitly or as expressed in their behaviour, gestures, actions.'[58] And he also describes 'the objective, often incompatible, values of mankind – between which it is necessary, often painfully, to choose'.[59] That suggests that Berlin is a moral realist.

A moral realist insists that moral values are objective: that is, that they are real and that they exist independently of the observer. In this context, Berlin explicitly states that 'there is a world of objective values.'[60] This statement has a certain direct appeal.[61] When we discuss moral questions, we tend to think that we are addressing something substantial, something with right and wrong answers attached, and so we attempt to find the right ones. We do not believe it is simply a matter of subjective perception, but instead that these perceptions are *about* something – something in relation to which our perceptions can be considered adequate or inadequate. Moral realism has a strong direct appeal because it seems to safeguard the experience of what we do when we pass moral judgements. Indeed, we regard moral judgements as cognitive judgements, as judgements that can be either correct or incorrect in relation to a particular set of circumstances. If someone says 'one should help the poor' or 'the mass extermination of the Jews was evil', the individual in question believes they are referencing something outside their own emotional state. After all, there is a difference between saying that 'the mass extermination was evil' and 'it is disturbing to think about the mass extermination'. That is why there can also be moral disagreement. If one thinks, for example, that we should *not* help the poor, then the contrary assertion is viewed as having an inherent truth value – even if one believes that the assertion is incorrect. One assumes that moral judgements entail truth and falsehood. If it were, on the contrary, just a matter of emotion with no objective mainstay, one could say that there was no real moral *disagreement*, just conflicts of feelings. A moral realist is a *cognitivist*, and what that essentially means is that moral values are cognitive ideas, that moral judgements express perceptions about moral facts, and that we can uncover moral facts through moral reflection or the like.

A moral realist will also typically be a universalist: he will believe that morals are universal entities. These morals are binding whether or not they are recognized by those who happen to live in a certain place at a certain time. There is, furthermore, no descriptive assertion here regarding what people here or there might happen to believe or want. Instead, it is a matter of what we should believe, want and value by virtue of our character as moral beings. That is to say that it is conceivable that morality actually exists, and that no one has succeeded in adequately recognizing it for what it is. In other words, morality is something about which we all can in principle be mistaken. Therefore the argument from disagreement is not necessarily relevant. Extensive disagreement about moral principles is logically compatible with a universal, moral realism, since it is possible that many people are simply wrong about what true morality entails. However, that does not mean that the argument entirely lacks force. If we compare ethics to the sciences, it is clear that there has been – and is – a substantial amount of disagreement in both spheres. The difference here is that, when it comes to the sciences, agreement is eventually reached; answers are eventually found, even if new answers will someday replace them. A scientific realist will say that agreement is reached because someone manages to provide a representation of what some independent reality 'actually' looks like. In the ethical sphere, meanwhile, one does not find such agreement. Indeed, it should be emphasized that a moral realist is not obligated to believe that rational solutions to moral disagreements can always be found – for example, because moral concepts hold too much vagueness or uncertainty. However, the moral realist will also argue that moral norms can usually be objects of rational consideration.

As previously mentioned, Berlin seems to be a moral realist in this vein, but there also appears to be a tension between his realism and his pluralism, as there is between his pluralism and his universalism. As Berlin explicitly argues, there are at least some human rights that are universal and are recognized by all cultures, and these constitute an empirical basis for living a good life.[62] As Stuart Hampshire further points out, there are definite limits to the conditions under which human beings and societies can flourish, and history has shown us numerous examples of these limits being violated.[63]

As a result, a pluralist like Berlin would never support a Platonic ideal state or the equivalent, but would content himself with saying that there are certain minimum conditions that every decent society must realize, and that this foundation can also support many diverse, legitimate and mutually incompatible societies.[64] As such, Berlin must be interpreted as viewing pluralism as part of *reality*, and not simply of our perceptions of reality, and furthermore as recognizing that certain fundamental rights exceed pluralism and are generally valid. On the basis of this universalism, his defence of negative liberty becomes less problematic than if he were a relativist, because we can therefore argue that negative liberty is not simply one freedom among many, but, on the contrary, that it encompasses certain fundamental conditions for living a good life – in every society.

Even though this observation cannot yield a fixed and universal rule for finding some balance between negative and positive liberty,[65] there will yet be a certain amount of negative liberty – defined through the fundamental rights – that under no circumstances can be rescinded with respect to positive liberty or some other good. Value conflicts will arise, and they cannot be resolved by simply calling on some neutral principle. If certain fundamental rights are in jeopardy, however, this will take precedence over other goods. The question then becomes which rights have such status.

7

A Republican Concept
of Freedom

In later years, the concept pair of negative and positive liberty has been challenged by so-called 'republican' theorists. In this context, 'republicanism' indicates a tradition within political philosophy that stretches back to Machiavelli and on to Thomas Jefferson and James Madison via thinkers such as Milton and Montesquieu. Many people will also extend that line back to ancient Rome and Cicero. In contemporary political philosophy, republicanism sees itself as a return to and an extension of classical republicanism, and it has cast an especially critical eye on liberalism and its focus on negative liberty.[1] The relationship between republicanism and liberalism is unclear. A number of thinkers, such as Montesquieu and Thomas Jefferson, are highlighted as central representatives of both traditions. Liberal thinkers today often consider republicanism as doing little more than emphasizing a component of the liberal tradition, and do not believe that it presents any real alternative as such.[2] Republicans usually acknowledge that a kinship exists there as well, but believe that republicanism does indeed pose a clear alternative to liberalism. Maurizio Viroli, however, has argued that they are not alternatives at all, and that liberalism is nothing more than a diluted and incoherent version of republicanism.[3] The dialogue between the two traditions is further complicated by the widespread use of caricatured description, such as when republicans represent liberalism as being solely based on a negative liberty concept – usually the Hobbesian variety – whereas the majority of liberal thinkers have a considerably more complex perspective on freedom than that. The point of this brief discussion of republicanism's freedom concept is not to settle the dispute between liberalism and republicanism, but simply to acknowledge the strengths and weaknesses of its freedom concept.

The two most central, modern republican theorists are Philip Pettit and Quentin Skinner.[4] Pettit and Skinner differ in their positions and certainly in their approaches – Pettit is more systematic and Skinner more history-oriented – but they are closely enough related that we can provisionally regard them as both advocating for one position.[5]

One way to approach the relationship between republicanism and liberalism is to consider them both representative for what Benjamin Constant termed, respectively, 'ancient liberty' and 'modern liberty'.[6] The first form of liberty is participative, where citizens have the right to directly influence politics through debate and by voting in government organs, and it functions best in relatively small and homogeneous societies. In contrast, the modern form of liberty is based on the constitutional state, civil rights and freedom from extensive government intervention in people's lives. In this case, people's influence on politics must necessarily be more indirect – due simply to the state's size – and take place through elected representatives. Constant concluded that ancient liberty is no longer possible in the modern world, but that does not mean that he rejects it entirely. On the contrary, he insists we keep both in view, because even if ancient liberty is a thing of the past, it still contains elements that modern liberty requires in order not to degenerate: 'The danger of modern liberty is that, absorbed in the enjoyment of our private independence, and in the pursuit of our particular interests, we should surrender our right to share in political power too easily.'[7] In short, Constant believes that modern freedom can easily become depoliticized, that as long as one is not being hindered from pursuing his interests, he will no longer concern himself with how the state is governed. We shall not follow Constant's argument further here, but will content ourselves with using his distinction to outline the difference between the two approaches to freedom, where one places the most weight on political participation and the other on rights.

Let us now turn to the republican critique of liberalism's freedom concept. A standard argument within republican theory is that a purely negative liberty concept is unsustainable, because it is compatible with the idea of a slave who is yet free. If a master essentially lets his slaves govern themselves and also gives them room to do as they please in their daily lives, and accordingly nothing hinders the slave from doing what he wants nor forces him to act against his wishes, the slave will be free according to a negative liberty concept. That is counterintuitive, to put it mildly: that a person who is someone else's property should be deemed free. As a result, any freedom concept with such implications has a serious blind spot.

Pettit and Skinner have instead suggested that freedom should be interpreted to mean that a person or a group of people are not being subjected to another's 'arbitrary power'. Such a freedom concept will not be forced to conclude that a slave is free; the slave would be subject to the slave master's arbitrary power, whether or not the slave master used that power to force the slave to act in a certain way. As Skinner writes:

> Slaves are never free, because they are never free of their master's will; their actions are invariably performed by the leave and with the grace of someone else. As a result, a slave's pattern of conduct is nothing other than a reflection of what their master is willing to tolerate. This in turn means that, even if there is almost no probability that such slaves will be subjected to interference in the exercise of their powers, their fundamental condition remains wholly unaffected.[8]

Meanwhile, it can be tempting to object that this idea is too unnuanced. It is one thing to argue that no slave is free – I regard that statement as uncontroversial – but is every slave *equally* unfree? If we compare slave X, who is unchained and can largely do what he wants on a daily basis, with slave Y, who is perpetually chained and never gets to do what he wants, it seems quite counterintuitive to suggest that the two are equally unfree. Both are obviously unfree in a critical sense, but it still seems logical to argue that Y is significantly more unfree than X, which is what the negative liberty concept would imply. In any case, the republican freedom concept does not contain this central aspect of freedom, whereas the negative liberty concept preserves it.

Furthermore, we must note that the republican freedom concept is also negative because freedom is interpreted to mean the absence of something. Pettit closely approaches a thought of Berlin's when he writes: 'What freedom ideally requires in the republican book is not just that the doors be open but that there be no doorkeeper who can close a door – or jam it, or conceal it – more or less without cost; there is no doorkeeper on whose goodwill you depend for one or another of the doors remaining open.'[9] The similarity to Berlin shows itself in the idea that freedom here depends on action alternatives remaining open and that there is another agent who can close the door. The republican freedom concept nonetheless distinguishes itself from Berlin's negative liberty concept by the stress it places on *what* freedom is the absence of: not concrete interference, but a certain type of power relationship. It is tempting for a proponent of the negative liberty concept to argue that the republican position does not actually add anything new to the negative idea of freedom as the absence of interference, and instead only specifies one dimension of that concept. In answer to this objection, the republican can argue that his freedom concept can be formulated more positively, such that freedom consists in being a citizen of a state where all are equal and no one is the master of another, and it seems clear that the republican freedom concept says something more here than what is entailed in the traditional negative freedom concept.

The question then becomes whether the republican freedom concept is more adequate than the negative one. As we have already seen, it deals with an institution like slavery in a more convincing way, even if there were some issues surrounding the idea that slaves in general are equally unfree. Meanwhile, other examples can be more problematic. Let us imagine a state where all citizens are equal and no one is the master of another – in short, a state where no citizen is subject to 'arbitrary power'. That is sufficient for freedom in the republican sense. However, freedom here also seems to allow people to live under conditions that appear to be quite unfree. The republican society we are describing has universal suffrage. Furthermore, all laws and rules are openly published, and they are not arbitrary because all citizens have helped to establish them, either directly or through representative democracy. Therefore the criteria for republican freedom is met. The example, however, can be extended to say that the majority regulates this society down to the last detail. For example, all citizens must dress identically, namely in ankle-length brown robes of hemp. Eating anything but organically grown vegetables is forbidden, and discussing religious questions in a public arena is certainly prohibited, because it can lead to social unrest. All citizens are required to remain updated on laws and rules, and these are made public in a daily radio broadcast at 9 p.m. to which all citizens must of course listen. Examples of such detail regulation in people's lives could go on endlessly. This society, which has next to no room for individual choice, is compatible with the republican freedom concept, but very few would claim that the citizens here have any measurable degree of freedom. Therefore the republican freedom concept also appears to be insufficient.

Republicans can attempt to solve that problem by defining 'arbitrary power' so as to preclude this kind of detail regulation. However, the problem here is that it is not clear what republicans actually mean by *arbitrary* power. Different power relationships encompass us and embroil us. The question the republican must, therefore, answer is what makes certain power relationships 'arbitrary', and therefore illegitimate, in terms of a republican freedom concept. Philip Pettit has tried to clarify the matter by arguing that power is arbitrary if it does not accord with the welfare and worldview of those it affects.[10] Unfortunately, it is not evident what this idea implies. When it comes to agent welfare, we might imagine it has something to do with an agent's enlightened self-interest – that is, the interests an agent should have if he or she is to be considered rational. However, those interests need not correlate with the agent's worldview. It is conceivable that the lifestyle described in the previous example, where a person eats nothing but organically grown vegetables and so on, will maximize the agent's enlightened self-interest because the mandatory diet is healthy, but what if the agent hates vegetables and thinks that organic production is ridiculous? In that case, there would be a conflict between the agent's enlightened or objective self-interests and his or her actual, subjective desires. This conflict can be solved, of course, if the agent's enlightened self-interests simply take precedence. At this point, we are in a situation where the agent's actual desires are disregarded by a well-meaning, paternalistic state, something that does not seem compatible with freedom. On the whole, it is difficult to see that, based on his theory, Pettit can formulate any principle limits to paternalistic interference in people's lives. One could, for instance, essentially ban all unhealthy food and all ostensibly harmful television programming without coming into conflict with Pettit's republican freedom concept. On the other hand, a society could privilege subjective desires and say that power is not arbitrary so long as agents are able to fulfil their subjective wants. The problem with this solution is that it is simply difficult to imagine a society whose citizens are granted their every subjective wish. Accordingly, every society will be permeated with arbitrary power and come into direct conflict with a republican freedom concept, which has now taken on an outright utopian character. A more moderate interpretation is that the individual's interests and desires must be taken into account in the political decision-making process, preferably through the introduction of universal suffrage. The problem with this interpretation is that we are back to the scenario where a minority can, in keeping with the democratic process, let its voice be heard – only to have it drowned out by the majority, who vote to regulate people's lives down to the smallest detail. 'Arbitrary power' is something a democratic majority can also clearly possess. This idea, for instance, seems evident from Pettit's following description: 'A person is dominated by those others in the sense that even if the others don't interfere in his or her life, they have an arbitrary power of doing so: there are few restraints or costs to inhibit them. If the dominated person escapes ill treatment, that is by the grace or favour of the powerful.'[11] It is, furthermore, worth remarking that in 1785 Condorcet had already warned against 'the maxim, too prevalent among ancient and modern republicans, that the few can legitimately be sacrificed to the many'.[12] Indeed, we can all interfere in each other's lives with 'arbitrary power'. To eliminate arbitrary power in such a broad sense would require a scope of intervention that lacks historical precedent even in the most totalitarian societies. In other words, republicans must limit their focus to certain types of arbitrary power.

Pettit himself gives a more precise formulation when he writes that a government authority does not exercise arbitrary power if it works to satisfy the avowable interests its citizens have in common.[13] He adds that this idea is still valid, even though an individual might sometimes desire something different, like to be exempted from a particular law. After all, if a law must have the support of every single citizen in order to make it compatible with freedom, and therefore legitimate, on a practical level every law would be illegitimate; there will always be *someone* who disagrees with a particular law's formation. Such a viewpoint, furthermore, would be so eccentric it would prove irrelevant to any political philosophy that wanted to stay in touch with real politics. Pettit realizes this, and therefore observes that a law's legitimacy is not weakened if some individuals disagree with majority opinion. The problem here is that there are no longer any limits to what a majority can legitimately pass that then affects the minority. Pettit tries to anticipate this objection be saying that the possibility for this type of development, where a majority simply decides to override a minority, 'testifies only to possible, not actual, dominance'.[14] This argument is untenable for the simple reason that history has shown us numerous – and very real – examples of precisely this kind of dominance.

Skinner, for his part, formulates it thus: 'we remain slaves when we are granted our individual freedom by the mercy of someone with arbitrary power; in contrast, we remain free persons when our freedoms can only be restricted with our consent.'[15] Unfortunately, this formulation does not solve the problem either. Skinner emphasizes that, according to this definition, an individual retains their status as fundamentally free even when jailed for a crime, so long as he has given his consent to the law by which he is judged. As a result, Pettit finds himself in the strange situation where he is forced to deny that a state deprives a citizen of his freedom by incarcerating him according to prevailing law.[16] The individual will certainly not lose his *republican* freedom here, because his incarceration does not represent arbitrary power, but it should be obvious that imprisonment does actually constitute a freedom deprivation, and accordingly, that there are central aspects of freedom that are not encompassed by the republican freedom concept.

As mentioned, Skinner attempts to solve this dilemma by arguing that it is not a freedom deprivation if a person has consented to the law by which he is judged. In that case, the following questions arise: what if one has not in fact consented? If an individual is judged by a law he strongly opposes, does that person lose his republican freedom? Say that I am stupid enough to think people should be allowed to drive with a blood alcohol level of .02, and that I get pulled over with a blood alcohol level of .0175. In Norway, the penalty for this is a fine and unconditional imprisonment. According to Skinner's formulation, it seems to directly follow that I have lost my republican freedom because I am being judged under a law I do not support. In contrast, if I had consented to current blood alcohol limits, my republican freedom would be intact. Obviously, that is not a conclusion that Skinner wants to draw, since it would invite complete arbitrariness when it came to freedom and the penal code. Instead, it would make sense to argue that consenting to the democratic process that led to the adoption of a particular law implies consent for that law. In that case, one person's support or opposition for the law would be irrelevant to the freedom problematic, and republican freedom would stay intact simply because one has participated in a democratic process. Unfortunately, that solution does not get us very far, since the problem with a majority dictatorship persists.

Maurizio Viroli offers another solution to this problem. He argues that I, as an individual, should only be bound by the laws I actually recognize, and that I have the power to veto any law of which I disapprove.[17] The problem with this approach is that republicanism loses its very definition and ends up resembling anarchism.

Whatever the interpretation, republicanism is beset with significant problems and seems to require other theories and freedom concepts to supplement it. This idea can also be illustrated by returning to the slave example. As mentioned above, republicans stress that even if a slave master does not consistently interfere in and try to control every detail of the slave's life, the very awareness that such interference could happen places the person in a state of unfreedom. However, we could replace 'slave master' with any other incarnation of absolute power, including that wielded by a democratic majority in an absolute democracy. In this scenario, a minority could occupy exactly the same position as Skinner describes with regards to the slave, namely, 'we become inclined to make some choices and avoid others, and that accordingly imposes clear limitations on our freedom of action, even if our rulers never interfere in our activities or never show the least sign that they intend to do so.'[18] The awareness of the majority's absolute power will cause the minority to constrain themselves, even if the majority actually leaves the minority in peace. Indeed, the republican argument that a slave is unfree due to ever-present uncertainty supports a negative freedom concept; it is by establishing a sphere in which the individual can absolutely make decisions that someone is given a freedom awareness. However, the republican freedom concept is unable to provide such a sphere, because it does not define a space free of general interference, but simply one lacking in exercises of 'arbitrary' power. Indeed, one can say that the necessity of operating with a negative freedom concept follows from Pettit's general definition of freedom: 'Freedom means having security against interference, and the measure of freedom is the quality of protection provided.'[19] In this case, negative freedom rights will be an unavoidable component in securing an adequate quality of protection. An alternative that is naturally open to republicans, however, is to include an element of negative freedom in their definition of 'arbitrariness', but it then becomes difficult to see that republicanism would pose any alternative to mainstream liberalism. Whatever the case, the liberal tradition has recognized the necessity of also operating with a negative freedom concept.

In conclusion, we can return to the question of the extent to which republicanism contributes anything new to standard liberalism from Locke onwards. For it is not readily evident that it adds anything to what Locke did not clearly articulate at political liberalism's onset:

The *natural liberty* of man is to be free from any superior power on earth, and not to be under the will or legislative authority of man, but to have only the law of nature for his rule. The liberty of man, in society, is to be under no other legislative power, but that established, by consent, in the commonwealth; nor under the dominion of any will, or restraint of any law, but what that legislative shall enact, according to the trust put it in. Freedom then is not what Sir Robert Filmer tells us, Observations, A. 55, 'a liberty for every one to do what he lists, to live as he pleases, and not to be tied by any laws:' but freedom of men under government, is, to have a standing rule to live by, common to every one of that society, and made by the legislative power erected in it; a liberty to follow my own will in all things, where the rule prescribes no; and not to be subject to the inconstant, uncertain, unknown, arbitrary will of another man: as freedom of nature is, to be under no other restraint but the law of nature.[20]

In this passage from Locke, we find that the negative and 'republican' freedoms appear to perfectly accord in a single freedom concept. And this is not something we find just at liberalism's commencement. In *Constitution of Liberty*, the philosopher Friedrich Hayek uses the very condition of being subject to another's arbitrary will to introduce his freedom concept:

The freedom of the free may have differed widely, but only in the degree of an independence which the slave did not possess at all. It meant always the possibility of a person's acting according to his own decisions and plans, in contrast to the position of one who was irrevocably subject to the will of another, who by arbitrary decision could coerce him to act or not to act in specific ways. The time-honored phrase by which this freedom has often been described is therefore 'independence of the arbitrary will of another'.[21]

As it turns out, the phenomenon of arbitrary power is not a blind spot in the liberal tradition after all. Instead, the thought here is that freedom can better be defined and protected by emphasizing those fundamental rights that no democratic majority can disregard. And the primary accusation liberals will level at republicans is that they themselves are blind to the arbitrary power a democratic majority could wield.

Actually, there are very few thinkers whose viewpoint on freedom exclusively operates within a negative freedom framework, as the matter is characterized and criticized by republican thinkers. Hobbes falls rather unproblematically into this category, as does Bentham, but not the thinkers who are commonly regarded as most central to the liberal tradition. We have already seen that Locke and Hayek do not conform to that picture. The same is obviously true of Berlin. For Kant, too, freedom in a very real sense entails not being subject to the will of another. In a marginal note to his early work on the beautiful and the sublime, he writes:

> In whatever state he finds himself, the human being is dependent on many external things. He always depends on some things because of his needs, on others because of his concupiscence, and since he surely is the administrator of nature but not its master, he must rather accomodate himself to coercion, because he does not find that it will alway accommodate itself to his wishes. But what is much harder and more unnatural than this yoke of necessity is the subjection of one human being to the will of another human being. There is no misfortune more terrible to him who would be accustomed to freedom – who would have enjoyed the good of freedom – than to see himself delivered to a creature of his own kind, who could force him to do what he wants.[22]

As is commonly acknowledged, Kant's ethics revolve around his autonomy concept, which further provides a springboard for his political and legal philosophies.

If we turn to John Stuart Mill, we certainly cannot label his freedom concept as purely negative in the Hobbesian sense. On the contrary, his conception of autonomy, which belongs to a positive freedom idea, must be recognized as central here.

All of these thinkers place great emphasis on negative liberty, and rightly so, even if they interpret negative liberty in slightly different ways. However, none of them believe that freedom itself can be reduced to a purely negative concept, especially not in the Hobbesian sense. As such, it is tempting to dismiss the republican critique of liberalism as a straw man argument. That would be rather premature, however, because even if the critique of liberalism is not entirely apt, republican thinkers nonetheless highlight certain aspects of the freedom problematic that are worth addressing.

I referred by way of introduction to Benjamin Constant's distinction between 'the ancient liberty' and 'the modern liberty', and pointed out that the former contains elements that modern liberty needs in order not to degenerate. Freedom requires institutions and social practices. It must be protected and regulated, and that presupposes activity on the part of citizens. Constant argues that modern liberty, which is liberalism's freedom concept, faces a danger of depoliticization if citizens do not concern themselves with how the state is governed, just as long as they are not being hindered in their private pursuits. By refraining from political participation, by not voting and letting one's voice be heard, a person renounces a substantial part of her freedom, and it is this important aspect of ancient liberty that republicans stress anew. For their part, republicans are in danger of neglecting elements central to modern freedom, such as civil rights and security from extensive government intervention in people's lives. Liberal rights are required to safeguard these elements. In the next chapter I will take a closer look at the stipulations for freedom that are not contained in the negative freedom concept, an idea I will approach through a discussion of the relationship between freedom and equality.

8
Freedom and Equality

A utonomy is more than negative freedom, because it requires more than the absence of obstacles. A world where all people are equally guaranteed a space of non-intervention can be a world where the ability to translate one's freedom into practice is nonetheless very unevenly distributed. What is the relationship between freedom and equality? Freedom is not equality and equality is not freedom, but freedom can be regulated with respect to equality and equality can be established with respect to freedom. Norberto Bobbio points out that there is an opposition between liberalism and egalitarianism when one interprets them as absolutes: a fully liberal society will not be completely egalitarian and a completely egalitarian society will not be fully liberal.[1] Egalitarian thinkers can leave room for freedom in their theories, but it will always be subordinated to the equality ideal. In the same way, liberal thinkers can prize widespread equality and work to reduce inequality in their society, but the acceptable measures for reaching that goal will always be limited by those rights that define an inviolable freedom space.

The philosophical debate on the equality concept is so comprehensive that it cannot possibly be done justice to in such a short chapter, and I will therefore content myself with focusing on those aspects I consider to be the most relevant for the freedom problematic.[2] I will not go so far as Ronald Dworkin and argue that every plausible contemporary political theory must have equality as its primary goal,[3] but I will at least insist that equality must in some ways be one of its most central values.

'Equality' is a complex idea that cannot be defined in any straightforward manner. As was the case with freedom, being 'for' equality is an uncontroversial stance – the controversy only arises when one tries to specify what type of freedom, or what type of equality, one is for. Equality distinguishes itself from freedom in the sense that one can, without a doubt, increase freedom in the world without simultaneously increasing unfreedom, while it is more uncertain that one can increase equality in one quarter without increasing inequality in another. As Marx underscored in his *Critique of the Gotha Program*, 'complete equality' is impossible because the introduction of one form of equality will only increase another form of inequality.[4] By giving two people the same wage for the same hours worked, you simultaneously create inequality by giving more to those people who work the most hours, and if you give the same exact wage to all workers you will also create inequality, because childless workers will have more to spend than a father with four children. Marx's point can be interpreted to mean that 'equality' and 'inequality' are abstract enough concepts that no comparably abstract net increase in equality is possible. Indeed, Marx concludes that a just distribution principle would mean that every individual shall produce according to their abilities and receive according to their needs. However, other than noting that this distribution principle is non-egalitarian, the idea shall not be pursued farther here.[5]

In this context, another example would be giving a 150-cm-tall poor person exactly the same amount of food as a 190-cm-tall poor person. The portions may be equal, but each individual's nutritional requirements would be unequally satisfied. If men and women in a medium-income or high-income country (the matter is not so clearly documented in low-income countries) are given qualitatively identical health services, women will live several years longer than men. Equal health-care opportunities do not yield equal life expectancies. If you wish to create equal life expectancies, you must offer unequal healthcare services, such that women receive fewer then men.

It is also generally true, for example, that one cannot have both full equality of opportunity and full equality of results. Equality of opportunity will necessarily yield result inequality, and to achieve equality of outcome, one must necessarily presuppose opportunity inequality. Equality and inequality must be visualized in concrete terms. In examining how to achieve a great measure of equality with respect to X, we must simultaneously take into account how that will lead to a great measure of inequality with respect to Y. Oftentimes, increasing inequality in one respect, in exchange for inequality in another, will be an excellent idea, but that obviously depends on the content of X and Y. Nonetheless, there is a danger that one is simply speaking empty words if one advocates for 'great equality' without specifying 'equality with respect to *what*'. And demanding 'absolute equality' is to demand the impossible. In addition, it should be pointed out that 'equality' and 'inequality' are purely formal modifiers that do not in themselves indicate to what extent it is desirable to have equality or inequality with respect to something. For example, it is not desirable for everyone to be equally miserable as the most wretched people on earth. In contrast, most people agree that there should be equality in the eyes of the law.

As Amartya Sen has pointed out, every normative social theory that has won a certain amount of support over time has demanded equality with respect to something or other, something that theory holds to be especially important.[6] That is not just true of theories that usually fall under the 'egalitarianism' category, but also theories that explicitly oppose a principle of equal distribution of material goods. For example, Robert Nozick's libertarian theory of the night-watchman state assumes that all individuals should have equal rights. Even utilitarianism is egalitarian in the sense that it believes all individuals shall count equally in the great benefit calculation. Therefore it is not especially illuminating if one simply argues for equality among men, since, practically speaking, everyone advocates for equality in one sense or another. The crucial thing is the answer to the question: equality with respect to *what*? It is only when one has clarified the *what* that it becomes clear whether one is saying something potentially controversial or at all informative.

A world without inequality simply cannot exist. If we, on a purely hypothetical level, imagined a world with complete material equality, where everyone had access to identical material resources, then non-material resources would still create inequalities. We perpetually distinguish in various ways between winners and losers. Allow me to illustrate this with a passage from Michel Houellebecq's novel *The Elementary Particles*, which describes the experience of one of the book's two protagonists, who lives at his mother's hippie collective, where material goods do not play a significant role: 'Here he was surrounded by the vulvas of young women, sometimes less than a metre away, but Bruno understood that they were closed to him: other boys were bigger, stronger, more tanned . . . From the first time he went to stay with his mother, Bruno knew he would never be accepted by the hippies; he was not and never would be a noble savage.'[7] Human costs will vary even in contexts where economy is irrelevant. My point here is not that we should not try to ameliorate the consequences of economic inequality or other forms of material inequality, but simply that we must be aware that reducing such inequality or eliminating it altogether will not solve all our problems. Equalization in one respect will increase variation in another.

If one would like to tackle the problem more radically and try to abolish not just economic, but all other forms of inequality, then one must resort to some type of repression to ensure that no one comes out ahead. Kurt Vonnegut's satirical short story 'Harrison Bergeron' introduces just this society, where a 'Handicapper General' is charged with making sure that no individual is more privileged than any other.[8] Extremely intelligent people must wear a radio receiver in their ear that emits a sharp sound every twenty seconds, thereby causing them to lose concentration and ensuring that they make no unfair use of their intelligence. Physically strong individuals bear weights so they cannot unfairly use their strength. And attractive people must wear ugly masks so that they do not gain unfair advantage through their beauty. Naturally, no one has ever advocated for this kind of equality in any society – it is a satire, after all – but that would be the logical consequence of any attempt to introduce equality of results into all spheres of life. Such a project would result in all people being treated differently, however, since some people would have their potential deliberately reduced, and no one would have any real freedom to speak of.

Distributive Justice

Most people will agree that there should be a fair allocation of goods in a society, but there are some who reject the very notion of distributive justice, such as Friedrich Hayek and Robert Nozick. According to Hayek, justice is a characteristic of individual actions, in keeping with whether they either agree with or contrast with the general rules for a society.[9] For example, a robbery would be unjust because it conflicts with general rules regarding ownership. As long as individuals do not break these rules, there is no justice or injustice. If we were to simplify Hayek's thought, we could say that the question of justice or injustice does not present itself on a societal level, but only on an individual level. One can object to Hayek, however, by saying that there are distribution patterns in society, and that these cannot be reduced to an individual level. This applies, for example, to taxation and public health and education expenditures. A distributive character naturally belongs to the levels on which these take place, and these levels will prove the objects of political decisions. It is, therefore, not illogical to argue that, when it comes to distribution, the question of justice is valid. Hayek leaves himself open to such objections, because he operates with a state that provides a number of welfare benefits and that also has a flat tax. Indeed, when it comes to Hayek's thought, it can seem self-contradictory to allow government interventions that also meet his definition of coercion, such as mandatory taxation. At the same time, Hayek argues that such initiatives are legitimate if they are based on a rule and if this rule equally applies to all citizens.

Robert Nozick opts for a different approach. Nozick argues that every man possesses ownership of self, a thought we also recognize from Locke's political philosophy. This ownership includes the individual's body, abilities and labour – and everything that can be considered a product of these. To own something is to have a right to it, to use it or dispose of it as one wills. These rights, furthermore, establish moral boundaries for others' actions. For example, they cannot murder you or harm you because that would imply a violation of your property rights. Nor can they force you to work against your will – no matter how beneficial it might be to yourself or others – since you are the rightful owner of your labour. From this starting point, Nozick proceeds to draw some controversial conclusions, the most famous of which is that taxation is a form of slavery.[10] The argument here is that by forcing you to pay an income tax, you are, in reality, being forced to involuntarily work for the state during the time in which you produce whatever value is taken from you through taxation. This is also an argument against redistribution, as it occurs, for instance, in welfare states. By granting some citizens the right to certain benefits, like social relief programmes, the state simultaneously grants them the right to reap the fruits of others' labour, which enables the former to be partially regarded as slave-workers for the latter. This situation, of course, is incompatible with the principle that every individual has self-ownership. According to Nozick, the welfare state is therefore an extremely immoral institution because it violates an individual's most fundamental rights.

In the meantime, Hayek and Nozick are two exceptions in the debate surrounding distributive justice, since they reject the very idea that such a thing exists. Most people accept the idea of distributive justice, but are in disagreement as to the scope and basis it should have. Usually the matter of equality enters into these discussions; that is to say, the answer regarding what exactly distributive justice entails largely follows from the equality concept one takes as a basis.

The most radical form of distributive justice advocates for absolute distribution equality or equality of outcome. It insists that all individuals, regardless of their needs or societal contributions, shall receive exactly the same amount of goods. Apart from François-Noël Babeuf, this conception of distributive justice has very few advocates.[11] One reason it does not enjoy much support is that the consequences it engenders are highly counterintuitive: for example, that a society in which everyone has next to nothing, but where that next to nothing is equally apportioned, is preferable to a society where everyone has much more, but where some have more than others. The ideal of equality of outcome also dictates that the first society, whose citizens are among the worst off and who accordingly have a lower welfare standard than in the second society, is still to be preferred simply because everyone enjoys the same amount of welfare: they are miserable to the same extent. In an article entitled 'Equality as a Moral Ideal', Harry Frankfurt has formulated a convincing critique of the conception of economic equality of outcome by demonstrating that such an equality will lead to a violation of more fundamental values.[12] He concludes that the morally relevant question is not whether all have the same amount, but whether all have *enough*. In a subsequent article, he explains that by 'enough' he does not simply mean that the basic needs are met, but rather 'enough for a good life'.[13] Obviously the question then becomes what 'enough' implies in this new context.

An alternative to equality of outcome can be resource equality, which means that everyone will be assigned the same portion of fundamental resources, but the results that can be achieved with these resources is left up to the individual. One obvious objection here is that resource equality would seemingly result in some pretty ridiculous inequalities. If John and Paul are assigned identical resources, but John, unlike Paul, is dependent on outrageously expensive medicine and aid, then this form of resource equality will occasion great inequality, because John must use most of his resources to achieve the level that Paul already occupied prior to the resource distribution. This objection could be countered, however, by regarding John's disorder and Paul's good health as a part of their resources.[14] The problem with this solution is that it leaves the door wide open to the idea that a person's every trait – such as talent or enthusiasm – is a component that must enter into the resource calculation, such that it must be compensated for, and at this point resource equality would be identical with equality of outcome. This requires that a principle or theory of resource equality be developed that lacks such implications and that provides a reasonable level for what resources people will be assigned, while at the same time preserving a person's responsibility for his own life.

Early on I defined personal responsibility as the responsibility *I* have for *me*, that is, that the subject and object of responsibility are one and the same person. Personal responsibility is a central reason that equality of results appears unjust because such equality is incommensurate with holding people accountable for the more or less predictable consequences of the choices they make. The intuition behind the ideal of equality of opportunity is that everyone should be guaranteed a certain level of resources, and that they are then responsible for their lives from that point on. If one denies the existence of personal freedom and responsibility, and believes that we are no more responsible for our lives than a salmon returning to a particular stream to spawn, then one can always maintain equality of outcome. But could we actually *live* with such a conception of ourself and others? As Ronald Dworkin points out, 'we cannot plan or judge our lives except by distinguishing what we must take responsibility for, because we chose it, and what we cannot take responsibility for because it was beyond our control.'[15] This answer supports the ideal of equality of opportunity because it creates a relatively uniform starting point, and thereafter underscores an individual's responsibility for administering that platform to the best of their ability. Indeed, one important reason that Dworkin believes that a person must bear the consequences of his own choices is that it will act as an incentive to make good choices and develop the self in a beneficial way.

A general moral intuition here is that people should be held responsible – and be rewarded – according to the effort they put forth. On this point, however, John Rawls argues that the willingness to make an effort is not to the individual's merit.[16] The argument runs that the willingness to make an effort is a product of one's heredity and environment, and so cannot be considered of the agent's own making. In short: if a person is a sluggard, it is because his hereditary characteristics and social environment have made him that way. Therefore that should have no consequences whatsoever for the person's economic intake. Let us imagine two waiters: the first is a hard worker who is attentive to his guests, has educated himself extensively about the food and wine list and does everything he can ensure that his guests have the best possible experience. The second waiter is lazy, inattentive, has hardly glanced at the menu or the wine list and for the most part lets his guests fend for themselves. At the end of the day, the first waiter has received $200 in tips, while the second has only received $50. According to Rawls's argument, they should in principle now divide the money, so that each gets $125, since the first waiter is not a hard worker of his own accord and the same is true of the second waiter's obvious indolence. Most people will intuitively conclude that this division is unjust. Rawls does not extend this argument to any sphere but the economic, but if the argument is sustainable, there is no reason it should not apply to all spheres of life. For example, all students should receive the same grade, because why reward diligent students any more than idle ones? After all, neither can take credit for being either industrious or lazy. Yet to sever the connection between what an agent *does* and what he *deserves* so starkly contradicts general moral intuitions that it requires stronger arguments than those Rawls mobilizes in this context.[17]

In reality, all relevant discussions of distributive justice will concern equality of opportunity, not equality of outcome. Equality of opportunity does not mean that everyone has the same possibility of winning a competition, only that they all have the same possibility of participating. Most people agree that our society should have equality of opportunity. However, that is only a surface agreement, because the concept covers some very different ideas. We can distinguish, in any case, between minimal, moderate and radical equality of opportunity. The minimal idea holds that such things as ethnicity, religion and gender should not play a decisive role in someone's right to an education, a job and so on. Competence should be the only relevant factor here. So weak an idea of equality of opportunity is something very few have difficulty in accepting, but many will believe that this is only the tip of the iceberg, and will also require that everyone have the opportunity to reach the same level of competency. That means that everyone, irrespective of social background and so on, should have the same opportunity to achieve a particular education or job according to the natural talents they possess. A gifted child from a poor, uneducated family should have the same real chance to earn a doctorate or become an executive as a child from a wealthy, well-educated family. In this sense, equality of opportunity is not found in any existing society. We can determine that fact by taking a look at social mobility, where it turns out that education and career choices are largely reproduced from one generation to the next. Equality of opportunity, as it is here represented, can seem like a great idea, but it would also require radical intervention. For example, family background plays so large a role in an individual's formation that presumably we would have to abolish the family as an institution and allow the state to take over the parenting role. However, some people will advocate for an even more radical form of equality of opportunity, which says that not only should everyone with the same natural talents have the same opportunities, but that the state should compensate for differences in talent: that is, every individual, independent of both social background and natural talent, should have the same possibility to attain a given position or the like. So radical a conception of equality of opportunity would require detailed regulation of the individual's life to an extent not seen in any totalitarian society. We can also observe that this idea of equality of opportunity is beginning to look a lot like equality of outcome.

A Minimum Standard

The model we find in liberal democracies falls somewhere between minimum and moderate equality of outcome, with different societies occupying different places on a continuum. The most widespread variant is a model that has a defined base, a minimum standard, where all citizens must be assured a certain level of health, education, material goods and so on, while other resources can be quite unevenly distributed. Today there is widespread agreement that all citizens have a right to a basic level of material goods, health services, education and so on, and that general access to these goods is a question of distributive justice. From a historical perspective, this thought is relatively new, and did not appear before the 1700s. There were certainly ideas about distributive justice before then, but, for example, an Aristotelian perspective suggests that the individual should receive according to *merit*. The idea that every citizen is entitled to certain welfare goods simply by virtue of the fact that he is a citizen would be utterly foreign to Aristotle.[18] This approach to distributive justice continued to dominate up until the end of the 1700s, and it is important not to impose a modern interpretation of distributive justice onto the earlier discussion surrounding the term, since that would only lead to a systematic misunderstanding of the concept.[19]

In the modern sense, distributive justice implies that the state will ensure that material goods and so on are distributed among its citizens so that all are guaranteed a certain level of benefits. The debate surrounding distributive justice largely focuses on the scope of the goods to be distributed, on the principles of distribution and on how much state intervention is acceptable in order to ensure that distribution happens.

The most important transitional figure from classical to modern understanding of distributive justice is Adam Smith. Smith follows the philosophical tradition's distinction between perfect and imperfect rights. Roughly speaking, perfect rights mean that one can judicially require that a perfect right be respected and, accordingly, use the law to enforce that respect. An imperfect right is unrelated to such a requirement.[20] As such, imperfect rights are in a class with voluntary ones. Since Smith further categorizes distributive justice as an imperfect rather than a perfect obligation, it seemingly follows that Smith leaves any effort on behalf of citizen welfare up to the individual citizen's discretion. Indeed, Smith also warns against using power to enforce imperfect rights, as this would constitute a danger to freedom, security and justice.[21] So far Smith does not distinguish himself from any of his historical predecessors. However, Smith also writes that certain beneficence obligations are of such a character that they approach 'what is called a perfect and complete obligation', and that in a civil state these can be rightfully enforced by power.[22] The thought that a government can rightfully impose obligations of charity on its citizens represents a decisive development in the history of distributive justice, and brings us significantly closer to the modern concept of such justice.

What is it that Smith more concretely hoped to accomplish? A well-known argument he makes is that education must be secured for all, something that depends on a redistribution of resources from the rich to the poor.[23] Furthermore, luxury vehicles should be taxed higher than freight vehicles, so that 'the indolence and vanity of the rich is made to contribute in a very easy manner to the relief of the poor'.[24] He also outlines other kinds of tax laws that will help the matter, and concludes that it is not unreasonable to ask the wealthy to contribute more toward public expenditures than the poor.[25] Both rich and poor must pay taxes, of course, but tax revenue shall go toward initiatives that will benefit the poor more than the rich. Smith's arguments mark a decisive shift in the viewpoint on poverty. His predecessors regarded 'the poverty problem' as a question of how to handle the bad morals and criminal tendencies of the indigent, and not as a question of how one could help them out of such a situation. Furthermore, to the extent that the poor should be helped, the question became one of charity, and not of the right all citizens have to certain fundamental goods. The thought surrounding charity was especially rooted in Christian ethics, but it is worth noting that this did not lay the groundwork for the welfare state – instead it was up to the individual's conscience whether or not to help ease the plight of the poor. Connecting poverty to the disadvantaged individual's moral fibre, furthermore, created the widespread conception that the poor were poor because of their bad moral character, and furthermore, that it was necessary for them to remain poverty-stricken if one were to persuade them to do anything at all – they had to be forced into activity by the yoke of necessity. One representative for this latter viewpoint is Arthur Young, who wrote: 'Everyone but an idiot knows that the lower classes must be kept poor, or they will never be industrious.'[26] Smith would think Young was mistaken, and he says that if anything, the poor tend to work too hard.[27] He also argues that wages should be sufficiently high for people to be able to provide for their families and guarantee them a reasonably good life.[28] Smith's economic theory was primarily motivated by concern for the poor, and his moral defence of capitalism rested on the idea that, in the long run, capitalism is the economic system best designed to better the plight of the most disadvantaged. Nonetheless, it must be said that what Smith recommends is a far cry from what we today would call a welfare state.

The next step toward a welfare state was taken by Thomas Paine in *Rights of Man, Part II* (1792) and in *Agrarian Justice* (1797). In *Rights of Man*, Paine advocates replacing traditional poor relief with a tax-financed social insurance scheme, and in *Agrarian Justice* he progresses even further in the direction of comprehensive redistribution. He also explicitly formulates this idea as a question of *rights*. The state's obligation to provide for the most disadvantaged is not 'a matter of grace and favour, but of right'.[29]

Paine argues in *Rights of Man, Part II* that a state that truly has the common good in sight will reduce or eliminate the tax burden on the poor, and will thereafter develop social services designed to mitigate the poor's dilemma. According to Paine, two groups stand out as especially in need of aid: families with a large number of children and the elderly. For the first fourteen years of a child's life, the family should receive a yearly sum of £4 from the state, so that the family will have the means to send the child to school and so on. Paine writes: 'By adopting this method, not only the poverty of the parents will be relieved, but ignorance will be banished from the rising generation, and the number of poor will hereafter become less, because their abilities, by the aid of education, will be greater.'[30] Newly married couples were another group he regarded as especially vulnerable to poverty, and each newly married couple should receive 20 shillings from the state and another 20 shillings for every newborn child. Paine also advocated establishing large factories for employment, where those who were willing to work would receive room and board in exchange for their labour.

These factories were not meant to provide permanent jobs, but would exclusively act as temporary solutions to get people over the hump of a difficult period. For the elderly, he suggested several different pension plans, and here it should be noted that the average life expectancy in Paine's day was substantially lower than it is today. Those who were still working at age 50 should receive a yearly sum of £6 from the state, and after 60 people should receive a public pension of £10 per year.[31] These social programmes anticipated the welfare state that was to come.

Such programmes would not simply be financed through tax increases. Paine advocated not just for raises in tax levels, but also for restructures in the entire tax system. Taxes that particularly affected the poor, such as those on basic necessities, should be eliminated completely, as well as on other products the poor consumed, such as beer.[32] Instead, taxes on luxury items should be increased; in particular, a high inheritance tax should be levied on large estates. At the same time, he insisted on upholding the right to private property, and rejected any redistribution proposal that would force the wealthy to give up said property.

Paine further developed these ideas in *Agrarian Justice*, where he repeated that the matter was not one of charity, but rather of the *right* to welfare.[33] As such, he writes that all citizens, whether men or women, rich or poor, shall receive an annual sum of £15 when they reach 21 years of age, and when they reach 50 years, they should receive an annual pension of £10. This would be financed through inheritance taxes on large estates and fortunes. In suggesting this idea, Paine was not trying to attain the greatest equality possible, but rather to establish a social security net that would prevent anyone from falling below a certain defined level. It did not concern him that one individual might have more than another. Instead, his focus was on the plight of the most disadvantaged: 'I care not how affluent some may be, provided that none be miserable in consequence of it.'[34]

Nonetheless, what it means to exist in 'misery' must vary with historical and social context. A *common sense* definition surrounding being miserable or poverty-stricken is: a person is poor when they do not have what they *need*. This statement does not really do much to clarify the idea, however, since human need will vary. However, as Smith observes: 'By necessaries I understand, not only the commodities which are indispensably necessary for the support of life, but whatever the custom of the country renders it indecent for creditable people, even of the lowest order, to be without.'[35] What a person needs cannot be determined at a single glance, for example, with reference to biological requirements.

Mankind has always needed more than the satisfaction of purely bio-logical requirements, because we are social beings, and that means that our needs are defined in keeping with social standards that exceed biological ones. Furthermore, the distinction between 'natural' and 'artificial' requirements is anything but straightforward. Instead, one can argue that the distinction between human needs that are consistent and 'natural' and those needs that are historically mutable will inevitably remain an abstraction that can never be concretely pinned down. As Theodor W. Adorno writes: 'What a person needs to live and what he does not in no way depends on nature, but is rather the product of the "cultural existence minimum."[36] Let us therefore keep in mind that when we argue that a person has or lacks something he or she 'needs', the implications of that statement will partially be determined by the individual's social context.

The Capability Approach

The most important contribution to the discussion of how to concretely interpret equality of opportunity has been made by Amartya Sen and Martha Nussbaum. Together they have formulated what is called the capability approach, which regards certain capabilities as fundamental to human development, and poverty as the inability to realize those capabilities.[37] The question basic to the capability approach is: 'What are people actually able to do and to be? What real opportunities are available to them?'[38] In this context, a capability simply indicates a minimum standard to be met, and says nothing about a possible redistribution of resources above that level.[39] Naturally, that does not mean that one cannot argue for more comprehensive redistribution, but just that the idea would not follow from the capability approach. Meanwhile, it has become clear that there are important distinctions between Sen's and Nussbaum's approaches, and Nussbaum has criti-cized Sen's approach for being too vague and indefinite. In contrast to Sen, Nussbaum has concretized the capability approach by providing a list of ten capacities, and we will return to this list below. Let us first take a look at Sen's approach.

Sen's theory distinguishes between two different approaches to justice. The first, which attempts to define the perfect institutions and rules for a society, he calls 'transcendental institutionalism'.[40] A theory of perfect justice, however, is neither necessary nor desirable.[41] It is unnecessary because we can create a better, more just world without embracing perfectionism as a norm, and it is undesirable because, in reality, it would be so far removed from all actual politics as to prove politically irrelevant.[42] Transcendental perfectionism is therefore flawed because the very pursuit of perfection can distract us from addressing concrete issues in the real world, such as assuring that women in developing countries have access to education. Another problem is that individuals living in an actual society will never agree upon a single ideal. Sen insists, however, that we do not need such agreement, because we can determine that B is better than A to a significantly larger degree than that X is the ideal to end all ideals. (I can further add that whenever the attempt has been made to realize political perfection in the real world, the results have nearly always been catastrophic, something to which I will return later.)

Turning to Sen's second approach, the comparative, we find that it focuses upon what kind of life that is actually realizable. This is the approach that Sen prefers. In this context, it should be noted that Sen's philosophical model is Adam Smith, and that he has devoted a large portion of his authorship to rescuing Smith from friends and foes alike. In particular, the *Idea of Justice* greatly emphasizes Smith's theory of the 'impartial observer', whose gaze is not omniscient but comparative. We can reach some sort of rational accord on the different forms of injustice to be opposed, Sen argues, without achieving total agreement on one single ideal of justice. Sen, the pluralist, further adds that there is not simply one set of principles for just institutions, but many.[43] It does not require a sense of perfection to tell us that A is better than B, just as we do not need to know the exact height of Mount Everest to determine that Galdhøppigen is higher than Glittertind.[44] Rational comparisons can be undertaken without ever knowing what 'perfect' actually is. For example, say that Kraftwerk's *Trans Europa Express* is the absolute perfect album. How in the world would that help me to figure out which of the three albums in David Bowie's Berlin trilogy – *Low*, *Heroes* and *Lodger* – is the best?

Sen concludes that the justice concept requires comparisons to be made between the real lives that people can live rather than being formulated in the quest for ideal institutions. That is what makes these comparisons relevant to the political discussion. A theory of justice must tell us something about the real choices we can make, and not just feed us ideas about some presumptively perfect world order.[45]

Though the capability approach is one such theory of justice, it is also a theory of freedom. A capability is a form of freedom, Sen writes, because it enables different lifestyles.[46] He then describes capabilities as synonymous with the freedom to live one kind of life rather than another. In an extension of this idea, he identifies development with the elimination of different forms of unfreedom. Having a capability, furthermore, is fully compatible with choosing not to realize it, but at least one has that choice. 'Responsible adults must be in charge of their own well-being, and it is up to them to decide how to use their capabilities. But the capabilities that a person does actually have (and not merely theoretically enjoys) depend on the nature of social arrangements, which can be crucial for individual freedoms.'[47] One example that Sen provides concerns a wealthy person who, should he decide to fast, can have the same calorie intake as a poor person who is starving; however, they have different capabilities, because the wealthy person can always choose to eat, whereas that particular action alternative is not open to the poor person. There can also be other reasons why a person might not want to realize a capability, however, such as when she chooses to go on a hunger strike to demonstrate against some injustice. To force a person to realize a capability is to deprive them of power, not only over their own body but also over the ability to influence others through their choices.[48] Accordingly, capability realization must be voluntary.

It is worth remarking that the individual, not the family or the group, is the basic unity in the capability approach; among other things, this is due to the fact that skewed distribution in families and groups is an important contributing factor in capability shortfalls. Let us take gender, for example: in a household consisting of two adults and two children, a boy and a girl, and where the household income is adequate, a systematic skewed distribution in the boy's favour can occur – something we know takes place, particularly in many Asian and African countries – so that the boy goes to school, but not the girl. As a result, the girl suffers from a capability shortfall, and in that respect is disadvantaged, despite the fact that the household has a sufficient income.[49]

In order for the individual to realize the life he desires – or to approach such realization – the resources necessary to ensure his freedom must be in place. An obvious example is a severely disabled person who suffers from a capability shortfall that can only be remedied by the application of resources that help to rectify the disability.[50] A person who is paralysed from the waist down, after all, is more likely to be confronted with serious obstacles in his pursuit of a particular lifestyle than others, if that person does not also have a wheelchair, an apartment designed for a person in a wheelchair, ramps next to the stairs and so on. In the same way, an illiterate person will lack a critical resource for functioning in a society like ours, where literacy is so fundamental. If freedom means being able to live one life rather than another, it soon becomes evident that non-interference is not enough – freedom also has material and institutional requirements.

On the other hand, a society cannot be structured in such a way that every citizen has access to all the resources required to realize the life he desires. To bring the point home: if someone wants to become a movie director, and the film he wants to make costs $200 million, it is obvious that that individual cannot legitimately demand those resources be assigned to him. Some basic level must be put in place. Furthermore, Sen argues, to be apportioned the resources that will establish such a fundamental existence is in no way synonymous with being deprived of the responsibility one has for one's life; in contrast, it is to be given the means to take such responsibility:

> The argument for social support in expanding people's freedom can, therefore, be seen as an argument *for* individual responsibility, not against it. The linkage between freedom and responsibility works both ways. Without the substantive freedom and capability to do something, a person cannot be responsible for doing it. But actually having the freedom and capability to do something does impose on the person the duty to consider whether to do it or not, and this does involve individual responsibility. In this sense, freedom is both necessary and sufficient for responsibility.[51]

Sen's freedom concept is positive, but at the same time it is pluralistic because it allows for a manifold of different actualizations. Therefore Sen's positive freedom is not encompassed in Berlin's critique of positive liberty. By positive freedom – or 'substantial freedom', as he terms it – Sen means the ability to realize oneself, to make choices regarding the type of life one wishes to lead and to be able to integrate oneself into one's environment.[52] Since freedom will always be a *degree* of freedom, however, positive freedom is not something one ever fully has or completely lacks. Sen, furthermore, does not believe negative freedom to be inconsequential. On the contrary, he assigns it intrinsic value, and insists that it is in fact a requirement for positive freedom.[53] Still, he also underscores that a purely negative freedom concept is insufficient. A person who does not experience any limitations on his negative freedom, but who, so to speak, lacks all resources (property, health services, education and so on), will lead an unenviable existence and have very few real options.

Where classical liberalism focuses on the formal conditions for freedom, the capability approach emphasizes freedom's material conditions, which it defines as a minimum standard. Though this idea can certainly imply a comprehensive redistribution of material resources, it does not suggest that extensive inequalities are unjust, just so long as everyone achieves the minimum standard. In this respect, the capability approach is in line with liberalism's traditional conception of equality of opportunity, in contrast to socialism's tendency to promote equality of outcome.

In this context, Sen questions whether we should also require equality of capability, and his answer is a clear no.[54] The reason for this is that even though we ought to assign equality of capability great relevance, it cannot simply trump other important considerations, among them equality. Furthermore, he argues that the capability approach only preserves one of freedom's many aspects, and, more specifically, that it does not preserve freedom's process aspect so well as it does its opportunity aspect.

Sen regards the capacity approach as a tool for evaluating life quality, while Nussbaum wants to utilize it to define a set of rights that ought to be recognized and implemented by all states.[55] Gender perspective is also more central to Nussbaum than to Sen. She has emphasized that women, by and large, have enjoyed more restricted freedom and fewer opportunities than men. Rights are obviously important, but a pure rights perspective is insufficient, since social justice also encompasses economic resources and social conditions. As she writes: 'To secure a capability to a citizen it is not enough to create a sphere of non-interference; the public conception must design the material and institutional environment so that it provides the requisite affirmative support for all the relevant capabilities.'[56] Real freedom requires more than the realization of a negative liberty concept.

In contrast to Sen, Nussbaum has devised a specific list of capacities that, in her opinion, are minimum standards that must be met in order for a person to lead a free and worthwhile life. What follows is her list of fundamental, human capabilities:

I LIFE
Being able to live to the end of a human life of normal length;
not dying prematurely, or before one's life is so reduced as to
be not worth living.

2 BODILY HEALTH

Being able to have good health, including reproductive health; to be adequately nourished; to have adequate shelter.

3 BODILY INTEGRITY

Being able to move freely from place to place; to be secure against violent assault, including sexual assault and domestic violence; having opportunities for sexual satisfaction and for choice in the matters of reproduction.

4 SENSES, IMAGINATION, AND THOUGHT

Being able to use the senses, to imagine, think, and reason – and to do these things in a 'truly human' way, a way informed and cultivated by an adequate education, including, but by no means limited to, literacy and basic mathematical and scientific training. Being able to use imagination and thought in connection with experience and producing works and events of one's own choice, religious, literary, musical, and so forth. Being able to use one's mind in ways protected by guarantees of freedom of expression with respect to both political and artistic speech, and freedom of religious exercise. Being able to have pleasurable experiences and to avoid non-beneficial pain.

5 EMOTIONS

Being able to have attachments to things and people outside ourselves; to love those who love and care for us, to grieve at their absence; in general, to love, to grieve, to experience longing, gratitude, and justified anger. Not having one's emotional development blighted by fear and anxiety. (Supporting this capability means supporting forms of human association that can be shown to be crucial to development.)

6 PRACTICAL REASON

Being able to form a conception of the good and to engage in critical reflection about the planning of one's life. (This entails protection for the liberty of conscience and religious observance.)

7 AFFILIATION

a Being able to live with and toward others, to recognize and

show concern for other human beings, to engage in various forms of social interaction; to be able to imagine the situation of another. (Protecting this capability means protecting institutions that constitute and nourish such forms of affiliation, and also protecting the freedom of assembly and political speech.)
b Having the social bases of self-respect and non-humiliation; being able to be treated as a dignified being whose worth is equal to that of others. This entails provisions of non-discrimination on the basis of race, sex, sexual orientation, ethnicity, caste, religion, national origin.

8 OTHER SPECIES
Being able to live with concern for and in relation to animals, plants, and the world of nature.

9 PLAY
Being able to laugh, to play, to enjoy recreational activities.

10 CONTROL OVER ONE'S ENVIRONMENT
a Political. Being able to participate effectively in political choices that govern one's life; having the right of political participation, protections of freedom of expression and associations.
b Material. Being able to hold property (both land and movable goods), and having property rights on an equal basis with others; having the right to seek employment on an equal basis with others; having the freedom from unwarranted search and seizure. In work, being able to work as a human being, exercising practical reason, and entering into meaningful relationships of mutual recognition with other workers.[57]

As Nussbaum herself points out, this list coincides to a large extent with the rights embodied in different human rights declarations.[58] All the capabilities on the list, furthermore, are regarded as equally valuable. That means that *all* the capacities on the list must be protected, thereby precluding the argument that over-emphasizing one capacity makes up for another going unrealized. Indeed, the minimum standard of justice on earth is attained only when *all* people have realized all ten capabilities.[59] And though the last decade has seen more progress toward this goal than ever before, we still have a long journey ahead. The list of capabilities is not carved in stone, however, and Nussbaum concedes that it can certainly be revised.[60] A number of problems nonetheless present themselves here, since this list can hardly be put into operation, and the question also stands open as to what is concretely required in order for a capacity to be considered met. The closest Nussbaum comes to an explanation here is in saying that the list should not set the bar so high that no state could ever succeed in its realization nor so low that it would sink below the limits of what is required for human dignity.[61] It is not difficult to agree with this statement, but the answer is still so general that it borders on the uninformative. The capabilities on the list also distinguish themselves from each other in the sense that some, like 'bodily integrity', are significantly easier to legislate than 'able to feel concern for animals'. Furthermore, there is reason to question whether all the capabilities on the list are equally important, and here Nussbaum differentiates herself from Sen, who believes that we *must* weigh rights against each other.[62] In the end, Nussbaum's ambition toward a rights fortification of capabilities certainly has its attractive aspects, but it is difficult to imagine that her specific list could realistically be fortified. It is also doubtful that all the capabilities on her list *should* be fortified, and a number of the capabilities that she suggests will not be included in the fundamental rights I outline in chapter Nine.

Be that as it may, it is clear that the capability approach provides freedom's liberal understanding with an important element, namely, the material and institutional conditions necessary for its realization.

Excursion: Utopias

Every genuine utopian project is based on the assumption that the old world must be destroyed in order to make way for the new. A complete utopia lacks all trace of the old world – every such trace would be akin to the rotten apple that ruined the fresh ones in the basket. Utopias claim to have the monopoly on truth, morality and salvation.

When one glances through the history of utopias, a few peculiarities tend to jump out, such as the fact that they do not contain people like you and me. There is hardly a sick person in sight and criminals are nearly always a thing of the past. In general, people do not lie and cheat. Instead, all citizens are model specimens. And that means that utopias have zero space for people who fall short of the ideal. As such, non-model individuals must either be eliminated or utterly transformed. In essence, there is no place for people like us – and that means that we must resist the utopian seduction.

If we want to examine political utopias, we must start with Plato, who in many ways authored the prototypical utopian society upon which later utopias are founded. For Plato, the ideal state must retain no trace of any previous society, any previous model, but must instead be built from the ground up. Accordingly, the state's rulers 'would take the city and the dispositions of human beings, as though they were a tablet . . . which, in the first place, they would wipe clean".[63] Rulers have the power to intervene in *every* aspect of citizens' lives; politics knows no bounds. Plato argues that the ideal state, however, must be built upon the idea of *justice*. The state is made up of individuals, a fact that proves conditional for the realization of the good and just life. The principle of justice is the same for the state as it is for the individual. The state exists to meet its citizens' needs; individual citizens are not isolated, but instead depend on each other for a good life. Everyone gathers together and shoulders the same load. Since we all have different talents, however, we are suited to best serve society in different ways, and division of labour is the most effective method to achieve this. To my knowledge, Plato is the first thinker to develop a theory around the division of labour. The state's citizens, he argues, should be separated into different groups, each with its own distinct task. Plato's reasoning for assigning diverse jobs to people is that everyone has their own natural talents.[64] Here Plato progresses from the thought that every man has a specific being that is suited to a given task, and he believes that every individual has a duty to the city-state to perform the task for which he is best adapted: 'each one must practice one of the functions in the city, that one for which his nature made him naturally most fit.'[65]

Children are raised with an eye toward the specific function they will perform in the state. Therefore the state is responsible for child-rearing – something that will become a common feature of later political utopias. The reason for this is simple: our family background influences us far more than almost anything else in life, and the state's unity, therefore, is threatened if children are raised in families. In particular, belonging to a family creates bonds of loyalty that are stronger than those to the state. Plato writes that children should never know their biological parents and vice versa. Weak and unsuitable children, furthermore, must be discarded for the sake of realizing the best possible offspring. There is no real sickness or crime in the ideal state, of course, because by definition that would not be ideal. All citizens are paragons: healthy souls in healthy bodies. In terms of education, a person must first be taught moderation. If one cannot control their desires and urges, after all, it is difficult to learn anything else. In fact, most people will not progress farther than learning to control these basic desires, and those who remain at this stage go into trade. Those who progress further learn to develop power; the ones who stop here become guardians. Finally, we are left with the cream of the crop, the philosophers, who shall attain insight into the good and become rulers. Those who make it to this last stage are between forty and fifty years of age, so education takes its time.

What Plato describes here is an *ideal* state, one he recognized could never be realized in its pure form. Towards the end of his life, therefore, Plato wrote *Laws*, the largest work he ever produced, and herein he describes what he calls the next best state.[66] In this state there is not much individual freedom, and even less religious freedom, since god-deniers are condemned to death. The state and religion are inextricably connected. Rulers must also conform to the letter of the law, and those who overstep it will be executed.

The perfection Plato sought in his political philosophy can only be realized through large-scale oppression, something that is also typical of most later utopias, no matter how based in liberty they claim to be. Meanwhile, one thing Plato lacks, and which has proven a central element to modern political utopias, is a progressive understanding of history. That first appeared with Christianity, and it is to this stage of utopian development that we will now turn.

John Gray suggests that 'modern politics is a chapter in the history of religion.'[67] To a certain extent, he is right. In modern times, political utopias are largely secular variants of Christian paradisiacal visions. That is also true of ideologies that claim to be scientifically based, such as Marxism and Nazism. In the context of this discussion, Gray relies heavily on Norman Cohn's work, especially the book *The Pursuit of the Millennium*.[68] In this work, Cohn demonstrates how Nazistic and Communistic ideologies adopt the same historical interpretation as that found in the so-called millenarianistic sects of the Middle Ages. The end time plays a crucial role in these visions, whose people are existing on the cusp of a conversion to a world without hunger, sickness and suffering, and where the powers of darkness have been defeated once and for all. Modern utopian movements envision a similar scenario, which dictates that all the world's ills will be overcome through a great transformation. However, the dawning of this new world requires radical intervention. The old world must be decimated to pave the way for this new, perfect society.

Medieval apocalyptic movements expected the return of Christ, who would then rule over a new kingdom. And though today the word 'apocalypse' calls to mind catastrophe, the word's Greek origin actually indicates the lifting of a veil, the revelation of divine mysteries, such as in the Book of Revelation. These ideas focus on salvation, not catastrophe. The salvation event, furthermore, is the goal of history – when it occurs, history is over. Along these same lines, Marx and Engels write in *The Communist Manifesto* that communism poses the solution to history's riddle.

Cohn identifies five characteristics of the salvation belief found in such medieval sects:

1. It is *collective* and experienced by a community.
2. It is *worldly*, since salvation first takes place here on earth and not in the beyond.
3. It is *imminent*.
4. It is *total*. That is, it is not just an improvement over the old, but is an utter transformation to a state of fulfilment.
5. It is *miraculous*. That is, it depends upon divine intervention.

Modern revolutionary and utopian movements share these beliefs, with one key difference: man takes God's place. Elements of the miraculous, for example, can be found in Marx's thought. After all, it is fundamentally unclear how communism's 'higher phase' – when the communist utopia, that is, is finally realized on earth – will be brought about from the transitional phase that, as Marx himself concedes, is no paradise.

Orthodox Christianity held that God's kingdom would first be realized in Heaven, and that prior to this event, Christ would return and defeat the powers of darkness. A few groups reversed this idea, however, and argued that, in the first place, God's kingdom would be formed on earth, and in the second place, that kingdom must be realized in order for the second coming of Christ to happen at all. For the sake of the kingdom's realization, a purification process must be set in motion. One of the most famous historical examples culminated in Münster in 1534–5.[69]

In 1534 the Anabaptists seized power in Münster and formed a theocratic state that in a variety of notable ways anticipated – and would prove a model for – the modern communist state. They christened this state the 'New Jerusalem'. The Dutchman Jan Matthys assumed leadership, believing that he had been chosen to achieve no less than world domination, and that it was his duty to purify the world of evil in order to prepare for Christ's second coming and the dawn of the new era. As a result, Matthys insisted the rest of the world would soon go under and that only Münster would be spared. Hordes of believers flocked to the city. Leadership then fell to the Dutchman John of Leyden, who persevered in and radicalized Matthys's vision. His first item of business was to purify the city of all unclean elements. To begin with, the Anabaptist leadership wanted to execute all Lutherans and Catholics, but they contented themselves with merely banishing them – into a snowstorm. Among others, invalids and the elderly met the same fate. Anyone banished was forced to leave behind their possessions. Soon thereafter, the private ownership of money was abolished, allowing the state to regulate exactly how much each individual would receive. Food was then confiscated from people's houses and the right to ownership essentially revoked. Finally forced labour was introduced. All books but the Bible were burned. Those who protested were imprisoned or executed for godlessness. Over time the death penalty became more and more commonplace, not just for murder and theft, but also for lying and various forms of insubordination. The city's leaders lived in increasingly greater luxury and its common citizens in increasingly greater poverty. In 1535 the city was finally conquered, the Anabaptists were tortured to death and Münster again became Catholic. The Münster episode would probably have been remembered as nothing more but a historical oddity, were it not for the way it so obviously pointed to modern totalitarian regimes.

The Christian concept of historical progress was secularized in modern times, something that takes an especially poignant form in Hegel, who was the most important philosophical inspiration for Marx. Hegel subordinates all of history's horrors to a historical course where every individual must be considered 'a means to an ulterior end', and where 'the cunning of reason' ensures that progress is guaranteed.[70] Hegel also describes history as a 'slaughtering bench'.[71] All victims on this 'slaughtering bench' are reduced to random flotsam governed over by a rational and benevolent totality. Ultimately, 'the claim of the World-Spirit' triumphs over all other considerations, and world history occupies a higher plane than human morality.[72]

In Marxism, Hegel's theoretical idea of history becomes a practical, forward-looking quest. Just as Hegel believed that he could legitimate earlier evils by considering history as a totality, Marxists believed it could be used to legitimate present and future evils. This idea is clearly formulated by Georg Lukács: 'Communist ethics makes it the highest duty to accept the necessity of doing evil. This is the greatest sacrifice the revolution asks of us. The conviction of the true communist is that evil transforms itself into good through the dialectics of historical evolution.'[73]

The political ideal reveals and vindicates both the historical process and its victims. Every action is justified with respect to this ideal, which, because it was understood as history's or nature's law, outweighed any concern for the individual. Of course, this Marxist version of the teleological suspension of the ethical – that is, the setting aside of morality in favour of a higher purpose – resulted in an estimated 100 million dead. The goal of historical progress obviously overshadowed every other moral consideration.

Communists – for example, the Anabaptists in Münster – existed before Marx. Like John of Leyden, Marx is also a representative of apocalyptic communism. He was severely critical of those who supported a gradual realization of the communistic ideal, who sought to improve conditions for factory workers and so on. Instead, he maintained that capitalism should be allowed to develop in the worst possible way, forcing a radical upheaval to take place. The point was not to improve upon the old, but to create a revolutionary new beginning.

In many respects, Marxist communism can be considered a religious ideology. This may seem like an unusual statement, since it would be hard to find a more militantly anti-religious ideology. However, Marxist communism duplicates Christian apocalyptic patterns of thought: God is simply replaced with history and humanity. Just as Christ's second coming marks the utopian end of days in one doctrine, communist thought anticipates the end of history when society finally reaches its so-called 'highest phase'.

Yet Marx wrote very little about how this utopia might concretely come into being. That was clever of him, since it preserves an air of mystery. A few hints are scattered here and there, of course, such as that society will take from each according to ability and provide to each according to need. It will also apparently be a society where people can develop themselves in a variety of different directions, rather than just being confined to one particular job, something Marx considered to be severely limiting. In a particularly famous passage, Marx criticizes the division of labour in a capitalistic society:

For as soon as the distribution of labor comes into being, each man has a particular, exclusive sphere of activity, which is forced upon him and from which he cannot escape. He is a hunter, a fisherman, a shepherd, or a critical critic, and must remain so if he does not want to lose his means of livelihood; while in communist society, where nobody has one exclusive sphere of activity but each can become accomplished in any branch he wishes, society regulates the general production and thus makes it possible for me to do one thing today and another tomorrow, to hunt in the morning, fish in the afternoon, rear cattle in the evening, criticise after dinner, just as I have a mind, without ever becoming hunter, fisherman, shepherd or critic.[74]

There are many ideals that sound just fine in theory, but that become more difficult when one begins to wonder how they might be put into actual practice. One good example is Marx's formulation: from each according to ability and to each according to need. The problem here is obviously that implementing this ideal would require a complete mapping out and strict control of all citizens, in short, a totalitarian state. In addition, it is difficult to imagine this society producing much of anything at all. We might note that none of Marx's job examples take place in actual factories and so on. A society that produces according to the principles for labour that Marx establishes here will experience a huge loss of production and will suffer a setback, several centuries' worth in terms of material living standards, something that will certainly lead to a significant decrease in life expectancy, an overall increase in infant mortality, instances of starvation and so on.

Marx characterized the transition period from capitalism to the communist paradise as a 'dictatorship of the proletariat' that might conceivably involve 'some unpleasantness', as he phrased it. Strict control would be necessary until the 'higher phase' was realized. Once the higher phase was reached, of course, there would be complete freedom, and the state itself would cease to exist. Getting to that point, however, required people's freedom to be suppressed. The problem, though, is that this utopia *cannot* actually be realized, and so the condition of unfreedom is permanent. In actual communist societies, the 'transition period' proved to be the perpetual order of the day.

In *State and Revolution*, Lenin argued that, under the dictatorship of the proletariat, it was unnecessary to use force against the masses, but only against the enemies of the State and the Revolution, since the regime, after all, existed to serve the masses.[75] The problem was that the masses were not exactly as Lenin, and later Stalin, envisioned them, and so the use of force and violence was directed with particular intensity against the very workers and farmers that the new regime was supposed to serve.

One could certainly object that this violence and oppression was largely a localized relic of the tsarist regime rather than something belonging to communism itself. However, that viewpoint is untenable. Execution was a fixture in the time of the tsars, of course, with around 14,000 deaths in the last 50 years, but in just the six years that followed the Revolution, the Bolshevik secret police, the Cheka, executed 200,000 people.[76] This represents a jump from an annual average of 280 to 33,000 executions, that is to say, about 120 times as many people killed. At most, the tsar's secret police numbered 15,000, while the Cheka had 250,000 members by 1921. Forced labour also existed under the tsars, but nothing like the scope it reached under the Bolsheviks. My point here is not to paint the tsarist world in rosy hues – there is no reason for that – but instead to stress the violent transformation that took place under the Bolsheviks. Extreme oppression was not something merely inherited from the tsars, but was a radical new product of the utopian vision.

Lenin explicitly stated that the people who would prove endemic to communism's higher phase would be nothing like the people who surrounded him on a daily basis. The communistic paradise could not tolerate such stock. In this respect, the communistic revolution was not about liberating people such as they are, but about eliminating them such as they are – or, at very least, radically transforming them. Utopia calls for a new brand of person. In contrast to what the Nazis put into play, furthermore, this was not a predominately racist project, though it did have its racist elements, an idea anticipated by Marx's anti-Semitism and then particularly radicalized during Stalin's time. Like Nazism, however, communism claimed that science would help create the new man, although what went on in both cases was actually an ideologically driven pseudo-science.

Immediately following the Russian Revolution, a class of people was targeted and stripped of their rights – something that could include the right to nourishment.[77] By 1918 five million people had already been 'declassed' in this way, a rather remarkable development, to put it mildly, considering that the Revolution was based on a presumptively egalitarian ideology. Be that as it may, by 1932 all Soviet citizens had to carry their passports with them at all times, and these passports did not just contain people's gender and age, but also their social class and ethnicity. Emptying large cities of undesirable elements was also a clear goal, and widespread deportation forced people into conditions that signified extreme deprivation and often certain death.[78] Under Stalin, these purges were substantially more ethnically and racially motivated than is generally recognized. Groups from the Caucasus and Crimea were especially targeted, but also Asians, Jews and so on. Nonetheless, ethnicity was just one criterion among many. A new group was always in the wings. A paranoid logic governed these purges, which dictated that the Bolsheviks were constantly under threat from subversive forces. In the Soviet Union, mass arrests particularly took off in 1937, due not least to the fact that people had begun to complain that their society did not in fact fulfil their expectations. This was no utopia. Instead of finding fault with the utopian ideal, however, the hunt for scapegoats began. Obviously regressive elements must be sabotaging things; appropriate measures had to be taken. Ideological indoctrination was, of course, a crucial factor in individual re-education, but the worst enemies of the Revolution (if not so hopeless as to warrant immediate execution) also required hard labour. Hard physical labour was a means to transformation. Gulags were the concentration camps that welcomed the individuals and groups who threatened the purity of the society – or rather, of the utopia.

As political circumstances and alliances changed, expressions like 'Trotskyist', which were used to denote enemies particularly dangerous to the Party, State and Revolution, shifted content as well – and it took ever less to be considered a 'Trotskyist'. The fact that the enemy lacked a concrete face, however, did not lead many in the Central Committee to question his existence. Instead, the increasingly imprecise criteria used to define the 'enemy' meant that more people simply fell into this category – and not only individuals, but also their family and friends. What is perhaps most surprising is that an overwhelming majority of prisoners in the Soviet Union came from the lower classes. In 1934 alone 93.7 per cent of prisoners had only a rudimentary level of education or none whatsoever, while in 1940 that number was 88.3 per cent. True proletariats were obviously unwelcome under the proletariat's dictatorship. And here we come to the heart of it: real human beings are simply not those described in utopias, and that means that we humans will always be on the losing side.

In general, all politics are a form of social engineering. Karl Popper, for his part, distinguishes between utopian and piecemeal social engineering as models for social development.[79] The utopian social engineer wants to see society transformed in one fell swoop. After all, the existing society is in such a sad state that gradual improvements cannot possibly save it. The old must simply make way for the new. One of the most significant problems with utopian social engineering is that it operates in totalities, and whatever deficiencies arise must therefore be chalked up to incompetence or betrayal, since the ideal is beyond reproach.

Yet the truth of the matter is that true utopias or paradises belong to the angels and saints – and we humans are neither of those. People are fallible – they *fail*. And flawed creatures have no place in utopias – or rather, utopias have no place for us. In addition to our fallibility, mankind is characterized by value pluralism, by the fact that we pursue goals that are not only different, but are at times incompatible. The point here is that a wealth of genuine values exist – for example, freedom and equality – that often conflict with each other. And conflicts of values are a part of human life. Indeed, it is important to recognize that these value conflicts not only play out between different groups, but also within the individual himself. In many cases, there will not even be one right answer, but rather a variety of right answers, to the question of which values should be prioritized. Since people will always have different values and ideals, furthermore, every society will contain the same conflicts. Given this fact, the utopian dream can only be actualized through mass oppression, since any utopia requires that all value conflicts cease to exist. Utopia is a society organized around one single ideal of the good life and this ideal is shared by all.

In short, utopias cannot live with fallibility or pluralism. Instead of striving for utopias on earth, we ought to attempt to promote the peaceful co-existence of groups and individuals with various and incompatible ideas of the good life, where it is assumed that a certain moral minimum standard is met. As Popper correctly observes: 'Work for the elimination of concrete evils rather than for the realisation of abstract goods. Do not aim at establishing happiness by political means. Rather aim at the elimination of concrete miseries.'[80] It is crucial to focus on the here and now, rather than sacrificing the present for the sake of some miraculous future to be. Of course, those who advocate for the opposite of utopian social engineering, namely, piecemeal social engineering, can certainly have ideals – can even dream of an ideal world with a rather utopian character – but these people will always be prepared to revise their ideals, to make compromises when they realize that the human costs for implementing their ideals is way too high and so on. Ideals can be advanced in piecemeal on the basis of a variety of societal forms, whereas utopia is the total package and requires imme-diate actualization. The utopian social engineer allows no room for compromise. The goal that lies ahead, a society where humankind can thrive like never before, is so seductive that no price seems too high. As Popper also observes: 'the attempt to make heaven on earth invariably produces hell.'[81]

In *Lady Windermere's Fan*, Oscar Wilde remarks that there are only two tragedies in this world: 'One is not getting what one wants, and the other is getting it. The last is much the worst.'[82] Experience dictates that the phrase 'your wildest dreams have come true' means that some-one somewhere has made an infernal pact. Nowhere has this truth been more accurately proven than in political utopias.

9
Liberal Rights

Liberalism is a theory of political freedom, and the theory existed well before it got its name. When John Locke wrote his *Second Treatise on Civil Government*, it was not because he wanted to found an ideology with the name 'liberalism', because at that point the word did not exist in any language. And though one should be ever wary of basing an argument on etymological considerations, it is relatively clear that 'liberal' and 'liberalism' are primarily associated with freedom.[1] There were no 'liberalists' in Locke's era, or rather, there was no one who would associate themselves with that term. 'Liberalism' comes from 'liberal', which in the fourteenth century was used to denote people who were free, in contrast to those who were not. In the fifteenth century the word's use was broadened to encompass freedom in several senses, including freedom of will, but was particularly associated with having certain prerogatives or privileges. The use of 'liberal' to denote a general political, non-class related viewpoint emerged in the eighteenth and nineteenth centuries. It was also during the 1800s that the idea of 'liberalism' appeared – long after many of the works generally accorded canonic status within the liberal tradition had been written. This is also the point at which a reasonably specific, political context grew up around 'liberal', and it was then used to indicate an ideology.[2] As a result, when we discuss liberal rights and liberalism in the context of earlier thinkers, we use the terms retroactively. What we observe is that the concept of liberal is particularly linked to certain prerogatives, which are transformed into what we recognize as 'rights'. These rights constitute a form of normative absolute that establishes inviolable boundaries that no government, group or individual can trespass. Essentially, these rights define a freedom space, or to use Mill's words: 'a circle around every individual human being' into which no one not authorized by that individual can step.[3]

When it comes to human history, the idea that all people, by virtue of the fact that they are human, possess such a space is the exception rather than the rule. The clearest example of this idea is slavery's broad scope. A typical estimate is that four out of every five advanced agricultural societies have their basis in some form of slavery. A substantial portion of the African population – at least one-third – were slaves even before the gruesome European and American slave trade was introduced. Ancient Greek and Roman economies were founded on slavery. Indeed, when we examine the historical origins of the philosophical discussion surrounding freedom, we find that it stems from the experience of slavery.[4] There was broad philosophical consensus as to slavery's acceptability in ancient Greece.[5] One of the few exceptions to this rule was the Sophist Alkidamas from Elea, who observed: 'God has left all men free; nature has made no man a slave.'[6] Though many people today believe that slavery is essentially a thing of the past, nothing could be farther from the truth – there are more slaves on the earth today than ever before. The relative number was greater in the past, but the absolute number has never been so high. If by 'slave' we mean a person who is forced to work without pay under threat of violence and without the possibility of escape, then right now there are around 27 million slaves in the world.[7] The greatest number of these are found in India and the African countries, but victims of the slave trade exist in our neck of the woods as well. Depending on where you are, the price of a slave varies substantially, but the global average is just under u.s.$100. For a mere $100 you can buy yourself a human being and dispose of him or her as you see fit. Slavery is the absolute contrast of everything we desire in our human life, and it is astonishing that, when it comes to the current political agenda, the problem occupies such a low priority. A slave is paradigmatically unfree because he or she lacks all rights and is utterly subject to another's will.

Rights are indispensable to a free life. One might even say rights are forced upon us, inasmuch as we cannot waive them even if we wish to. An individual cannot choose whether or not to have rights. A person could certainly decide not to avail himself of freedom of expression, but he could not irrevocably renounce the right to freedom of expression for all time. The most extreme example of an individual's waiving of his rights would be a person deciding to sell himself into slavery. Some theoreticians have argued that a person actually does have the right to permanently renounce their right to freedom by selling themselves into slavery,[8] but here I tend to agree with John Stuart Mill, among others, who writes:

> In this and most other civilized countries, for example, an engagement in which a person should sell himself, or allow himself to be sold, as a slave, would be null and void; neither enforced by law nor by opinion . . . The reason for not interfering, unless for the sake of others, with a person's voluntary acts, is consideration for his liberty. His voluntary choice is evidence that what he so chooses is desirable, or at least endurable, to him, and his good is on the whole best provided for by allowing him to take his own means of pursuing it. But by selling himself for a slave, he abdicates his liberty; he foregoes any future use of it, beyond that single act. He therefore defeats, in his own case, the very purpose which is the justification of allowing him to dispose of himself. He is no longer free; but is thenceforth in a position which has no longer the presumption in its favor, that would be afforded by his voluntarily remaining in it. The principle of freedom cannot require that he should be free not to be free. It is not freedom, to be allowed to alienate his freedom.[9]

Exactly *when* the rights idea occurred to man is a matter of some debate. In the broadest sense of the word, it is difficult to imagine any society without certain rules allowing individuals and groups to act in some ways and prohibiting them from carrying out other acts on each other. Without rules of this kind, however rudimentary, 'society' would not exist. In the meantime, that rights concept is so broad that it tells us practically nothing. If we look at when we began to consider 'rights' in an objective sense, we find that the idea occurred in ancient Greek and Rome, where a society could be 'organized around justice' and where an individual could receive a 'right'. This objective understanding of a 'right' nonetheless sharply distinguishes itself from what we today conceive of as rights. For example, in this context, a person could receive his 'right' if he was executed for a crime. A person's right, interpreted to mean something that belongs to that person as a subject and which implies that she has an inviolable space for self-determination, is a much newer phenomenon.

The story of liberal rights used to begin with Locke at the end of the seventeenth century, but there is relatively widespread agreement that we must actually go back to Hobbes and Grotius earlier in the century. Some thinkers will extend that line back to Ockham in the fourteenth century, but that move is more controversial. Obviously, the framing of the Magna Carta (1215) was an important step in the development of the rights idea. However, we would be on fairly safe ground if we argued that it was only the late Middle Ages before the idea that human beings had certain inherent rights really began to emerge.[10]

As Locke saw it, all people are born free and equal, and they have certain rights that are valid irrespective of what positive laws exist in different societies across the globe. Every individual has the right of ownership to – and therefore the right to dispose of – his own life, and the state's most important undertaking is to preserve these rights. By submitting to the law, people enable this protection to occur, and the law does not limit, but instead increases human freedom. The purpose of establishing a law that can be sanctioned by a government authority is to protect what Locke calls 'the natural law', which states that because everyone is born equal and free, no one may cause injury to another's life, health, freedom or property. Here, at the very inception of the liberal tradition, it is already clear how central the idea of rights is. Liberalism's development is inextricably entwined with that of rights; the freedom that liberalism champions is enshrined in a set of rights.

It should be stressed that the rights of which we are speaking must be guaranteed to every individual, irrespective of ethnicity, gender, religion and so on. As such, we can use the expression 'human rights'.[11] These rights, furthermore, should be considered to be inherent, equally possessed by all and valid everywhere. When we use the expression 'liberal rights' instead of the more specific 'human rights', it is because the latter tends to be strongly associated with the specific set of rights embodied in the Universal Declaration of Human Rights (1948) and the European Convention on Human Rights (1950), the UN's International Covenant on Civil and Political Rights (1966) and the UN's International Covenant on Economic, Social and Cultural Rights (1966). Liberal rights partially coincide with human rights, but also differ from them in a number of important ways. In the first place, liberal rights have a narrower scope – they usually focus on a few fundamental rights. In addition, human rights, as they are understood by the above conventions, are binding for states, but not individuals.

Rights in the classical, liberal sense cannot be violated by states alone, but also by individuals and groups, and the protection of individual rights against violation from other individuals and groups is the cornerstone of the state's existence.

In the past, liberal thinkers tended to focus on a small number of rights. As we move forward in history, what perhaps strikes us most is the way in which the terms 'rights' and 'liberalism' grow increasingly broader. That is, increasingly more ideas fall under the category of 'rights' and the scope of what we interpret as 'liberalism' becomes steadily greater. Yet this tendency, which we have seen particularly in the last ten years, can also threaten the status of rights as normative absolutes.

The Scope of Liberal Rights

Liberal rights enjoy a wide acceptance, though paying them verbal homage does not always translate into political practice. There are also critics of the rights idea, particularly within Marxism. Marx attacked the concept of absolute human rights – such as freedom, security, the right to property, the freedom of religion and so on – because they were ostensibly based on an untenable view of humanity and obscured society's real problems. He believed that emphasizing human rights would only bolster man's egoism, and would in reality lead to a greater lack of freedom.[12] True freedom entails the forcible preclusion of property ownership and religious practice. One might say that, according to Marx, man did not have a *right* to freedom, but rather a *duty* to freedom, and that freedom was normatively understood as originating in a particular ideal. The Marxist viewpoint on rights, however, proves an exception to the widespread belief that rights are indispensable. Indeed, the rights idea has proven so appealing to a majority across the political spectrum that the tendency has instead become to baptize an increasing number of interests in the name of rights. Yet a classical, liberal standpoint would regard this development as detrimental.

One can always argue that, as an ideology, liberalism is in constant flux and that the formation of an increasingly comprehensive set of rights is nothing but the evolution of liberalism's social aspects, given that it now encompasses more interests than before. However, this assertion underestimates the extent to which this tendency attacks liberalism at its very core. The point here is that the more rights that shelter under the liberal flag, the more that liberalism ceases to be a theory of the right and instead becomes a theory of the good. Many thinkers, myself included, will therefore argue that one of the most attractive aspects of liberalism as a theory of political freedom is that, in contrast to most other ideologies, it succeeds in upholding a distinction between the good and the right. Therefore the rights increase is problematic.

When it comes to the number of rights with which it makes sense to operate, there is no clear and straightforward answer, and this is partially due to the fact that the issue is tied to the question of what status these rights should occupy. Rights are powerful, normative forces. As Ronald Dworkin has expressed it, to have a right is to have a kind of trump card[13] – that is, the fact that we can engender a good if we do this or that will be trumped if someone has a right that suggests that we should not perform that particular action. When 'everything' is a right, however, that normative force is weakened. If rights are trump cards, in Dworkin's sense, it is reasonable to suppose that we should only operate with a limited number. Indeed, if one significantly increases the number of rights, it seems only logical that they must also receive a lower status. For example, the right to work appears in the Universal Declaration of Human Rights. Article 23 states: 'Everyone has the right to work, to free choice of employment, to just and favourable conditions of work and to protection against unemployment.' Yet it seems obvious that 'right' here is subordinate to, for example, the right to life. Indeed, one can debate whether the 'right to work' is really all that meaningful, but that would lead us too far astray.[14] Suffice it to say, in latter years the tendency to assimilate more ideas under the term 'human rights' has only increased.

On the other hand, nothing in the *concepts* of either rights or liberalism clearly imposes limits on the class of liberal rights. No conceptual analysis will answer the question regarding which rights are fundamental and which should be excluded. Furthermore, it appears clear that the scope of rights will vary according to historical context, for example, as technological innovation poses the problem of the private sphere's exact status. When it comes to liberalism, the number of rights will, in a certain sense, always remain an open question. Nonetheless, from a liberal standpoint one can certainly argue against an extreme increase in the number of rights, in particular because many of these subsequent rights largely differ *in kind* from the liberal rights and, in fact, pose a threat to them.

Classical, liberal rights are *individual* rights, whereas many of those that have been added fall into the category of group rights, that is, rights that are neither individual nor strictly universal. Furthermore, the classical, liberal rights are more negatively than positively oriented, though they cannot strictly be placed within a negative liberty framework. For example, the right to education is a positive right. A number of rights can also be formulated both positively and negatively (like 'the right to nourishment' and 'the right to freedom from hunger'). Nonetheless, it is clear that classical, liberal rights are overwhelmingly negative, since they guarantee a person freedom from certain types of intervention in his or her life, while the increase in rights has particularly tended toward the positive pole, such as the right to work, to leisure time and to various welfare benefits.

Let us first examine group rights. In this context, it should be noted that disagreement persists on whether group rights are at all legitimate. Roughly speaking, there are three different positions on the matter:

1. Group rights exist that cannot be reduced to individual rights.
2. Group rights exist, but they are simply an aggregate of individual rights.
3. Group rights do not exist; all rights are individual.

The most significant distinction here is between the first position and the other two, since (2) and (3) agree that what we actually have is individual rights. However, (2) suggests that in certain cases it is useful to approach rights on a group level, just as long as these rights lead us back to individual rights. One example of (2) might be that citizens in a state can be regarded as a group and, according to Locke, that group has the right to depose one government and appoint another. The classical, liberal viewpoint clearly falls between (2) and (3), whereas (1) has no place here. Within a liberal framework, however, group rights are problematic because they can threaten individual rights, whether those individuals are inside or outside the group. A group might recognize a right and then wield it against individuals within the group to regulate their lives. This idea is especially precarious if the group is so constituted that individuals have not chosen to be a part of it, but belong to it by virtue of their ethnicity or such. Some thinkers have attempted to solve this problem by suggesting that group rights should only be applied externally, that is, to groups and individuals on the outside.[15] However, it is difficult to see how this limitation could be put into practice. Furthermore, there is reason to be concerned over possible conflicts that might arise between group rights and individual rights, even though the individuals are not actually a part of the group. The main purpose of recognizing individual rights is to protect individuals from various forms of force, including those from different groups. If we operate with group rights as well, we could run into a case where group rights trump individual rights, thereby diminishing the individual's protection.

One solution here is that we indeed accept certain group rights, with the caveat that individual rights take absolute priority when it comes to conflicts. After all, liberalism aims to protect legitimate differences. That means that the liberal must accept ways of life that are not his own, among them those that value tradition and community above individualism and autonomous choice. Nonetheless, liberalism also insists that the individual take precedence over the group, because individual rights are inalienable and establish a space for the individual to determine his own life course – though it can certainly be a more collectively and traditionally oriented one.

If we now turn to positive rights, we could say that, from a liberal standpoint, their increase is largely due to a confusion of interests and rights. Society never attains what we can call homeostatic equilibrium – it holds individuals and groups with diverse interests that all attempt to define and control the society in keeping with their various interests. And politics fundamentally concerns itself with negotiating between these interests. Rights, however, cannot be the object of such negotiations, because rights are by their very definition absolute. Yet if every imaginable interest is rebranded a right, the rights idea becomes diluted and the space for political action narrows. Indeed, the situation becomes especially muddled when various rights – those belonging to groups, individuals or a group and an individual – collide. Within a liberal conception of the political, having space for political negotiations is crucial, though it is also important to establish absolute boundaries regarding what can legitimately be an object of such negotiation.

There are many goods that must be viewed as political objectives rather than as rights. In this context, rights serve to limit the measures that are acceptable in our attempts to reach these political objectives. When 'everything' is a right, however, rights are severely hampered in their role as border guards for political exercises of power. Instead, what we have is a myriad of rights in constant collision, which would then require us to resort to various pragmatic solutions. In this case, we might as well give up the rights discussion entirely, and instead start thinking in terms of various interests to be weighed against one another. However, that would be synonymous with abandoning all absolute principles.

There is such an accordance between an idealistic broadening of rights and an unprincipled pragmatism that both tend toward the destruction of the unique status of liberal rights. In addition, the rights increase obscures the important difference between, on the one hand, various interests, which are more or less legitimate, and, on the other, those absolute rights that every society claiming political freedom for its citizens ought to validate.

So What Are the Liberal Rights?

I am in complete agreement with William J. Talbott here, who writes:

> The fundamental idea behind rights is that all adult human beings with normal cognitive, emotional, and behavioral capacities should be guaranteed what is necessary to be able to make their own judgments about what is good for them, to be able to give effect to those judgments in their lives, and to be able to have an effective voice in the determination of the legal framework in which they live their lives.[16]

What this means, in short, is that liberal rights should guarantee the opportunity conditions necessary for human autonomy. Liberal rights protect and enable individual freedom. Therefore the list below contains no 'right to freedom', since every right to be found there is in some way just that.

We could now attempt to explain liberal rights consequentialistically, which means focusing on the fact that they tend to increase well-being, and there is indeed a wealth of empirical data that shows that a society that respects these rights, and whose citizens accordingly enjoy political freedom to a greater extent, will also have higher measures of material well-being. The risk with this strategy is that we can also take a society, such as modern-day China, which has seen a substantial increase in well-being without also respecting liberal rights. As such, a consequentialist account will be burdened with a weighty contingency.

Another strategy, which is the most common, is simply to argue that beings with autonomous capacity must also have the opportunity to develop and practice that autonomy, and this is possible only to the extent that the liberal rights are guaranteed. This is the particular strategy that I have chosen.

The rights listed below are meant to apply to every autonomous person who has reached legal majority. In saying this, I do not mean to imply that people who are either not of age or fully autonomous should lack rights, but that they will, to a certain extent, have other rights. For example, a small child, by definition, is not entitled to the right to freedom from paternalistic intervention, nor should they have voting rights, but they will presumably have stronger welfare rights than adults.[17] Other rights will be common to both groups, such as the right to bodily integrity. However, I will not address children's rights here, nor will I take up animal rights, which must correspond to only a small extent with liberal rights or human rights.[18]

1. The right to security. This mainly encompasses the right not to suffer harm at the hands of another, and accordingly not to be murdered, abused, raped, tortured, etc. Furthermore, it is the right to avoid being imprisoned or chained (when not legally sanctioned) and to avoid being forced to do something against one's will through physical or psychological coercion. In addition, it is the right to avoid any threat of the above.

2. The right to be recognized as a subject of rights, to be equal in the eyes of the law and to be protected by the law, as well as not to suffer arbitrary imprisonment, arrest or expatriation.

3. The right to privacy and informational privacy.

4. The right to freedom of expression, which includes freedom of the press.

5. The right to freedom of ideas and freedom of religion.

6. The right to own property and to be protected from arbitrary seizure (or wilful destruction) of the same.

7. The right to democratic participation, to participate in a nation's government either directly or through elected representatives.

8. The right to freedom of organization and freedom of assembly.

9. The right to education and to the opportunity to develop one's cognitive and emotional abilities. This right must be defined according to a minimum standard, since there is no 'ceiling' as to how much education and development a particular individual might desire.

10. The right to adequate nutrition, shelter and health. This right must obviously be defined according to a minimum standard, preferably in keeping with the capability approach, since there is no 'ceiling' on these benefits. The right to adequate nutrition cannot be interpreted as the right to goose liver and champagne and the right to shelter is not the right to a palatial residence. Additionally, the right to health cannot at all be interpreted as a right to meet the World Health Organization's (WHO) health definition: 'Health is a state of complete physical, mental and social well-being and not merely the absence of disease or infirmity'.[19] The fact of the matter is, this definition *cannot* be realized, and so a *sufficient* level must instead be established. This right also has environmental implications, because widespread pollution, etc. will represent a health threat.

11. The right to individually determine what gives life meaning and value, and to translate that viewpoint into practice without being hampered by paternalistic interference.

All these rights are individual and designed to promote autonomy. They do not clearly fall within Isaiah Berlin's definition of negative or positive liberty. With the exception of 11, almost identical or related rights can be found in the 'Universal Declaration of Human Rights' (1948), though the latter contains a number of rights not included on my list, because I believe they either directly follow from the rights I have listed (like the right not to be a slave, which follows from number 1) or would be good candidates for a supplemental list that would vary from state to state (like the right to work, to paid holidays or the right to enjoy art). Number 11 on my list is the most unusual addition.[20] Its importance, however, cannot be understated, because it is key to living out an autonomous life.

This list, of course, is not meant to be exhaustive. It does not include all the rights that should be accepted and protected by a given society, and it ought also to be supplemented with a number of other rights. However, what rights these are will vary from society to society and will depend upon that society's traditions and developmental *niveau*. In short, the eleven rights on the list should be considered universal, while the supplemental rights will vary. As such, the list establishes an absolute minimum that must respected in *every* society. It also places limits on which rights should be considered critical, since the supplemental rights must give way if they come into conflict with the fundamental, liberal rights. Obvious candidates for an expanded list would be, for example, the right not to be discriminated against with respect to gender, ethnicity, religion, sexual orientation and so on, as well as the right to a safe workplace.

In the next chapters, I shall not address all of the fundamental, liberal rights in detail, and will instead examine those rights that in recent times have come under particular pressure in liberal democracies: the right to informational privacy, to freedom of expression and to not be the object of paternalistic interference.

10

Paternalism

Intervention aimed at ensuring that an individual acts in accordance with what others have determined to be that individual's enlightened self-interest is called paternalism. Paternalism comes in many different forms. What they all have is common is that a person's right to selfdetermination is overridden in the belief that the person is not capable of acting in his or her best interests. The main problem with paternalism is that it denies an essential human characteristic: our innate ability to take control of and shape our own lives, whether for good or ill. For paternalists, judgement and self-control are faculties we should be spared from exercising. Paternalists will even claim that it is only in the presence of such limitations that we can attain true, positive freedom, because only then is the individual liberated to conform to the paternalist's idea for what an individual should be. After introducing the traditional forms of paternalism, I will concentrate, for the most part, on the idea of so-called 'libertarian paternalism', which has achieved broad political support in the last few years.

Liberal thinkers have always been rigorously anti-paternalistic. This is clearly formulated by Kant, for example, who writes:

> A government might be established on the principle of benevolence toward the people, like that of a father towards his children. Under such a *paternal government* (*imperium paternale*), the subjects, as immature children who cannot distinguish what is truly useful or harmful to themselves, would be obliged to behave purely passively and to rely upon the judgement of the head of state as to how they *ought* to be happy, and upon his kindness in willing their happiness at all.

Such a government is the greatest conceivable *despotism*, i.e. a constitution which suspends the entire freedom of its subjects, who thenceforth have no rights whatsoever.[1]

With this thought in mind, Isaiah Berlin observes that paternalism 'is to treat men as if they were not free, but human material for me, the benevolent reformer, to mould in accordance with my own, not their, freely adopted purpose'. This approach is despotic, because 'it is an insult to my conception of myself as a human being, determined to make my own life in accordance with my own (not necessarily rational or benevolent) purposes, and, above all, entitled to be recognized as such by others.'[2]

Along these same lines, John Stuart Mill also argues: 'The only freedom which deserves the name is that of pursuing our own good in our own way, so long as we do not attempt to deprive others of theirs or impede their efforts to obtain it. Each is the proper guardian of his own health, whether bodily *or* mental and spiritual.'[3] Mill formulates three main arguments against paternalism: (1) The individual is best situated to evaluate what is to his own best advantage, and total happiness in society will be maximized if the individual is allowed to act according to his own evaluations – a utilitarian argument. (2) All coercion is an insult to human dignity – a rights-based argument. (3) Being able to make choices, both good and bad, is prerequisite to the development of individuality – a virtue ethical argument with an individualistic twist. As we will see, behavioural economics has given us good reason to call (1) into question, while (2) and (3) have remained consistently persuasive.

Forms of Paternalism

There are many different kinds of paternalism, many of which can be organized into opposing pairs.[4] Let us briefly examine the most important:

Hard and soft paternalism: soft paternalism is usually understood to mean that one is justified in preventing someone from carrying out involuntary actions that one considers dangerous for them or to hinder them temporarily while determining whether the given action is voluntary.[5] Voluntariness here is usually interpreted using Aristotle's two criteria: the action must be controlled by the agent and the agent must have sufficient knowledge of what he or she is about. According to the soft paternalist, an agent must be allowed to carry out an action if the criteria for both knowledge and control are met. John Stuart Mill provides a famous example of this type of paternalism: if a person wants to cross a bridge that looks dangerous, another person has the right to stop him because it is uncertain whether or not he intended to put himself in danger.[6] If, after being made aware of the danger, the first person still wishes to cross the bridge, he must be allowed to do so unhindered. In contrast, hard paternalism does not pause to consider whether an action is voluntary or not, but exclusively focuses on whether or not a given intervention will further a person's well-being, happiness, interests, values and so on. If the agent chooses a sub-optimal action alternative, the hard paternalist would consider intervention a legitimate way to secure the best results for the agent.

Weak and strong paternalism: a weak paternalist believes that intervention becomes legitimate when it enables an agent to choose means that are adequate to their ends. If a person believes personal security is more valuable than a sense of freedom, it is proper to intervene if the individual chooses not to wear a bicycle helmet. On the other hand, if a person instead values a sense of freedom, the weak paternalist would let him ride without a helmet. That is to say that the weak paternalist focuses exclusively on the *means* an agent uses to meet their goals, though it is completely left to the agent to determine what those goals might be. A strong paternalist, however, believes that a person can have the wrong goals in life or that they might prioritize less important goals over more important ones, and that it is therefore legitimate to prevent them from carrying out actions designed to realize their mistaken goals. For example, a strong paternalist recognizes that both personal security and a sense of freedom are important values, but believes that personal security is clearly the more significant. Therefore it is legitimate to force people to use bicycle helmets. While the weak paternalist only wants to govern the means to a given end, the strong paternalist believes that both the end and the means must be governed. Weak paternalism is desire-neutral, while strong paternalism is desire-oriented.

Broad and narrow paternalism: the broad paternalist is concerned with all sources of paternalistic intervention, whether these stem from public authorities, religious communities, other individuals or the like. The narrow paternalist is exclusively focused on intervention from public authorities.

Social paternalism: this is a less common term that, in a sense, focuses on 'social' as opposed to 'state-driven' factors. That is to say that this kind of paternalism stems from an individual's social environment

– for example, from family members or a religious community – rather than from public authorities. In this context, social paternalism indicates the non-state-driven aspects of broad paternalism. Some people, however, will interpret 'social paternalism' to mean that a person's right to self-determination must be overridden for the sake of people other than the individual himself.[7] In my opinion, that is nothing but a category error, since by definition paternalistic intervention must be justified with respect to the individual. If intervention is justified with respect to others' well-being, we are no long talking about paternalism, but just your everyday coercion. (At the same time, it is clear that paternalistic intervention can certainly be motivated out of a concern for both the individual and for others, but it is the focus on the individual that determines whether or not paternalism is involved.)

Libertarian Paternalism

Richard Thaler and Cass Sunstein's theory of libertarian paternalism has been the object of extensive debate in the last few years. The theory was first presented in the articles 'Libertarian Paternalism' (2003) and 'Libertarian Paternalism Is Not an Oxymoron' (2003), and was introduced to a wider audience through the book *Nudge* (2008).[8] The libertarian paternalist wants to shove or nudge people in a certain – welfare-maximizing – direction without depriving them of the option to select other alternatives. As such, the theory seems to satisfy the social-democratic impetus for centralization and the liberal desire to safeguard people's freedom of choice. In what follows, I will attempt to show that, in many ways, this brand of libertarian paternalism is unattractive, and my critique of this variant will touch upon stronger varieties of paternalism as well.

Given the liberal opposition to paternalism, 'libertarian paternalism' sounds like an oxymoron. As the title of Sunstein and Thaler's article indicates, however, they insist that this is not the case. Instead, they believe that they have developed a form of paternalism that will be acceptable to liberalists and libertarians alike.[9] As they write: 'We elaborate a form of paternalism, libertarian in spirit, that should be acceptable to those who are firmly committed to freedom of choice on grounds of either autonomy or welfare.'[10] In this discussion, I will focus more on their theoretical assumptions than on the concrete, paternalistic measures they suggest. However, I will first briefly examine some of libertarian paternalism's behavioural economic premises.

Much of today's behavioural economic research is based on the findings of psychologists Daniel Kahneman and Amos Tversky. In the beginning, Kahneman and Tversky did not place any undo emphasis on economic considerations in their studies. However, it quickly became clear that their results were quite significant to the field of economics. I will not detail this research here, except to remark that, as it turns out, our decisions are not so rational as we might like to believe.[11] These findings pose a contrast to classical economics, which holds that agents act rationally with respect to their desires, as long as agents possess the relevant information needed for decisions. Now, not many classical economists would argue that people really *are* that way. Instead, the idea is a methodological simplification, much in the same way that a physicist might operate with a ball rolling along a friction-free surface in a vacuum – even though these conditions do not exist in the real world. What behavioural economics uncovered, however, does not merely depart from the idealizations present in the classical economic model, such as one might find in an actual physics experiment involving a ball rolling along a smooth surface, but instead found that agents do not at all reason and act as one originally supposed in classical economics. Over time, a significant amount of literature has emerged to document that fact.[12] Among other things, behavioural economics has shown that minor and often irrelevant factors influence the individual's preference of one action alternative over another. For example, the fact that it takes two minutes to fill out a form can be enough of a disincentive that an individual will opt out of something that seemingly would yield great benefits. In this context, Thaler and Sunstein suggest that having good default rules can neutralize and overcome such disincentives and lead to better overall choices. They also point out that people often avoid the trouble of evaluating complex subjects with too many alternatives, and that 'a thoughtfully chosen default rule, steering them in sensible directions, is a blessing.'[13]

As Sunstein and Thaler also write: 'The presumption that individual choices should be respected is usually based on the claim that people do an excellent job of making choices, or at least that they do a far better job than third parties could possibly do.'[14] Here we find a substantial weakness in their argument, since it presumes that enemies of paternalism have, generally speaking, based their opposition on the assumption that human beings are *Homo oeconomicus*. That same weakness affects Daniel Kahneman, who in his most recent book, *Thinking, Fast and Slow*, advocates for Thaler and Sunstein's libertarian paternalism.[15] Kahneman then proceeds to attack the apparent 'libertarian' conception that human beings are rational agents (in the narrow sense of *Homo oeconomicus*) – agents who, due to their presumptive rationality, do not need protection from their own choices. Yet Kahneman's reasoning here lacks precision. There are certainly a number of libertarians who put their faith in *Homo oeconomicus* and champion the thought that people always know what is best for themselves, but there are also important thinkers who, though often categorized as 'libertarians', explicitly reject this understanding of mankind. In fact, if we turn to the central theorists of classical liberalism, we find that most of them do not base themselves on *Homo oeconomicus* at all. This is true, for example, of Kant, Humboldt and Mill. And anyone who thinks that Adam Smith identifies man with *Homo oeconomicus* has simply failed to read what he has to say.

Friedrich Hayek clearly makes this point in his classic essay, 'Individualism: True and False', where he suggests that man is a 'very irrational and fallible being' and that 'individual errors are corrected only in the course of a social process'.[16] The fact that Smith is at all associated with an anthropology based on *Homo oeconomicus* is, furthermore, due a widespread misconception:

> Perhaps the best illustration of the current misconceptions of the individualism of Adam Smith and his group is the common belief that they have invented the bogey of the 'economic man' and that their conclusions are vitiated by their assumption of a strictly rational behavior or generally by a false rationalistic psychology. They were, of course, very far from assuming anything of the kind. It would be nearer the truth to say that in their view man was by nature lazy and indolent, improvident and wasteful, and that it was only by the force of circumstances that he could be made to behave economically or carefully to adjust his means to his ends.[17]

In keeping with this observation, one can perhaps say that behavioural economics does not actually represent a *new* synthesis, but rather picks up where earlier economics left off, at a time when there was not such a sharp distinction between economics and psychology. Indeed, it is not unreasonable to call Adam Smith a behavioural economist, since he developed his economic theories with man's psychological virtues and vices always in the back of his mind – something that becomes quite obvious if one reads *The Wealth of Nations* and *The Theory of Moral Sentiments* in context of each other – and he accordingly anticipates later behavioural economic insights on any number of points.[18]

The rejection of *Homo oeconomicus* is not only a feature of the older liberal tradition, however, but also of much of the newer. Hayek himself is a clear example of this:

> Another misleading phrase, used to stress an important point, is the famous presumption that each man knows his interests best. In this form the contention is neither plausible or necessary for the individualist's conclusions. The true basis of his argument is that nobody can know *who* knows best and that the only way by which we can found out is through a social process in which everybody is allowed to try and see what he can do.[19]

The liberal tradition has always been anti-paternalistic *despite the fact* that we humans do not always know exactly what our best interests are, and only very seldom does the claim turn up that in reality we must be considered 'rational agents'. As Hayek remarks in *Constitution of Liberty*, most political theories assume that people are actually quite ignorant. As he also points out, those who argue for real freedom 'differ from the rest in that they include among the ignorant themselves as well as the wisest'.[20] Therefore the basic premise is not that the individual knows best, but rather that *no one* knows best.

Another weakness in Thaler and Sunstein's argument for libertarian paternalism is that, on a practical level, it does not take into account liberal theorists. A notable exception, which can be found in a footnote to 'Libertarian Paternalism Is Not an Oxymoron', is worth examining in this context:

> Some of the standard arguments against paternalism rest not on consequences but on autonomy – on a belief that people are entitled to make their own choices even if they err. Thus John Stuart Mill, *On Liberty* . . . is a mix of autonomy-based and consequentialist claims. Our principal concern here is with welfare and consequences, though . . . freedom of choice is sometimes an ingredient in welfare. We do not disagree with the view that autonomy has claims of its own, but we believe that it would be fanatical, in the settings that we discuss, to

treat autonomy, in the form of freedom of choice, as a kind of
trump, not to be overridden on consequentialist grounds.[21]

Sunstein and Thaler's argument against anti-paternalism here is
skewed, because it refutes an assumption that is not actually fundamental to anti-paternalism. In point of fact, it is the autonomy conception and not *Homo oeconomicus* that essentially forms the basis
for anti-paternalistic thought. By privileging welfare maximization
and assigning autonomy a secondary role at best, Sunstein and
Thaler actually depart from most of what the liberal tradition has
to say and certainly from the tenets that libertarianism holds central.
Furthermore, they provide no argument as to why consequences must
trump autonomy, other than stating that it is 'fanatical' to suggest
otherwise.

Thaler and Sunstein also believe there to be a standard, defined by
'choice architects', to which every individual must conform in order to
be regarded as rational. Of course, people can still behave 'irrationally'
if they choose – but the standard itself is set by a system of experts.
And now we come to it. Sunstein and Thaler, as it turns out, have
quite a bit in common with Frazier, the founder of Walden Two in B.
F. Skinner's novel of the same name. Frazier assumes that, given a
functional knowledge of human behaviour and, furthermore, knowing the true recipe for the good life, it would be irrational not to use
that knowledge to everyone's best advantage. Frazier thinks he has the
monopoly on what is in every individual's interests, and thereby feels
justified in using behavioural techniques to force people to realize his
particular vision of the good life. The same is true of Thaler and
Sunstein. They, too, believe that they hold the good life norm, and they
will use behavioural techniques to force people to realize that life in
keeping with this norm. Obviously they advocate for a much less radical form of intervention than does Frazier, but they also underscore
how powerful the choice architect's tools are. If anyone were to suggest
that the norm Thaler and Sunstein want to establish is dead wrong,
and would prefer a different kind of life, Thaler and Sunstein would
simply say that they are mistaken. They would not 'force' anyone to
live according to their norm, but would simply 'influence' or 'nudge'
them in that direction.

At this point, we come to what is perhaps the most curious aspect
of Thaler and Sunstein's libertarian paternalism, given the behavioural
economic premises upon which it is based: they do not for a single

moment question their own use of *Homo oeconomicus* as a positive norm for all agents, and instead claim that, though agents make inferior choices, they would change them 'if they had complete information, unlimited cognitive abilities, and no lack of willpower'.[22] In particular, *Nudge* follows a consistent pattern: first describing the irrationality of ordinary people's choices and then examining what a rational agent would have done instead, only to conclude by showing that, with one relatively easy intervention, agents can be guided toward more rational results. By 'rational results' here, Sunstein and Thaler mean results that maximize the individual agent's welfare. In other words, the point of libertarian paternalism is to encourage people to do what *Homo oeconomicus* would have done. And although Sunstein and Thaler follow behavioural economics in its rejection of *Homo oeconomicus* as a reliable model of actual human conduct, libertarian paternalism nonetheless embraces *Homo oeconomicus* as its rational norm.

The privileging of agent welfare, however, is also rather arbitrary. Given Thaler and Sunstein's standard for rationality, for example, it would be irrational of me to act on moral grounds if that action did not maximize my well-being. Yet Amartya Sen has pointed out that this viewpoint on rationality is untenable.[23] The fact is that people consistently choose alternatives that they know will not personally benefit them because they think it to be morally right in a given situation. For instance, agents deliberately uphold obligations to family, friends, organizations and so on, even if the welfare cost is greater than simply ignoring that obligation. A person who never behaved in that way could hardly be described as anything but a psychopath.

People have values that cannot be neatly reduced to personal welfare concerns. Let us imagine that Paul has a serious disorder that will result in a painful death if left untreated. Paul's doctor tells him that there are two possible treatments, X and Y. While there is a 90 per cent chance that X will cure him, Y only has a 50 per cent chance. At this point, X seems like a much more rational alternative than Y. However, there might be other reasons for Paul to choose Y over X – reasons that do not touch upon Paul's own well-being. Perhaps there are economic considerations. X might be so expensive that, if Paul were to choose X, he might cause his family to lose everything and end up on the street. In this case, Y is the logical alternative. By choosing it, Paul elects to take a greater health risk in order to reduce his family's economic risk. Then again, Paul's concerns might be exclusively moral. Perhaps he has spent his whole adult life fighting for animal rights and therefore cannot accept *X*, because production of that medicine is tied to extensive animal suffering, while *Y* entails nothing of this kind. If Paul accepts a greater health risk because he does not want to abandon his moral principles, the choice is a rational one and he must be allowed to make it.

The absolute privileging of individual welfare as a normative ideal is nothing less than an economistic prejudice that Thaler and Sunstein do not call into question. This is one of the most fundamental problems with Thaler and Sunstein's libertarian paternalism. As a result, their theory is not necessarily any more palatable, from a liberal standpoint, than various other forms of paternalism.

Libertarian Paternalism Is Still Paternalism

Libertarian paternalism is a wide-ranging concept, since it throws the door wide open to paternalistic intervention from every conceivable source, both governmental and non-governmental. However, Sunstein and Thaler's work places the most emphasis on the benefits to be had from governmental regulation. In essence, libertarian paternalism seems more related to the soft and weak forms of paternalism than the hard and strong forms. As they write:

> The libertarian aspect of our strategies lies in the straightforward insistence that, in general, people should be free to do what they like – and to opt out of undesirable arrangements if they want to do so . . . We strive to design policies that maintain or increase freedom of choice. When we use the term *libertarian* to modify the word *paternalism*, we simply mean libertypreserving.[24]

Voluntariness is a prerequisite here, and a person's choice must be respected even if, in the paternalist's eye, it is not in the person's best interest. It should be simple to opt out of the paternalist's standard solution, and ideally one could do it with 'a click'.[25]

At the same time, Thaler and Sunstein insist that there is no reliable or acceptable alternative to paternalism; therefore we should focus on the pragmatic question of which form of paternalism is preferable rather than the moral question of whether paternalism is inherently good or evil. Accordingly, they consider a comprehensive anti-paternalism to be pointless. After all, their argument runs, every situation that involves choice will have a standard rule that influences agents in one direction or another, and this means that paternalism is unavoidable. In contexts where people make choices, furthermore, opting for a non-intervention policy is synonymous with accepting the status quo with all its attendant biases, and so non-intervention is a paternalistic choice along the same lines of intervening in people's decision-making contexts.[26] And yet such a broadly stated definition of paternalism encompasses every single choice that influences another person's decision, whether one wishes to influence them in a way they consider to be positive or negative for the agent – and indeed, every single choice that happens to influence other agents, even when one is utterly indifferent to the agents' welfare. To put it mildly, that is an unconventional take on paternalism, seeing as the term is usually reserved for actions that are specifically designed to override another agent's choices when one believes that these choices are not in the agent's own best interests. According to the usual interpretation, paternalism is in no way inevitable – something Thaler and Sunstein can hardly claim, since they define 'paternalism' so broadly that they actually break with normal language usage.

In the meantime, they have also given paternalism a narrower meaning, in the sense that one deliberately sets out to influence an agent's choices in a way the agent himself would interpret as *positive*.[27] That viewpoint is also rather unconventional, since it includes all helpful behaviour whatsoever. Suffice it to say, this also contrasts with normal language usage, which once again understands 'paternalism' to mean cases of intervention where an agent's choices are overridden because one believes that agent is not acting in his own best interests. The libertarian paternalist, on the other hand, takes the stage as a 'choice architect' whose mission is to maximize the individual person's welfare. And yet 'choice architecture' is so loosely defined that it includes every single action that happens to alter people's circumstances in such a way that it somehow or other affects their decisions. For example, a café proprietor who puts fruit in front of desserts in a display case so that people will buy more fruit is a choice architect. Indeed, Thaler and Sunstein also characterize the designers of Apple's iPod and iPhone as outstanding choice architects.[28] Or for that matter: if, after painting a handrail, I set up a sign that says, 'WET PAINT', then I, too, am a choice architect. Indeed, not only am I a 'choice architect', but I am actually a 'paternalist', since I am attempting to steer people clear of wet paint. On the other hand, normal language usage would not deem that action paternalistic, but would consider it helpful. If we turn to the other end of the scale and look for an intervention that would fall under the category of libertarian paternalism, we could imagine a default rule calling for all people to be implanted with a radio transmitter such that they could be located at all times – the justification being that this would help locate lost or missing individuals – but where individuals could also elect not to have the implant or to have it removed. That would fit Thaler and Sunstein's paternalism concept, and would also satisfy its *libertarian* component, since individuals could always opt out of the default rule. However, that intervention clearly exceeds the bounds of what any liberal society would willingly entertain. Ultimately, Thaler and Sunstein's understanding of 'paternalism' is so broad – encompassing anything from a wet paint warning sign to our hypothetical implant example – that it obscures rather than clarifies important distinctions.

Preference Neutrality

According to Thaler and Sunstein,

> Libertarian paternalism is a relatively weak, soft, and non-intrusive type of paternalism because choices are not blocked, fenced off, or significantly burdened. If people want to smoke cigarettes, eat a lot of candy, to choose an unsuitable health care plan, or to fail to save for retirement, libertarian paternalists will not force them to do otherwise – or even make things hard for them. Still, the approach we recommend does count as paternalistic, because private and public choice architects are not merely trying to track or to implement people's anticipated choices. Rather, they are self-consciously attempting to move people in directions that will make their lives better. They nudge.[29]

In contrast to what Thaler and Sunstein claim, liberal paternalism should not be immediately associated with soft paternalism. A truly soft paternalistic approach would content itself with establishing the extent to which an action is voluntary or not, and if it is voluntary, the rest is up to the agent – a presumptively irrational choice would be respected just as much as a rational one. Thaler and Sunstein's libertarian paternalism, however, seeks to go further and to promote rational choices and prevent irrational ones. They assume that agents, by and large, act in ways that are contrary to what they really want or should really want. For example, most people want a financially secure retirement, but they do not save enough during their working years to meet that goal; and they want to be thin, but instead consume one calorie bomb after the next. One can, however, always question whether an agent is doing what he or she 'really' wants. For example, the weakness of will phenomenon has been the object of extensive philosophical debate from antiquity up to the present day – and we are no closer, in my opinion, to devising a convincing explanation for the phenomenon than Aristotle was. Often it is extremely difficult to establish what an agent 'really' wants. For example, an agent is not necessarily acting contrary to his 'real' desires when he *does* something other than what he *says* he is going to do. Even though an overweight person claims to want to lose weight, he is not necessarily acting contrary to desire by eating french fries or foie gras. It is entirely probable that the actual inclination to consume french fries or foie gras is stronger than the desire to lose weight. The problem of pinpointing exactly what a person's 'real' preferences are will prove a challenge to any type of paternalism that sets out to maximize these desires. Nonetheless, Sunstein and Thaler believe intervention is called for in order to assure that agents act in keeping with their 'real' preferences, something that, as we shall see, puts them on a level with the hard paternalist. The major difference between their brand and hard paternalism is that Thaler and Sunstein argue that paternalistic intervention should never – or only to the smallest possible extent – take on a coercive character: agents should always be able to select a different alternative to what the paternalist considers optimal.

There is an ambiguity in the expression 'real' when we talk about an agent's 'real preferences', because it can mean both (1) an agent's actual preferences and (2) the welfare-maximizing preferences an agent ought to have. This ambiguity is also present throughout Thaler and Sunstein's thought. However, it is important to distinguish between the two ideas as clearly as possible, because they correspond to two different types of paternalism: weak and strong. Weak paternalism is preference-neutral, while strong paternalism is preference-charged. A weak paternalist does not take into account his own preferences or those of a third party, but exclusively focuses on maximizing the actual preferences an agent has. In contrast, the hard paternalist tries to maximize the preferences an agent *ought* to have – according to what health experts consider optimal, for example – whether or not those particular preferences actually belong to the agent. Weak, preference-neutral paternalism gives agents complete freedom to pursue their own life goals, whereas hard, preference-charged paternalism uses existing standards to establish goals for the agent.

One example of the difference between the two paternalism types concerns the risks of smoking. A weak paternalist might consider it up to public authorities to appropriately educate the populace, though in as objective a way as possible, on the real dangers of smoking, because one assumes that everyone wishes to make an informed decision about whether or not to take those risks. On the other hand, if one institutes a monopoly on tobacco in order to decrease its accessibility and thereby use – since, after all, that is what is best for the smoker's health – then one has entered the realm of hard paternalism. The same is true if public health authorities decide to manipulate people by exaggerating the risks of smoking, because in that case an agent's ability to make a free and informed decision is impaired. And the same is presumably true of price hikes designed to decrease the use of tobacco products for the sake of people's health. However, it is also clear that those same fees can be used to cover the various negative externalities caused by smoking, for example, the increased use of health services, but such cases are entirely removed from the paternalism problematic. As John Stuart Mill observes:

> To tax stimulants for the sole purpose of making them more difficult to be obtained, is a measure differing only in degree from their entire prohibition; and would be justifiable only if that were justifiable. Every increase of cost is a prohibition, to those whose means do not come up to the augmented price; and to those who do, it is a penalty laid on them for gratifying a particular taste. Their choice of pleasures, and their mode of expending their income, after satisfying their legal and moral obligations to the State and to individuals, are their own concern, and must rest with their own judgment.[30]

Mill does not argue that it is illegitimate to tax drugs. Instead, he suggests that taxing drugs more highly than other commodities, which have more the character of necessities, can be fully legitimate since it will provide the state with additional revenue. However, he insists that imposing taxes to change an individual's behaviour for his own sake, that is, on paternalistic grounds, is illegitimate. Meanwhile, Thaler and Sunstein are of another opinion, and they claim, for example, that a smoker would be benefited by higher taxes on tobacco, since that would provide an incentive not to smoke.[31]

Unfortunately, Thaler and Sunstein do not adequately distinguish between preference-neutral and preference-charged paternalism, but instead vacillate back and forth between them. This is significant, because it is only the preference-neutral variety that would be acceptable to liberalism's mainstream.[32] Still, what grounds do we have to argue that Thaler and Sunstein's libertarian paternalism is not also preference-neutral? Their stated goal is to influence agent choice for the sake of a better result; a result, moreover, that should be evaluated as objectively as possible. The purpose, after all, is to maximize agent welfare, something which must be distinguished from the agent's actual desires.[33] They argue, furthermore, that the libertarian paternalist will not attempt to anticipate an agent's actual preferences, but will instead 'move people in directions that will promote their welfare'.[34] Of course, their argument is worded in such a way that it does sometimes give the impression that the agent's actual preferences are what ought to be maximized, such as when they state that choice architects should influence an agent's decisions so that the agent himself will believe he is getting a better result.[35] They also maintain that choice architects will 'influence people's behavior in order to make their lives longer, healthier, and better'.[36] More precisely, choice architects are consequentialists whose focus is on welfare maximization. It is at this point, however, that we find a misconception concerning the relationship between objective knowledge and desire-neutrality. Supposedly, the choice architect will base himself on experts who offer presumptively objective knowledge on a given subject. In this way, those who are, in reality, desire-oriented – since desires are external with respect to the agent – can create the appearance of being desire-neutral. And it is precisely because Thaler and Sunstein attempt to establish an objective method to evaluate welfare that they depart from preference-neutrality, since a preference-neutral approach bases itself exclusively on an agent's subjective desires. The problem, moreover, is that the individual agent might not necessarily think that maximizing his or her welfare is the most important item on the agenda. An agent, for example, can be a proponent of absolute equality of outcome, and that means ensuring that everyone receives exactly the same amount of welfare, rather than one individual trying to secure the highest amount possible for himself. Another agent might believe that the most important goal is to maximize personal freedom. A third might believe that it is crucial to ensure that certain moral standards are met. The point here is that the premise that an individual agent's welfare ought to be maximized is not without controversy.[37] In the end, Sunstein and Thaler repeatedly demonstrate their strong adherence to a conception of *Homo oeconomicus*, simply taking it as a given that we are all primarily out to maximize our own individual self-interests. However, that is not the case – our motivations are far more complex than that.

Another problem with Thaler and Sunstein's 'default rules' is that they are based on one ideal standard of welfare, whereas people themselves are different. Furthermore, what exactly this welfare standard implies continues to remain essentially vague. 'Welfare' is a problematic concept that says different things to different people. In this context, it would, perhaps, be tempting to turn to so-called 'happiness studies'. Perhaps happiness – or more precisely, subjective well-being – is the standard we ought to adopt here. If we examine some of the more typical results that happiness studies turn up, for example, we find that more money leads to a slight happiness increase, though in rich countries this amount is not overwhelming. In fact, too much focus on material goods acts as a depressant. You should apparently have friends and either be married or live together, though children seem to reduce happiness. Most people report being happier at work than any other place, and people who work more report being happier than people who work less. Women score higher than men. Age plays an important role: on average people are happiest when they are 27 years old, and thereafter the happiness level decreases until it hits rock bottom around 69 years old, before it again increases by a tiny amount. You should live in a country with a substantial amount of individual freedom. Activism-minded individuals who are engaged with various issues and work hard to make the world a better place do not score any higher than people who couldn't care less. In general, being educated or well-read does not affect the happiness index. So, if we want to adopt subjective well-being as our standard, we do have some cues about the directions in which people can be nudged. There is not much we can do about age and gender, but, for example, we can encourage people to work more and get married. Many people would agree with that kind of nudging. Yet what about prompting people to remain childless? Or nudging people to abstain from reading and education, since these pursuits do not register on the happiness index? Ostensibly, people should be doing something else with their time, something that actually counts towards happiness. Nudging people in these directions, however, would hardly win us any broad support. On the other hand, they follow from an approach that exclusively bases itself on subjective well-being. Yet the different characteristics that statistically achieve the highest score in subjective well-being evaluations do not necessarily result in what some – or perhaps most – people would consider to be the optimal lifestyle. We could imagine a life that would top the charts in every conceivable way, at least where subjective well-being was concerned – and still it would not necessarily be a life we would want to lead. Furthermore, it should be emphasized that happiness studies can only tell us what makes the average person feel content, but the average person is also a pure construct. The average person may well find that having a life partner increases their subjective well-being more than a large sum of money, but for some people the exact opposite is true. It is up to you to determine the category that best suits you – no happiness researcher can tell you that. As a result, we can presumably discard happiness studies as an authoritative source for establishing the ideal welfare standard that Thaler and Sunstein posit, but do not really specify.

What about taking more objective criteria than subjective agent well-being, such as health, life-expectancy, economic security and so on? The problem here again is not everybody interprets welfare values in exactly the same way. One person might consider good health to be the most important value. Another might prefer habits that are unhealthy in the long run. Some parents will want their children to eat as healthily as possible, while others will want their children to eat what they like. Even the pro-apple, anti-cake standpoint cannot be termed preference-neutral. In this context, the libertarian paternalist ought to keep in mind John Stuart Mill's important observation:

> The practical principle which guides them to their opinions on the regulation of human conduct, is the feeling in each person's mind that everybody should be required to act as he, and those with whom he sympathises, would like them to act. No one, indeed, acknowledges to himself that his standard of judgment is his own liking; but an opinion on a point of

conduct, not supported by reasons, can only count as one person's preference; and if the reasons, when given, are a mere appeal to a similar preference felt by other people, it is still only many people's liking instead of one.[38]

More recent liberalism tends to be value-pluralistic. It recognizes that we humans pursue goals that are not only different, but are often incompatible. And that is not just true of the relationship between different people and groups, since value conflicts also take place within the individual himself. That is, the individual is often torn between many genuine values – like welfare, freedom and equality – that cannot necessarily be maximized all at once and whose innate significance cannot be measured according to any presumptively neutral scale. However, when it comes to value pluralism, Thaler and Sunstein do not even broach the topic, but resort to a dogmatic value monism that is solely welfare-based. Value pluralism is only compatible with preference-neutral, not preference-charged paternalism.

Thaler and Sunstein, on the other hand, do underscore that people's preferences are often unclear, and of course they are correct, but it is still not obvious how this idea would support a preference-oriented rather than a preference-charged paternalism.

Practical Problems

At this point, one can object that the distinction between preference-neutral and preference-charged paternalism is of little consequence to the *libertarian* paternalist, because the individual always has the option to select an alternative other than what the paternalist deems optimal. The problem with this objection is that the libertarian paternalist has powerful measures at his disposal that he can use to control agent actions, something Thaler and Sunstein often stress.[39] Indeed, they underscore that an agent's desires can deliberately be altered without the agent himself being aware that coercion has been applied. What is that if not a form of manipulatory paternalism? Thaler and Sunstein do anticipate this objection, and champion John Rawls's public principle, which they interpret to mean that authorities should not institute policies that they are either not capable or not willing to publicly justify.[40] Presumably that would exclude outright lying. And yet there is nothing wrong with launching a severely manipulative anti-drug campaign, according to Thaler and Sunstein.[41] What, then, is to prevent us from carrying out equally manipulative campaigns against smoking and unhealthy food options? Campaigns like these slip through Thaler and Sunstein's not particularly tight net, just as long as the authorities are willing to justify them publicly, by saying, for example, that although these campaigns might be exaggerated, smoking poses such a serious health risk that fighting it requires extreme measures. As a result, people's desire for the reliable information that would allow them to make autonomous choices is superseded by the libertarian paternalist's emphasis on welfare-maximizing consequences.

In order for libertarian paternalism to function according to plan, furthermore, choice architects must either be experts themselves or must base themselves on experts who are not substantially influenced by the irrational factors that figure prominently in behavioural psychological studies. This stipulation is problematic, to say the least, as Sunstein and Thaler's own examples readily demonstrate: if you are told that a certain surgery has a 90 per cent survival rate, you are more likely to choose that operation than if you are told there is a 10 per cent mortality rate. The problem is, you find the same tendency among *medical doctors*, that is, among those experts who supposedly know better than the 'average' person.[42]

Choice architects will very likely suffer from many of these same cognitive defects. Looking at behavioural economics, one could also draw the exact opposite conclusion: that having insight into human 'irrationality' renders paternalistic intervention even less attractive than it was before. Given that irrationality applies to both paternalists and agents, one can argue that the individual agent will have stronger incentives to correct those mistakes that affect his or her desire fulfilment than an external paternalist would, and therefore that it is more likely that the agent would better succeed at preference maximization.[43]

Thaler and Sunstein stress how significant selecting one default rule over another can be in terms of the influence it can have on people's behaviour. As such, they come close to admitting that there is a *public choice* problem.[44] Choice architects, who are only human, after all, can often be suspected of designing default rules to promote their own interests instead of those belonging to the agents who are supposedly the objects of the paternalistic intervention.

Concluding Remarks

If Thaler and Sunstein end up giving the impression that their brand of libertarian paternalism is a model that nearly everyone, regardless of ideological standpoint, can accept, it is because they have either avoided or smoothed over most of the ideological debate. When one takes a closer look at their theory, however, it quickly becomes clear that the old, ideological problems surface anew.

One problem with the construction 'libertarian paternalism' is that 'paternalism' in particular – though 'libertarian' as well – is used in such a nebulous and imprecise way that there are no real limits as to what the category might contain. Much of what they describe as 'paternalism' should rather be termed 'helpful'. And since the umbrella term 'paternalism' is applied so broadly that it obscures distinctions between utterly harmless and potentially extreme interventions.

Libertarian paternalism certainly has its problems. Thaler and Sunstein, however, argue that these problems pose no serious draw-backs, because the default rules that influence people's behaviour will be there in any case, whether those rules are deliberately put into place or established somewhat arbitrarily. Since default rules of some kind are unavoidable, libertarian paternalism, they maintain, is preferable to other alternatives. It preserves an agent's freedom of choice, after all, and seeks to maximize his welfare.

It is difficult to disagree with Thaler and Sunstein when they argue that we should use our knowledge of human behaviour to help us develop solutions that will benefit people. Still, that is a far cry from manipulating people into leading the kind of life the paternalist deems best, rather than one the agent would choose for himself. Libertarian paternalism, or course, is more attractive than most other forms of paternalism – assuming that one takes a liberal viewpoint – but, in essence, no paternalism, or at the very least a preference-neutral paternalism, would be most preferable.

Because Thaler and Sunstein base their theory on such an extreme ideal for rational agents, namely *Homo oeconomicus,* who has 'complete information, unlimited cognitive abilities, and no lack of willpower',[45] we all fall short. At the same time, any well-meaning politician, bureaucrat and so on has an almost unlimited playing field for intervening in nearly every aspect of our lives. Libertarian paternalism is an ideology of beneficence that would control the population using an extensive network apparatus, where people to an ever-increasing extent would be organized under an administration made up of various expert systems.

Even though the term 'libertarian paternalism' clearly did not exist in Alexis de Tocqueville's day, he warned against the very political approach that libertarian paternalism represents:

> Over these men stands an immense tutelary power, which assumes sole responsibility for securing their pleasure and watching over their fate. It is absolute, meticulous, regular, provident, and mild. It would resemble paternal authority if only its purpose were the same, namely, to prepare men for manhood. But on the contrary, it seeks only to keep them in childhood irrevocably. It likes citizens to rejoice, provided they think only of rejoicing. It works willingly for their happiness but wants to be the sole agent and only arbiter of that happiness. It provides for their security, foresees and takes care of their needs, facilitates their pleasures, manages their most important affairs, directs their industry, regulates their successions, and divides their inheritances. Why not relieve them entirely of the trouble of thinking and the difficulty of living?
>
> Every day it thus makes man's use of his free will rarer and more futile. It circumscribes the action of the will more narrowly, and little by little robs each citizen of the use of his own faculties. Equality paved the way for all these things by preparing men to put up with them and even to look upon them as a boon.
>
> The sovereign, after taking individuals one by one in his powerful hands and kneading them to his liking, reaches out to embrace society as a whole. Over it he spreads a fine mesh of uniform, minute, and complex rules, through which not even the most original minds and most vigorous souls can poke their heads above the crowd. He does not break men's wills but softens, bends, and guides them. He seldom forces anyone to act but consistently opposes action. He does not destroy things but prevents them from coming into being. Rather than tyrannize, he inhibits, represses, saps, stifles, and stultifies, and in the end he reduces each nation to nothing but a flock of timid and industrious animals, with the government as its shepherd.[46]

II

Informational Privacy

The potential abuse of information is often used as an argument for the protection of informational privacy. This consideration is certainly relevant to the discussion, but there is another argument for informational privacy that is more deeply rooted in mankind's existential condition. Even if we could say, for argument's sake, that our information would never be abused, limits should still be set on the information that can be retrieved and the ways it can be used that are in keeping with the consequences it has for the forming of relationships to others and to ourselves.[1] Therefore the argument involving information's potential misuse ought to be supplemented with arguments drawn from the private sphere's significance to the building of relationships to others and, most notably, to the development of personality.

Every declaration of human rights would be incomplete without an article that included protecting the right to privacy and to informational privacy, simply because these are prerequisites for an individual's being able to realize a good and free life. Having a sphere of one's *own* is not a luxury, but a necessity. As Friedrich Hayek writes: 'Freedom thus presupposes that the individual has some assured private sphere, that there is some set of circumstances in his environment with which others cannot interfere.'[2] A private sphere shielded from intervention is a requirement for negative freedom and for the development of personal autonomy,[3] and autonomy entails that a person exercise a certain amount of control over his surroundings. A portion of this control is secured by laws that guarantee personal freedom of action, which means that each individual has a space where his own decisions prevail. However, freedom also requires more than non-intervention, more than the individual not being forced to act against his will – it also requires a space for self-formation that completely lacks 'soft' power's surveillant gaze.

'Privacy' and 'informational privacy' are not analytically well-defined terms. If we look for some definition that contains the necessary and sufficient conditions for these concepts, we will, in all likelihood, come up empty-handed or end up with a definition that encompasses too many or includes too few aspects.[4] Instead, it would be more useful to begin with a few paradigmatic cases and evaluate the extent to which other cases exhibit relevant similarities.[5]

Informational privacy is specifically connected to a person's ability to control the information related to them, whereas the right to privacy also includes a number of non-informational aspects. There will always be some data that very few people would consider private or especially sensitive, but that nonetheless should be included under the terms of informational privacy. This is because modern technology has made it possible to store an immense quantity of information. And whereas some individual pieces of information might seem completely harmless, when taken together these pieces can reveal a surprising amount about a person – just as a dot on a canvas seems meaningless when taken alone, but forms a naturalistic image when combined with other dots. Information that is unproblematic in one context can be problematic in others, since a change of context can give it entirely new meanings. And there is no real limit to how much data can be gathered about a person, how long it can be stored or how subtly it can be analysed.

When beginning a discussion concerning the limits to personal and informational privacy, one complicating factor is that these limits are historically variable. As habits, traditions, social structures, technology and other resources change, the concept of privacy varies as well. The meaning of 'privacy' alters with time and place, and it appears that every culture has its own viewpoint on the subject.[6] In philosophy, the debate concerning the relationship between the private and the public has been raging since antiquity, but it would take us too far off course to pursue the matter here.

One important factor driving these changes in recent times has been technological development. That was already a major concern for Warren and Brandeis, who in their classic article from 1890 emphasized the extent to which photography and the press had invaded the private sphere, as well as how a number of other technological innovations threatened to make it possible to broadcast to all corners of the earth anything a person might utter within a small private context.[7] Of course, technological development has exploded since Warren and Brandeis's time. We should not blame innovation itself, however, for undermining informational privacy, since we are the ones responsible for limiting it. A given technology can be used in different ways to different purposes – or we can refrain from using it at all.

Social norms are also in constant flux. In particular, the boundaries between the private and the public spheres have shifted as more of what was once strictly private is introduced into the public forum. Indeed, for many people *not* being observed is an even more terrifying scenario than being kept under total surveillance. The boundaries that do exist here are defined, among other things, by our *expectations* of which spaces should be free from surveillance. These expectations, however, can change according to the actual amount of surveillance present. If we begin to expect that more aspects of our lives will be monitored because, in fact, they are *being* monitored, then the boundaries around privacy and informational privacy will continue to contract. In short, if we establish limits based on what we would be willing to accept, then a total surveillance society could in principle be legitimized. However, the fact that a given amount of surveillance is acceptable to the majority does not adequately justify permitting that exact amount. This is a significant distinction between an absolute democracy and a liberal democracy, since the latter imposes limits on what the majority can decide.

An important argument for imposing limits on what data the state has a right to collect and/or compile is that this information can be abused and can also be used to undermine democracy itself. One could object here, of course, that in most Western countries democracy is under no real threat and that the governments of these countries would not misappropriate information in order to sniff out critics and dissenters. Even if that is true of the situation today, however, rules must be established and boundaries must be set in case of worse times to come. Traditionally, the state has been regarded as the foremost threat to informational privacy, since up until now it has primarily been government agencies that have had the necessary resources to carry out extensive surveillance programmes. Undoubtedly that threat is still present, but technological developments have also opened the door to countless other agents here. The potential for non-governmental agencies and other individuals to abuse information must also be taken into account when establishing such limits. This rationale is *instrumental* in nature, since it seeks to curb information access on the grounds that abuses of information could result in other evils. The question, however, is whether this rationale really gets to the root of things. Cannot the loss of privacy and informational privacy be considered an evil *in and of itself*, even if we assume that our information would not be subject to such misappropriation?

It is a matter of some controversy whether or not the right to privacy can be considered fundamental or derived and whether it concerns one right or a handful or rights. In an influential article, Judith Jarvis Thompson has argued that the right to privacy is not itself a fundamental right, but rather a handful of rights all related to the right to dispose of one's own property and person.[8] According to Thompson, it is our right to ensure that no one can view something we own – for example, a photo album – unless we have opened it up to the public. Furthermore, we have the right not to be an object of observation or eavesdropping, as long as we have not facilitated the situation, for example, by standing and talking next to an open window. Thompson claims that what we term the right to privacy *is* nothing more than the right to one's property, including one's own person. Therefore she believes that the right to privacy is a superfluous concept, since it carries no additional explanatory or justificatory power.

In order to refute Thompson's argument, all we must do is to provide a counterexample that exhibits a violation of the right to privacy and not the right to property. Let us imagine that Paul has stolen an MP3 player that is full of illegally downloaded material, which means that Paul's property rights do not extend either to the player or to its content. Many people would nonetheless think that it was a violation of Paul's right to privacy if John took the player without Paul's permission to see what Paul had been downloading. In that case, Thompson would conceivably respond that, by definition, there has been no violation of the right to privacy if there has not also been a violation of the right to property. It is difficult to see how the discussion could progress from here.

The relationship between property rights and privacy rights has also proven central to many important court decisions. Since no private person can claim ownership of public space, a defence of privacy based on the right to property seems to imply that one's right to privacy cannot be violated in public space. In the famous case *Katz vs. United States* (1967), which concerned the extent to which a telephone booth could be tapped without a warrant, Supreme Court Justice Potter Stewart stated that the Fourth Amendment 'protects people, not places' and that what a person 'seeks to preserve as private even in an area accessible to the public, may be constitutionally protected'.[9] Supreme Court Justice John Harlan concurred, and argued that only two requirements must be met: 'first that a person have exhibited an actual (subjective) expectation of privacy; and second, that the expectation be one that society is prepared to recognize as "reasonable"'. This justification makes the right to privacy a separate issue from the right to property, though the question remains as to *why* the right to privacy is so important to us.

James Rachels argues that all the interests assembled under the privacy concept have intrinsic value.[10] This value, according to Rachels, is rooted in the close link between the ability to control who has access to us – and this includes access to information about us – and our ability to create and develop different social relationships with others. Privacy enables us to distance ourselves from some people in order to form closer bonds with others. Forming relationships, moreover, entails choosing when to reveal different sides of ourselves and allowing others to approach us in various ways. However, if every single thing there was to know about us was potentially out there for all to see, the difference between a lover, a friend and a stranger would disappear. After all, we manifest in different ways to family members, friends, colleagues, public officials and so on. And some things we just want to keep to ourselves. Other things we are willing to share with family and friends in a sphere where we can express ourselves without pretence. And then there will be those things that we intend to share with a broader public. Everyone will have different ideas concerning where to draw the line between the private and the public, and it must be mainly left to the individual to decide what to share and with whom. A massive surveillance society, however, robs us of the opportunity to control these things on an individual basis.

The objection can still be raised, however, that Rachels's analysis does not go far enough, because perhaps the most fundamental relationship we will ever form is to ourselves. Privacy helps promote the idea that we all have an individual personality. It creates a space where the individual can reflect, express himself and relax – a space in which to develop that personality. The private sphere is a place where we can do what we want without fearing the reactions of those to whom we have not granted access. However, it is not just a matter of avoiding other people's potentially critical gaze, but also of having a space where we can avoid other people's eyes altogether, and where we can also abstain from self-observation. For it is when we are conscious of being watched that we tend to watch ourselves. And certain aspects of our lives depend upon us being left to our own devices. The point here is not that people must have something to hide, but rather that each person requires a personal zone where he has no need to question whether there is anything that needs to be hidden.

Erving Goffman defines the self as a set of roles that each individual plays out in different situations before an audience consisting of one's fellow man.[11] The self is then constituted as the individual assumes, develops and performs these roles before others. Therefore the self is not intrinsic and given, but instead materializes in social situations before onlookers. All such self-presentations also take place within the framework of social conventions, which the individual – for the most part – attempts to uphold. As a result, Goffman's self is constantly on the alert to make sure it is playing its roles correctly, and this watchfulness extends down to the smallest bodily detail. A typical critique of Goffman's theory is that the self then vanishes into social contexts, becoming an empty shell, a self without depth that is simply devoted to playing whatever role is strategically advantageous to a particular situation – and that perspective on humanity is entirely too reductive. To a certain extent, I do agree with this critique of Goffman, but I also believe he has several important points to make. As social creatures, we do in fact play roles for each other and we also watch ourselves to make sure that we are playing our roles correctly and that we are conforming to social norms as we do so. As T. S. Eliot puts it in *The Love Song of J. Alfred Prufrock* (1915), you 'prepare a face to meet the faces that you meet'.[12] Before we go out into public, we modify our appearance, change our clothes and so on. We don a face that we shed when we come home again. That does not mean that we are being false, but simply that we reveal different aspects of ourselves to different people, and this requires perpetual self-reflexivity on our part. However, we also need a space that frees us from playing these roles, where we do not need to monitor ourselves because we ourselves are not being monitored by others.

Surveillance is a part of the modern world in which we live. In Chaplin's film *Modern Times*, the cameras placed throughout the factory, including in the restrooms, which enable the factory director to keep an eye on his employees at all times, are symptomatic of this fact. The point is not for him to actually see what each and every employee is doing at all times, but rather to remind the workers that someone *can* watch them, so that they will adjust their behaviour accordingly. It is an idea Chaplin took from Jeremy Bentham, who designed a prison he called the Panopticon, where a guard could observe the prisoners without the prisoners ever knowing it. The idea was that the prisoners would thereby be encouraged to conduct themselves according to the warden's wishes, because they would never know when they were going unobserved. Bentham described this concept as 'a new mode of obtaining power of mind over mind, in a quantity hitherto without example'.[13] And he was right. When we know that other people are watching us – or that there is a good possibility that it is the case – our relationship to ourselves change: we begin to monitor our own behaviour.

Although the prisoners and workers in the above examples had no desire for this kind of surveillance, today we are surprisingly willing to submit to it. In this sense, our submission becomes a kind of voluntary enslavement. For it is indeed a form of enslavement, since we thereby give up a significant portion of our freedom. A characteristic of living a free life is having spontaneity, a lack of caution and calculation – or a kind of self-naturalness, if you will. Having to constantly assess our actions, even in the most banal respects, restricts our space for freedom of action in general. When we monitor ourselves because we think we are being monitored, we lose our very spontaneity – our casual unrestraint. That is exactly why informational privacy is so important to the protection of individual freedom.

We all know the experience of suddenly discovering that we are being watched, after being certain we were unobserved. It sends a shock wave through you, even if you were doing nothing wrong, because suddenly your conduct must be fit to be seen. The consciousness of being observed prompts us to observe ourselves in order to assure that everything is as we want it to be; our relationship to ourselves is thereby externalized. The point here is simple: if everything you do can potentially be observed and documented, you will be forced to take constant care. Without a sphere free of others' insight and interference, freedom and individuality cannot be created and maintained. A person who is constantly the object of public scrutiny, and who is also conscious of this fact, will lose much of their individuality and will largely become a creature of social convention. Of course, it cannot be denied that such social disciplining has its positive aspects, since we could not coexist without it, but it can also become an all too encroaching entity. Nonetheless, we humans are social beings who develop our personality through our relationships to others. It is only against this social backdrop that privacy has any meaning. One leaves the private sphere and one returns to it. It is a phenomenon that belongs in a social context.

One idea central to the liberal tradition is that freedom means having the opportunity to realize the good life in one's *own* style. That requires privacy, because privacy creates a sphere where this sense of *ownness* can be developed. The etymology of the word 'private', which comes from the Latin adjective *privus*, supports this idea. Originally, the term was used in the sense of singular or unique, but later pertained to something special or one's own. Warren and Brandeis seized upon this idea as well when they described the right to privacy as 'the right to one's personality'.

Torbjörn Tännsjö, however, rejects the idea that people in a society have a right to privacy, as well as the concept that limits should be imposed on the kinds of surveillance to which people can be subjected.[14] His reasoning here is that the overall benefits of having complete transparency in people's lives are so great that this becomes the only morally correct option. He also defends the idea of making all personal information, such as medical and financial records, freely available on the Internet. Furthermore, people's genetic codes should be registered. Tännsjö's utopia is, therefore, a complete surveillance society, and he believes that this utopia is already well on its way to realization, since today people are already subjected to extensive surveillance from all sides. However, he also insists that transparency in people's lives be met with equal transparency on the part of those in power. For example, the military, police and intelligence agencies should only be allowed to keep information confidential for a maximum of five years. There is, however, no compelling grounds for reciprocity here. One can be an ardent supporter of government transparency, for example, without believing that authorities should have equal insight into people's lives. And the fact that people today are subjected to such extensive surveillance is no argument that this monitoring should be extended even further. What Tännsjö calls 'the open society' is, in reality, the exact opposite of Karl Popper's idea when he coined the phrase. Popper knew that personal freedom requires that the individual have a certain amount of control over his surroundings, and this includes being able to control the flow of his personal information. Ultimately, Tännsjö's reflections regarding his open society seem neither philosophically sound nor politically convincing.

A typical argument from those who wish to see surveillance extended and, accordingly, informational privacy weakened is: 'If you have nothing to hide, you have nothing to fear.' This argument assumes that whatever you have to hide is in some way immoral or illegal. And this is the argument's weakness, since it in no way follows that the right to privacy in general and to informational privacy in particular is based on a desire to hide anything *wrong*.[15] That conclusion is based on a false dichotomy: either you have done something wrong and, accordingly, should be exposed or you have done nothing wrong and, as such, exposure would be harmless. As with other false dichotomies, there is at least one missing element here. In this case, it is simply the fact that you can still be harmed by personal exposure, even if you have done nothing wrong. We all have something to hide. What we have to hide may not be illegal or immoral, but it is usually something that we consider to be somehow so intimate that we do not want other people knowing about it. And though it may be something we find embarrassing or unpleasant, that is still no reason to view it as *wrong*. For example, a German survey from 2008 found that half of those asked would not use a telephone to contact a psychologist, marriage counsellor or drug counsellor because of the EU's Data Retention Directive.[16]

You can still have something to fear, even if you have done nothing wrong. Any reduction in informational privacy brings with it a reduction in personal freedom, but not necessarily in a way that is immediately obvious. It imposes no evident physical restraints on your ability to act, and you are apparently as free as you were before. Only apparently, however, because now you begin to censor what you say and do.

In totalitarian societies, of course, people live in fear of state authorities, whereas in modern welfare states the state is considered to be a source of security. To enable the state to carry out its mission as effectively as possible, citizens are willing to grant it access to large swathes of the private sphere that, according to the liberal tradition, are well outside the state's domain. After all, the modern welfare state cannot exist without having an enormous amount of information about its citizens ready to hand, and one could assume that the more the state knows about its citizens, the more efficiently it can carry out its tasks. It lies in the nature of the state to desire the greatest expansion possible – both from good and not so good intentions.

There is an expectation here that the state could continue to deliver more services more effectively, if only it had access to more information. Therefore the need for general privacy and informational privacy conflicts with the need for security and efficiency. With more information at their disposal, the police will presumably have an easier time tracking down suspects, tax authorities will better be able to ferret out fraud, health authorities can better orchestrate and improve patient treatment and so on. In a world where law enforcement officials know exactly where everyone is at all times, murderers, rapists and thieves could be easily identified. And yet there is also a real tendency to overestimate the usefulness that wholesale surveillance can have when it comes to, for example, fighting crime. London is one of the most camera-monitored cities – or perhaps the most camera-monitored city – on earth, but these cameras are only estimated to have helped solve about 3 per cent of London's street robberies.[17] And even if that rate was 30 or 50 per cent, that is still no reason to believe that society would be served by such massive surveillance. Nonetheless, representatives for the British police have argued that these cameras should be outfitted with microphones, so that, in addition to seeing them, one can hear what people are saying.[18] As it turns out, cameras with microphones have already been employed in the Netherlands. If microphones are adopted in Great Britain, one will presumably impose the same restrictions on them as in the Netherlands: namely, that they cannot be used to eavesdrop on private conversations out on the street, but solely to prevent crimes and apprehend criminals. And yet, how does one know that a conversation is private unless one eavesdrops . . .?

The demand for freedom – which includes general privacy and informational privacy – will always be met with counterarguments that centre on security and benefit. Today's ideological climate is such that the principal arguments for liberal rights seem to come up short in light of a whole series of pragmatic measures designed to solve apparently pressing problems – and where there is no time for adequate reflection on how these measures might alter the society in which we live. Perhaps the clearest expression for this kind of unprincipled pragmatism is Tony Blair's famous declaration that the threat of global terrorism means that traditional civil liberties arguments are not so much wrong as made for another age.[19] In making this statement, Blair went straight to the heart of the problem, even more so than he himself was aware. Do we really live in an era where liberal rights can no longer claim absolute validity? For my part, I do not believe that to be the case, nor do I see that the problems confronting us today hold those implications. Indeed, it is clear that if we were to give up these rights, the world would look very different from how it has been until now – and the change would not be for the better. As mentioned, privacy concepts vary with time and place. What is at stake now is privacy's *liberal* interpretation, which has been a corner-stone of our social understanding for centuries, even though it has also come under pressure in past times of crisis. To abandon this sense of privacy, which includes informational privacy, is to begin existence anew in a completely different kind of society. As Isaiah Berlin writes:

> The desire not to be impinged upon, to be left to oneself, has been a mark of high civilization on the part of both individ-uals and communities. The sense of privacy itself, of the area of personal relationships as something sacred in its own right, derives from a conception of freedom which, for all its reli-gious roots, is scarcely older, in its developed state, than the Renaissance or the Reformation. Yet its decline would mark the death of a civilization, of an entire moral outlook.[20]

12

Freedom of Expression

L iberal democracy is based on critique; on the fact that all people have the right to express their opinion about the direction in which their society is headed and about what things they consider unacceptable. Liberal democracies never reach absolute equilibrium: they contain individuals and groups with varying interests who all seek to shape and control the society with respect to those interests. Functional public arenas must exist where these disagreements can play out in a nonviolent manner, and that is only possible on the basis of freedom of expression. A culture of critique demands tolerance. The tolerance concept, however, has undergone a transformation in recent times and it now threatens to undermine freedom of expression rather than promote it.

The idea behind freedom of expression is simply that one should be able to express oneself publicly. Yet every rational discussion of freedom of expression will concede that it has its limits. There has never been – and probably never will be – a society with absolute freedom in this regard. At the same time, every rational discussion of expressive freedom in our time will also deem its existence crucial, since it is a cornerstone of liberal democracy. Accordingly, anyone who wants to do away with expressive freedom will also seek to abolish liberal democracy, and that viewpoint is so marginal that we do not need to include it in the following discussion. Our focus will be on *which limits* freedom of expression should have.

Whenever expressive freedom is addressed, emphasis is usually placed on the role that government sanctions can and should play. There are, however, other threats to freedom of expression. For example, John Stuart Mill stresses social sanctions, which can cause people not to express an opinion for fear of the reaction from others in the society. When a solid social consensus has been reached on a given topic, the personal cost of promoting an alternate viewpoint can be severe. Another threat is pressure from non-governmental organizations, where an individual, for example, can face loss of economic support if he expresses an opinion contrary to that of the organization. Nonetheless, in this chapter I will largely limit myself to *government sanctions* that are vested by law, and evaluate these according to Mill's so-called harm principle.

Justifications for Freedom of Expression

When it comes to the history of expressive freedom, one could begin by turning to Socrates' Apology in 399 BC or the Magna Carta in AD 1215. Or, for that matter, the pluralism and tolerance that characterized Muslim culture in the 700s and 800s. However, it is also rather anachronistic to try and impose a modern rights issue onto earlier cultures. The principle underlying expressive freedom belongs to a more modern context: the time period following the Protestant Reformation and all the religious and political conflicts it unleashed. The first really meaningful treatise on freedom of expression was written by John Milton, who in 1644 published *Areopagitica*. This tract was a reaction to the British parliament's attempt to halt publication of any content they deemed undesirable for whatever reason. In answer, Milton composed a number of arguments for expressive freedom. Among the most important was the simple observation that we can only discover the truth by considering the wealth of different viewpoints out there, and that no individual alone is wise enough to proclaim the truth for everybody else. A multitude of opinions is necessary for reason to develop as it should, namely, to seek out the truth. Milton, therefore, wrote that 'he who destroys a good book, kills reason itself.'[1] Since reason inherently seeks out truth, this argument endows freedom of expression with instrumental worth.

We can draw a rough distinction between consequentialist and deontological arguments for freedom of expression. A consequentialist holds that no action 'in itself' is good or evil, moral or immoral. The extent to which an action is good depends entirely upon its consequences. Accordingly, no action is inherently evil, and every action can be termed 'good' as long as the consequences are better than the alternative. With such a broad formulation, 'better consequences' can apply to just about anything, but the idea is usually specified to mean happiness, well-being and the like. In this sense, the argument holds that the consequences of protecting expressive freedom are better than the alternative. For consequentialists, furthermore, the value of freedom of expression is purely instrumental, defined in light of achieving certain goals. One consequentialist argument, for example, is that freedom of expression is a necessary condition for a functioning democracy. People must have the ability to express, read, hear, agree with and oppose a variety of perspectives – including those they find unacceptable. Without freedom of expression, *participatory* democracy is impossible. Of course, we could always have a pseudo-democracy where citizens were allowed to vote, but without the freedom to formulate and express opinions, it would hardly be a true democracy, since it would lack the very *process* that is at democracy's core. The drawback to the consequentalist argument, however, is that as soon as someone comes along and demonstrates that better consequences can be had by rescinding freedom of expression in individual cases or on a general basis, the defence for this freedom fails.

Deontological arguments, on the other hand, will typically maintain that people have a *right* to freedom of expression, and that we have a duty to respect that right regardless of any consequences. Often these arguments will base themselves on people's autonomy. Rights are weighty, normative entities. As mentioned earlier, they are a kind of trump card,[2] and that means that they outweigh any potential good that might result by acting to oppose to them. The drawback to these deontological arguments is that it can appear counterintuitive to dismiss consequences, no matter how terrible, as utterly irrelevant.

An intermediate position, which can be termed *weak consequentialism*, argues that rights should typically take absolute precedence, but concedes that sometimes there are consequences that might outweigh them. An idea fundamental to liberal democracy is that all citizens are equal and that *everyone* has the right to express their opinion about what society is and should be, and that also includes opponents of liberal democracy. We can also imagine situations, however, that demand a departure from this principle: for example, if an expression poses a substantial and imminent threat to the liberal democracy's continued existence.[3] In general, a weak consequentialist will hold that freedom of expression should be absolute in a political context, but will at the same time be open to the possibility that a consideration of consequences *can* overtrump that right if the reasons are especially compelling. Of course, the weak consequentialist will not have a clearly defined framework for *how* serious those consequences must be in order to outweigh all other considerations. In my opinion, we should be talking about a *specific* and imminent threat to the state's or to an individual's security. A similar idea was clearly expressed in the u.s. Supreme Court's decision in *Brandenburg v. Ohio* (1969), which upheld freedom of expression as inviolable except in those cases where a given expression 'is directed to inciting or producing imminent lawless action and is likely to incite or produce such action'.[4] According to this principle, the state cannot take 'precautionary' measures and censure expressions that in the long run might be considered harmful; it must be *likely* that the expression can directly incite 'lawless' actions and the threat must be *imminent*. One can also imagine, however, that a weak consequentialist would believe that expressions that would *eventually* present a similar threat should not be protected by expressive freedom.

However, it is often the case that arguments for freedom of expression do not clearly fall under either a consequentialist or a deontological approach, but instead consist of an amalgamation of the two. For example, one will often argue that democracy cannot exist without universal freedom of expression, thereby making it a *means* to the end of democratic development, while at the same time insisting that everyone has a *right* to freedom of expression, even if it can be used, for instance, to oppose democracy itself.

Mill's Freedom of Expression Defence

One of the most famous apologies for freedom of expression was given by John Stuart Mill in *On Liberty* (1859). Officially, Mill's liberalism, including his defence for freedom of expression, is consequentialistic-ally based, but it is reasonable to regard his perspective as a mixed bag of utilitarian and deontological elements – with a decided virtue-ethical slant. Still, it is Mill's freedom concept, not his utility principle, that is the true cornerstone of his political philosophy. In *On Liberty*, Mill argues that people must have the greatest possible freedom to air and discuss every idea, no matter how immoral it might appear.[5] We should have absolute freedom to express ourselves on any topic, whether it be scientific, moral or theological.[6] And it does not matter whether an opinion belongs to the many or the few: 'If all mankind minus one were of one opinion, and only one person were of the con-trary opinion, mankind would be no more justified in silencing that one person than he, if he had the power, would be justified in silencing mankind.'[7]

For, as Mill observes, we can never be entirely certain that the viewpoint we are trying to stifle is actually false.[8] In the second place, even opinions that are basically wrong can yet hold a kernel of truth. Indeed, even completely wrong ideas can be useful, since they prevent true ideas from stagnating and becoming dogmatic.[9] Mill's thought here is basically fallibilistic: all knowledge is error-prone. We can never be certain that what we believe to be true *is* actually true.[10] As such, critical evaluation is necessary to ensure that our ideas are rational, and that requires measuring them against other ideas. And even if our particular viewpoint happens to be the clear victor in the confrontation, still we cannot relax, because the possibility always exists that we are mistaken.

As a result, Mill can directly give the impression that he does not believe freedom of expression should have any limits. That is not the case. He does believe that freedom of expression has its limits, and like the restrictions on other freedoms, they are set according to his so-called *harm principle*: 'The only purpose for which power can be rightfully exercised over any member of a civilized community, against his will, is to prevent harm to others.'[11] Mill's formulation of what is probably his most familiar principle is not especially clear, because it does not specify what is meant by 'harm'. If we interpret 'harm' broadly, there are hardly any bounds to what could be considered injurious to another person. For example, I could stop you from badmouthing a piece of music so dear to me that it pains me to hear anything negative said about it. Obviously, such an absurd viewpoint is not what Mill had in mind. The principle does not encompass all forms of harm. Although what exactly Mill includes in his harm principle is a matter of some debate, the idea is commonly interpreted to imply that an injury must somehow encroach on someone else's rights.[12]

In many cases, it is obvious that a particular expression is harmful because it represents a rights violation, such as when a lawyer or a doctor breaks confidentiality. Often a concern for informational privacy imposes clear boundaries on freedom of expression. However, there are plenty of other cases where the matter is not so clear, because any potential rights violation depends upon the context into which a given expression falls. That is to say, an expression that is unproblematic in one context can be punishable in another. Mill's own example is that it should be considered legal to publish something in the newspaper about a corn dealer who lets the poor starve, but that it is punishable to say the same thing to a raging mob gathered outside the corn dealer's house.[13] In praxis, it becomes a matter of judgement. As with his example, however, Mill explicitly states that every expression can lose its 'immunity' when circumstances are such that a given expression constitutes a positive inducement to harmful action. Furthermore, it is clear that Mill's freedom of expression concept does not include anything that amounts to criminal deception or extortion of others.

Ultimately, Mill's harm principle suggests that there should be an extensive framework for freedom of expression, and some would call this 'freedom of expression fundamentalism', since this freedom takes precedence over so many of the other values that we also prize within the structure of a liberal democracy. The harm principle, furthermore, rests upon the belief that freedom, including freedom of expression, is the lifeblood of the liberal democracy, and therefore cannot be dismissed for the sake of other beneficial objectives.

The Logic of Critique and Violation

Democratic development takes place through the process of debate and critique. However, being an object of critique can be quite an unpleasant experience. It can feel like an injury or a violation, perhaps (or particularly) in those cases when a person feels that the critique is apt. 'Critique' has its etymological origins in the Greek verb *krinein*, which means to separate, organize, distinguish, decide, judge, investigate and so on. Critique is not just the laying out of arguments, but is rather a practice designed to separate what is tenable from what is untenable. Critique is often *negative*, focusing exclusively on the untenable side of the equation as it attempts to identify errors and deficiencies in people, groups, institutions, ideas, expressions and practices.

To strongly criticize another, however, is not contrary to the thought that all men are equal, but is inextricably linked to it. If I refrain from criticizing a person or a group for what I consider to be a serious mistake, simply because I believe that the individual(s) in question are unable to take the critique, then I am not treating them as equals. There is no real objective criterion, furthermore, that can tell us when a critical expression qualifies as injurious. As such, it can be tempting to resort to a purely subjective criterion, which means that if someone *feels* violated, they *are* violated. Such a criterion is obviously out of the question, because there is hardly a critical remark that cannot be interpreted as injurious in some way or other. For example, if I say that 'Marx's theory of surplus value is unsustainable', someone who strongly identifies with Marx's ideas might feel themselves injured, though of course I have not overstepped any bounds. Let us now take some more strongly worded examples: 'Manchester United is a shit club', 'Jazz is crappy music' or 'Right-wing extremists are brain-dead.' These statements are guaranteed to offend football fans, jazz enthusiasts and right-wing extremists. The question then becomes whether it is right to say that a violation has occurred; and if, after reasonable evaluation, the expression can be termed injurious, whether that fact should have any bearing on its protection under expressive freedom.

Obviously, the question of whether statement X is injurious is tied to the target's emotional response to X. Like other emotional responses, this one must be evaluated in terms of its relationship to its object, whether the relationship, that is, is rational or irrational, since we consider some responses to be adequate and others inadequate.[14] Furthermore, the feeling of being injured is usually accompanied by a sense that a person has a *reason* to feel that way. This reason introduces an element of rationality into the discussion that eclipses the purely subjective aspects of the response and allows it to be examined from a more third-person perspective. It also highlights a characteristic of the statement that helps to demonstrate that the sense of injury is rational. At this point, we have moved out of a purely subjective sphere and over into a more objective, or at the very least an intersubjective, space. With this idea in mind, we can argue that statement X should be regarded as truly injurious only if X's 'injurious' aspect can be accepted by a community as genuine. A further problem that arises here, however, is that different communities within a society can disagree on the extent to which X is damaging. For example, a religious community can consider X to be injurious, whereas the secular portion of the population might disagree. However, this is a discussion I shall not pursue further in this context. The point is that more is required here than just a person's *feeling* as though they have been injured by X. The person must also provide a *reason* for the fact that X is injurious, and that reason must also be acceptable to others.

Every idea is open to critique, and although that critique might be particularly damaging, it still does not mean that it should not be protected by freedom of expression. Even the lowest and most hateful expression imaginable, which lends not a single ounce of value to the public debate, but instead demeans it – even that should essentially fall under freedom of expression. Some people, of course, think that hate-speech belongs in a special category all of its own, and that it should not be protected. In my opinion, the fact that a statement is hateful or injurious should not be used to determine its degree of permissibility, no matter *how* hateful or injurious it actually is.

On the other hand, freedom of expression can conflict with other rights, from copyrights to informational privacy, and sometimes it might have to yield ground. Meanwhile, any violations here are only comprehended by the harm principle if we actually have a right *not* to be injured. If we lack that right, which in my opinion is the case, then there is no true rights conflict where injurious expressions are concerned. Expressions simply do not represent the kind of harm that we should enact laws to prevent. The world would undoubtedly be a better place without many hateful expressions; at the same time, a world where such things were prohibited would be much worse than it is now.

Protecting others' feelings is not the most important element in interpersonal communication. Violations, whether or not they are considered harmful, should not necessarily be avoided. Freedom of expression is often injurious, and it often targets ideas that should be violated, because they are untenable. Concern for others' feelings is certainly relevant, and it is doubtless immoral to hurt someone's feelings simply for the sake of the injury, but issues of immorality should stay outside a legislative framework.

Tolerance

A solid critique-oriented culture of expression, like the one I have sketched above, can often seem intolerant, and tolerance is one of liberal democracy's most prized virtues. The word 'tolerance' comes from the Latin *tolerantia*, which means to abide or to endure. Whether implicitly or explicitly, tolerance is judgemental in nature. One can only show tolerance for something that one believes to be wrong, or at the very least inferior. Tolerance is based on the assumption that, after critical evaluation, a person has deemed something to be insupportable or untenable. As as result, you cannot tolerate your own ideas, and certainly not other people's conceptions that coincide with your own. If everyone in the world was in perfect agreement, the world would lack tolerance, simply because the concept would be superfluous. In addition, one cannot tolerate things one has not evaluated critically; in that case, one is simply indifferent to them. Tolerance requires three things: 1) that an individual take a negative view on something; 2) that it is in the individual's power to do away with or to oppose it; and 3) that the individual refrains from doing just that. Instead, the individual chooses to abide or endure it.

Tolerance involves accepting other people's right to live those lives, think those thoughts and express those opinions that are different from our own. It certainly does not require that we endorse each and every one, but simply that we avoid compelling others to live, think and express themselves as we do. On the contrary, tolerance is entirely compatible with a strong critique of whatever it is that we are tolerating. A famous aphorism attributed to Voltaire puts it this way: 'I disapprove of what you say, but I will defend to the death your right to say it.'[15] What this idea suggests is that we must respect other people's right to express themselves – which is entirely different from respecting the expression itself. However, the tolerance idea has degenerated in our day, until now it is interpreted to mean some form of approval, or at least 'recognition', of that which one tolerates.[16] This is completely to confuse the logic of tolerance, however, since tolerance is based upon a disapproval of its object. Indeed, it is extremely intolerant to demand that we support every lifestyle and viewpoint under the sun. And though tolerance will always have an element of judgement to it, it nonetheless rests on a deep, basic understanding that a plurality of convictions and lifestyles guarantees the continued existence of individual freedom and liberal society.

Tolerance is never total in any society, however, because certain ideas or expressions have always been deemed intolerable. John Locke, who with his *Letter Concerning Toleration* (1689) was a key advocate for religious tolerance early on, is a striking example of this.[17] He underscores that the law's mission is not to distinguish truth from falsehood, but rather to ensure people's security. In keeping with this idea, he argues that religious convictions should not be objects of political regulation – with two notable exceptions. According to Locke, Catholics and atheists cannot be tolerated, because Catholics swear allegiance to a foreign power and atheists do not recognize divine will, which is the source of all rights and morals. In Norway today, one cannot argue that Catholics and atheists are tolerated, because no one would consider forcing either group to abstain from faith or lack thereof. In both cases, tolerance is superfluous. At the same time, Norway cannot be said to tolerate blasphemous expressions, since a blasphemy paragraph is still on the books. As such, legal sanctions could conceivably be brought against certain expressions. Granted, the paragraph is 'sleeping', but in principle sanctions are still possible.

A liberal society should not institute limits on what religious convictions, or critiques thereof, are permissible. That does not mean, however, that a person has the right to express himself in any way possible. For example, a religious community can be barred from broadcasting their message via loudspeaker at the local community centre, not because one dislikes the message, but simply because the loud noise would irritate other people. The right to self-expression does not entail the right to express oneself by any means in any context.

In recent years, there have been a number of instances in which religious groups have claimed that certain expressions, whether it be novels, plays, movies or caricatures, have violated their religious sensibilities. In terms of the harm principle, the important question becomes the extent to which a person's religious sensibilities and convictions are rights-protected and therefore inviolable. These groups argue that freedom of expression is only valid insofar as no one's beliefs are being injured. There is little doubt as to how this issue plays out in the context of Mill's harm principle. The argument can perhaps be made that, broadly speaking, any violation of religious or moral sensibilities falls under the 'harm' category. Yet, as we recall, the harm principle requires that any violation must be rights-related, and hurt feelings or injured sensibilities does not translate to a violation of rights. Accordingly, expressions that might have that effect should not be prohibited.

What about racist expressions? Racism is a phenomenon that essentially conflicts with fundamental liberal ideas regarding mankind's equality. As such, one might assume that liberalism would support the prohibition of racist expressions, and even deem them punishable. As a liberal democracy, after all, we have a duty to promote the concept of equality, and so we ought to oppose racism wherever we find it. The solution, however, is not to *ban* racist expressions, but to expose them as groundless. There can also be situations, of course, where the nature of a racist expression poses a rather clear threat to one or more ethnic minorities, but in that case it would lose its immunity under the harm principle.

We must ultimately make a distinction between moral and legal tolerance, between things we disapprove of but will not pursue through moral critique or legal sanctions respectively. Rights violations, on the other hand, should be tolerated neither morally nor judiciously. Other types of violations, for example, of someone's religious sensibilities, should be tolerated judiciously, but not necessarily morally, depending upon the goal and consequences of a given expression. Some violations should be tolerated both judiciously and morally. The important political question centres on the limits of legal tolerance, while the limits of moral tolerance is for the individual and civil spheres to determine.

Freedom of Expression and Critique of Expression

A comprehensive expressive freedom principle, such as that found in Mill and in this chapter, is not without cost. People will be hurt and offended, and serious conflicts might arise. Some people will argue that these costs are too great, and that we must be pragmatic and 'weigh' the various considerations against each other. The issue then becomes how expressive freedom can be 'weighed', for example, against religious sensibilities. What kind of scale should we use? For a religious fundamentalist, the matter is pure and simple – religion will always come first. The problem is that we have then abandoned liberal democracy. In a truly liberal society, certain freedoms will have the status of absolute rights that cannot be 'weighed' in the same way as we take different considerations and interests into account in the context of other questions. Absolute rights are not upheld because they are 'beneficial'. Within the framework of a liberal democracy, furthermore, we need to have principles that regulate value conflicts. The existence of the liberal democracy depends upon the presence of certain fundamental ideas that are not open to negotiation – that cannot be 'weighed', and perhaps discarded, when unpleasant conflicts arise.

Even though I support legal tolerance for hateful expressions, I am just as firm a proponent of moral intolerance where they are concerned. A defence of expressive freedom is entirely compatible with a sharp critique of both specific expressions and of a particular culture of expression. Liberal rights ensures that rights-holders have room to make choices, and within certain limits: the right to make immoral choices. The right to freedom of expression means that people can express themselves in ways that harm or violate others, and even though no good can come from those expressions. Expressive freedom essentially demands evaluational neutrality. The fact that an expression, by all accounts, is untrue or immoral is fundamentally irrelevant for the question of whether it should be protected under expressive freedom. One cornerstone of a liberal society is maintaining the important distinction between law and morality. It should not be illegal to be immoral, though immoral conduct will always be just that: immoral. We can certainly aim an arsenal full of moral critique at all hateful expressions, but they should also exist outside a legal framework.

In the end, people should have the right to fully engage in false or heinous expressions, but others are completely within their rights to call these expressions by their true names. Critique of expression is entirely compatible with holding the principle of expressive freedom to be inviolable. In short, we must simultaneously keep two ideas in mind: that we can both defend the right to express something *and* criticize the expression itself.

PART III
THE ETHICS OF FREEDOM

13

Realizing Freedom

The freedom concept presented in Part II, 'The Politics of Freedom', is not moralized. Though it does outline some of the frameworks necessarily for the free realization of a good life, it does not provide a recipe for the good life itself. A variety of good lives are possible within these frameworks, but there are also many lives that are unquestionably not so good. Ultimately, the value of political freedom lies in the contribution it makes to a person's, to an individual's, freedom. We cannot set an equals sign between political freedom and personal freedom, because political freedom is only part of, and one of many requirements for, personal freedom. If this section of the book is entitled 'The Ethics of Freedom', it is because I will now address how we ought to live, and will also take a closer look at freedom's connection to morality and meaning in life. In short, we are going to consider how we can give freedom actual substance in our daily lives.

The conditions for personal freedom have undergone tremendous change. It is a recent development that a living standard marked by a surplus of time and material resources – which makes freedom of choice one of the most central factors in a person's life – was not reserved for just a small minority. In earlier societies, most people's lives were dominated by another kind of necessity and struggle for survival. In the late modern society, where the fundamental material requirements are met for most people, the search for identity has become one of our chief occupations. Whom exactly, we ask, should we use our freedom to become? Charles Taylor writes:

> There are questions about how I am going to live my life which touch on the issue of what kind of life is worth living,

or what kind of life would fulfill the promise implicit in my particular talents, or the demands incumbent on someone with my endowment, or of what constitutes a rich, meaningful life – as against one concerned with secondary matters or trivia. These are issues of strong evaluation, because the people who ask these questions have no doubt that one can, following one's immediate wishes or desires, take a wrong turn and hence fail to lead a full life.[1]

A strong evaluation is an evaluation of the kind of person one ultimately wants to be. Central to Taylor's thought is that the fundamentals of strong evaluation have changed decisively in modern societies. In premodern or traditional societies, one could say that strong evaluations are, to a certain extent, self-evident, since they are essentially determined by one's social context. Traditional societies provide a much more unambiguous understanding of what should matter most in life, because tradition limits the availability of choices and does not often provide much knowledge of other lifestyles. There is obviously less autonomy to be had in such societies, but it is easier to find the meaning of life because one does not need to seek it out. In modern societies, however, social context is significantly more pluralistic – or fragmented – and therefore strong evaluation lacks the element of self-evidentiality. Instead, it is largely subject to explicit individual choice. Group belonging continues to form a decisive part of one's identity, but the modern individual belongs to significantly more groups than the premodern. Today you can be a Norwegian citizen, the child of Vietnamese immigrants, a resident of Belgium, a physicist, a creationist, a social democrat, a Black Metal enthusiast, a homosexual and a philatelist. All these things contribute to your identity and link you to various groups. As such, the framework for strong evaluations has become significantly looser and undefined, and it is much less obvious what kind of person one should become. That does not mean, however, that all choices are equally good. There are better and worse evaluations for establishing both an identity and a meaningful life. And it is no easy matter to determine what kind of life one ought to live. As Viktor Frankl puts it: 'Unlike an animal, man is not told by instincts what he *must* do. And unlike man in former times, he is no longer told by traditions what he *should* do. Often he does not even know what he basically wishes to do.'[2] Precisely because the matter is so indefinite, late modern man has become focused on – it is tempting to say obsessed with – self-realization. The constant and explicit search for self-realization also testifies to the fact that the individual often fails in his pursuit of self. As Frankl also aptly observes: 'As the boomerang comes back to the hunter who has thrown it only if it has missed its target, man, too, returns to himself and is intent upon self-actualization only if he has missed his mission.'[3]

The modern individual may have been liberated from tradition's sway, but that means he also bears a new kind of responsibility for himself, in particular for his own *self-becoming*. As Nietzsche remarks, 'You should become who you are.'[4] The individual's relationship to himself is self-reflective. A certain level of reflexivity characterizes members of every society, of course, but this reflexivity is radicalized in societies whose members are not so extensively bound to traditions that dictate who they are.[5] That means that individuals must increasingly construct their self-identity from the materials they have to hand, rather than the self simply appearing as something that is already given. The self becomes something to be created, governed, maintained, transformed and so on.

This idea is central to Michel Foucault's late philosophy. He rejects the thought that any given self can function as normative. There is no 'essence' upon which to fall back, and therefore it is our job to shape ourselves like an 'artwork'.[6] It is not about *finding* oneself, but rather about *inventing* oneself. This self-construction takes place, among other things, through what Foucault calls 'askesis', which means that the subject continues to work on themselves in order to achieve self-mastery.[7] This work takes place in the midst of countless forms of power that establish structures for the self's development. These structures, however, are not something out of which the subject can simply break. For Foucault, individuality is a social construction, but it is also a construction that possesses a self-fashioning capability. Of course, one weakness of Foucault's discussion is that it lacks any principles or norms for self-shaping. On the contrary, he rejects the concept that there is anything resembling universal morality or a certain set of practical principles with general validity. Instead, what any given self will or should become is entirely open – and the question is whether it is *too* open. Indeed, the closest Foucault comes to defining a norm here is to allude to *lifestyle* as an attractive concept for self-shaping.[8] He doubts, however, that we can ever truly 'mature'.[9] Since there are no norms associated with self-shaping, moreover, the self basically lacks all sense of direction and identity, all sense of where it is headed and who it is; instead, it is a self in perpetual motion away from itself, a self that views liberation as the endless project of precluding the phenomenon of self-sameness.[10] As a result, the self will never succeed in becoming itself, because it simply does not know – nor have any vague conception of – what it actually should be. Ultimately, it cannot even produce a coherent self-narrative, because its future self is completely up in the air.

As Paul Ricoeur has pointed out, however, a prerequisite for self-understanding is the ability to produce a relatively coherent narrative about who we have been and who we will become.[11] To be a self is to be able to explain oneself in terms of who one has been, who one will become and who one is now, at the intersection of past and future. And integral to this narrative is the question: what do you care about?

Meaning and identity can only be established to the extent that one *cares* about something. Of course, explaining what it means to care about something is no straightforward task. In this context, I will proceed along the lines of Harry Frankfurt. To care about something means that we value it, that we regard it, broadly speaking, as something we desire, and that desire, furthermore, is a desire that we desire to have. This desire is no passing fancy, but rather something with which a person identifies and considers to be an expression of who he is. The act of caring makes the world a meaningful place and gives our lives a direction. We shape ourselves in the process of deciding that a particular desire is, indeed, an expression of ourselves.[12] Those things we most care about, of course, are things that we *love*. As a result, Frankfurt writes, love is the foundation of practical reasoning and the ultimate source of human values.[13] It is also the reason we can assign value to other things. Frankfurt takes up Aristotle's point here, namely, that it is only in pursuing something for its own sake that everything else achieves meaning. Purely instrumental activities assume significance by being subordinated to activities that have their own intrinsic worth.[14]

In caring about something, however, it is important that we should not be too self-conscious about it. If I care about X simply so that I can call myself a person who cares about X, then I care about X for all the wrong reasons. For example, if I volunteer to help homeless animals, that is an inherently worthy task. I could be doing it, however, for several different reasons: because I know that animals are in need; or because I want to see myself as a person who helps animals in need. Given our considerable penchant for self-deception, we can easily vacillate from one to the other, but there is a fundamental distinction here. In the first case, the object I care about is the centre of my attention, and in the second case, I myself am the focus. Bernard Williams has pointed out that, in the second case, I am actually not sufficiently self-oriented.[15] That can seem paradoxical, since it is the very act of orienting on one's self that proves destructive. The paradox vanishes, however, when we realize that the problem in the second instance is that, instead of actively being present in my own life, I have adopted an external, observational perspective, as if I were studying another agent. As such, the action's ability to contribute meaning and identity to my life is severely diminished. In order for X to yield meaning and identity, I must be explicitly committed to the idea that X will do so.

A person who cares about something identifies with whatever it is he or she cares about. According to Frankfurt, caring about something means allowing ourselves to be guided by it, both on an individual and a general level, so that it functions as definitive for who we are. In keeping with Heidegger's notion of 'care' (*Sorge*), the act of caring for something brings together all the ways in which we are involved in the world and in ourselves.[16] Caring about something is constitutive for the self and all of its projects. If I truly care about something, moreover, it places limits on my conduct, because there are certain things that I cannot imagine doing under any circumstances. These limits, which are established by my inability to imagine carrying out certain actions, also provides boundaries for who I am, for my identity. In contrast, a person without such limits would essentially be a person without identity, because whatever he or she did at any point in time would be determined by circumstance. As Frankfurt writes of such an individual:

> Any stable volitional characteristics he may have are products of impersonal causal influences. They are not consequences of his wanting to be a person of a certain sort or to devote himself to a certain kind of life; they are not fixed by his will itself but by contingencies external to it. In other words, his will is governed entirely by circumstances rather than by any essential nature of its own. None of his volitional characteristics is necessary to him, since none derives from his own nature.
>
> This means that he lacks a personal essence, which would comprise the necessary conditions of his identity. For this

reason, there is no such thing for him as genuine integrity. After all, he has no personal boundaries whose inviolability he might set himself to protect. There is nothing that he is essentially. What he is at any given time is no more than what he happens then to be, which is merely accidental.[17]

Frankfurt argues that we humans are the only beings capable of taking ourselves seriously, and by that he specifically means that it is crucial that we 'get it right', that we find out who we are and live our lives according to this insight.[18] As emphasized above, identity and the faculty of caring about something are inextricably entwined. Part of 'getting it right' is discovering what you *should* care about. Frankfurt's take on the matter is simply that you should care about whatever you actually care about. However, according to Frankfurt, what you care about is not really up to you, since it is ultimately determined through 'volitional necessity'.

Volitional necessities are such that one cannot avoid caring about them. To the extent that one is subject to them, they ensure that there will be certain things one can neither fail to do nor refrain from doing.[19] What one cares about, Frankfurt believes, is determined by our biology and other natural circumstances, and there is very little we can do to alter the situation.[20] And while some volitional necessities are universally human, while others are strictly individual, Frankfurt generally believes that all people tend to care for the same things because there is little variation in terms of the biological, psychological and external causes that shape people's wills. If we cannot choose what we care about, however, there does not seem to be any normative grounds to hold people accountable for the objects of care in their lives. We simply lose the logical space in which to undertake such rational evaluations of meaning and morality.

This idea is further problematized by the fact that Frankfurt tends to regard morality as something derived, as being based in the act of caring about something. However, there are a multitude of different things we can care about. Frankfurt wishes to avoid moralizing here, because he wants to explore the opportunity conditions for a *meaningful* life, and it is certainly not obvious that a meaningful life must be a *morally good* one. A concentration camp commander, whose existence is, morally speaking, one of the worst imaginable, can still love his job and live an extremely meaningful life. However, to be morally good is another form of meaningful living, and even if the moral life is not necessarily any more meaningful than the immoral, it at least makes for a morally better existence.

It should be uncontroversial to state that certain actions and lifestyles are to be preferred above others, for example, that Raoul Wallenberg's life was morally better than Adolf Eichmann's. It is not that Wallenberg's life necessarily was any more meaningful or that he cared more than Eichmann did about things. On the contrary, Eichmann was exceptionally devoted to the task of administering the transportation of Jews to Nazi concentration and extermination camps.[21] As Frankfurt himself puts it: 'The Nazi may find in his devotion to Nazi ideals an ability to transcend himself, opportunities for self-sacrifice, for absorption into a large community of like-minded people who devote themselves in selfless and courageous ways to something they think is important.'[22] Indeed, Frankfurt argues that there will always be sufficient causes for who you are and what you do, which means that you could not have been otherwise or acted otherwise, given the existent causal chain. Freedom, for Frankfurt, accordingly consists in being wholehearted, in performing an action because you desire to perform it, provided that the desire is one that you wish to have. When you are wholehearted, when your will is undivided, when you care utterly and completely about something, you enjoy a special kind of freedom.[23] More freedom than that is not humanly possible, Frankfurt argues.[24]

From Frankfurt's perspective, then, the only conclusion that we can seem to draw is that both Wallenberg's wish to save as many Jews as possible and Eichmann's wish to facilitate the transport of as many Jews as possible to Nazi camps must be regarded as instances of volitional necessity. According to this logic, both Wallenberg and Eichmann 'got it right', since both wholeheartedly embraced their respective desires. Indeed, for those familiar with Wallenberg's and Eichmann's biographies, there is little doubt that both men cared a great deal about what they were doing; both were wholehearted, and this wholeheartedness gave their lives meaning and identity. However, it should be indisputable to suggest that Wallenberg got it infinitely 'more right' than Eichmann, and any theory that obliterates this basic distinction is difficult to take seriously. Does Frankfurt's theoretical framework allow for any normative evaluation of Wallenberg's life as being any better than Eichmann's life? Frankfurt recognizes that certain behaviours are unacceptable for moral or other reasons, but at the same time it is hard to see how the basic distinction between acceptable and unacceptable behaviours fits within the framework of his theory on freedom.[25]

Frankfurt is quite sceptical of the idea that a person can ever take an active role in determining about what he or she will care.[26] Therefore he is equally sceptical of the normative question of what it is we *should* care about, partly because we do not decide for ourselves whether to care about something or not, and partly because the question, to his thinking, cannot be answered in a non-circular fashion.[27] As a result, he concludes that 'the most basic and essential question for a person to raise concerning the conduct of his life cannot be the *normative* question of how he *should* live', because in order to be meaningful, the answer must be based on the prior matter of what a person *actually does care about*.[28] The evaluation of what is important to us, of what we do care about and should care about, will not ever start with a clean slate.[29] And, furthermore, it is logical to suggest that the evaluation of what we *should* care about must follow from a clarification of what we actually do care about. Frankfurt also discriminates between what is 'worth' caring about and what is not, but it is not obvious how he can even draw that distinction.[30]

Frankfurt is correct in saying that this normative question cannot start from a clean state, that every examination of the kind of life one should live can only take place based on an already existent store of conceptions and wants. If one were destitute of these things, choices would be completely random because they would then be made without any *reason* for preferring one thing over another.[31] A choice must establish some difference, and in order for it to be a meaningful choice, it must establish a meaningful difference. Meanwhile, this assumes that we already have some conception of what is meaningful, which again presupposes that we already care about something. However, that does not imply that the normative question cannot be raised and answered legitimately – and can even function correctively in terms of the life one is actually living, as well as in the determining of what it is one actually cares about. At this point, Frankfurt simply observes that since the question of what we *should* care about depends on the question of what we actually do care about, 'any answer to the normative question must be derived from considerations that are manifestly subjective.'[32] If that is the end of the matter, we have once again abandoned all rational basis for moral praise and censure.

As we discussed earlier, Frankfurt defines freedom as an agreement between first- and second-order desires. Basically, this agreement is established when one's first-order desires are brought into accordance with one's second-order desires or when one's second-order desires are brought into accordance with one's first-order desires. Frankfurt primarily concurs with the second alternative, because he believes that we do not really determine what we care about or love.

Is he correct? Even if an agent happens to experience a second-order positive identification with his first-order desires, and then acts accordingly, it is by no means convincing that he is necessarily free because of it. I will argue here that, in addition, freedom requires that a person could conceivably find that he did not identify with that desire; that he then could have acted contrary to it if he saw that there were good reasons to do so; and that, ultimately, he could have even modified his desires. Frankfurt leaves the door open to the possibility that a person might consciously change what he cares about, but he is silent as to how this change might take place, something made even more problematic by the fact that such an alteration is beyond the will's control.[33]

What we care about can always vary. The fact that an individual cares about something at one point in time does not mean it needs to coincide with what he cared about earlier or what he will care about later.[34] At the same time, it is crucial to Frankfurt that what a person cares about is not directly subject to his will and that it cannot be altered without further ado. The objects of an individual's most fundamental devotion must be things about which he cannot *avoid* caring.[35] It is only in the presence of this kind of necessity, he argues, that caring can serve as a foundation for substantial meaning in our lives.

Aristotle asserts, on the other hand, that while it is true that no man can avoid acting in accordance with his own character, in a certain sense this is still voluntary, because we ourselves partially originate our character.[36] Frankfurt, for his part, explicitly rejects the Aristotelian theory, and argues instead that being responsible for one's character – and the actions to which it gives rise – is not a matter of occasioning or shaping that character, but rather of 'taking responsibility for it'.[37]

Frankfurt's volitional necessities bind the will, however, since a person cannot will other than what he actually does. Nonetheless, the person does not feel compelled by this fact, because he also does not want to will other than what he actually does. In Sartrean terms, one could say that Frankfurt's theory has a copious amount of facticity and very little transcendence. A more existentialist or libertarian approach would concede that the self is largely a given and that, in a certain sense, the individual must take ownership of that self, must make it his *own*, by applauding its autonomy, but the libertarian will nonetheless argue that the agent must also have the ability to exceed what is given, to reshape and to redefine himself, on the basis of radical choice. As Frankfurt views it, the possibility for this kind of radical choice is in no way a prerequisite for autonomy, but rather something that undermines autonomy's possibility. In a situation where the self was not already a given, where one might imagine that human will had no limitations on it whatsoever, a person could not orient himself and would be without all criteria for self choice. The problem with Frankfurt's formulation here is that he sets it up as a sharp dichotomy, where the self is either completely given or totally independent of all givenness.

No one can create themselves from scratch. We all have a variety of conceptions about the world and ourselves, not to mention an abundance of values and desires. And very few of those conceptions, values and desires can, with any rationality, be said to have been *chosen*. Of course, we do have the ability to cultivate and change many of the above – for example, we can rid ourselves of a bias or learn to like a certain food dish – but again, that is something we do only by taking other given desires, values and conceptions as our starting point. Creating oneself *ex nihilo* is simply not an alternative we have, and if one thinks that, in order to be free, the self must be completely self-chosen, then they expect the impossible. Every formation and modification of self will be based on something already present. We can modify not only our first-order desires, but also our second-order desires – but always on the basis of our third-order desires. And these third-order desires, too, will be rooted in something that is given. You will never make an unconditional choice that is not based on conceptions and desires that are already present.

Anyone who wishes to create himself from scratch will be in the same situation as Dostoevsky's underground man, who thinks that freedom entails independence for every conceivable power or force.[38] For him, an action is only free if it cannot be attributed to any influence. Since he believes that his emotions and reason are the products of such influence, however, genuinely free actions must be independent from them as well. Accordingly, a truly free action must be unanchored in an agent's appetites, desires and values. However, that is a far cry from what we ourselves interpret as a free agent who engages in free actions. If I am a free agent, my actions must in some way spring from myself and be an expression of who I am. Meanwhile, who I am cannot be deciphered in the context of myself alone, as entirely divorced from my surroundings. As Charles Taylor puts it: 'I can define my identity only against the background of things that matter. But to bracket out history, nature, society, the demands of solidarity, everything but what I find in myself, would be to eliminate all candidates for what matters.'[39] Ultimately, freedom is the ability to devote oneself to what one cares about, and what you care about did not simply emerge in a vacuum. However, you also have the ability to reflect on what you care about, to question whether you should actually care about it and to consider how you might devote yourself to it. That is how you define who you are.

If we now compare Frankfurt's theory to Taylor's, it is clear that Taylor's theory is much more open to a deliberate *choice* of values, of what we should be caring about, without, for that reason, supposing that such choice would have to take place from a clean slate, as Frankfurt represents the alternative to his own position. Taylor's viewpoint is actually related to Foucault's, who underscores that the subject clearly did not originate all the practices it deploys in active self-shaping.[40] Instead, a subject's culture, society and social groups 'impose' these practices upon him. Still, the subject's work with himself is an expression of his freedom. By disciplining itself through 'askesis', the ego liberates itself from those appetites and desires that form a part of the self, but that the self interprets as foreign, as something it *should not* possess. The process of questioning whether or not to accept or reject different sides of the self is the way a person uncovers his self-identity. That is how we define and take responsibility for who we are.

Virtually everyone – even the most self-satisfied among us – has an idea not only of who they are now, but also of a future self that would make for a better version. Of course, it is not inconceivable that there are people so lacking in self-insight that they believe themselves to be perfect, with no room for any improvement. People who exist in certain extreme situations, such as at the edge of starvation, will hardly spend much time reflecting on how to better themselves. And toward the end of life, some people might conclude that it is only downhill from here, that they will become a steadily worsening version of themselves, as their bodies and senses fail. Most of us, however, are mindful that we have a way to go before we become who we should be – and that we will never truly reach that goal. We might even say we feel committed to this kind of self-scrutiny. As Kant formulates it, man is the only being who is capable of achieving self-cognition and who has the duty to seek self-cognition in order to become a *better* person.[41] Kant also believes there is ample reason to assume that a sober and honest self-scrutiny will yield disappointing results for most of us. However, according to Kant, man also has a penchant for self-deception, which prevents us from achieving true insight into how wretched we are.[42] Self-deception, on the other hand, will seldom be so total that we cannot recognize the distance that exists between who we are and who we should be.

Frankfurt insists that morality's significance to the questions of what has value and how we ought to live our lives has been severely overestimated.[43] Perhaps he is correct in that, and it is certainly true that there are other values besides moral ones and that not all values can be reduced or subordinated to moral ones. For example, an art-work can have a directly negative moral value, but have a great aesthetic value – indeed, a moral defect can prove an aesthetic strength. If you eliminated all the moral defects from, for example, Jean Genet's or Louis-Ferdinand Céline's literary works, you would simultaneously reduce their aesthetic value. And recognizing the aesthetic perspective in a work or an action does not mean invalidating the moral perspective. There is nothing to prevent a person from regarding a morally reprehensible act as a sublime work of art, while also believing that the action should be morally condemned or punished. And though it requires keeping two ideas in mind at once, there is no contradiction between the thoughts. As a result, we must concede that Frankfurt is partially right when he argues that we must recognize other values besides moral ones in our discussion of life's meaning and worth. Still, that does not entail setting aside moral values – they are unavoidable.

Personal freedom means having the freedom to realize certain life values, and you must take direct responsibility for what values you choose to implement. A free life does not need to be particularly meaningful, because an individual can elect to exercise freedom in relatively meaningless ways. Likewise, a meaningful life need not be particularly free, because an individual can also find meaning in lifestyles that leave very little room for freedom. Let us imagine a woman who has undergone a religious transformation. Upon reflection, she finds that her previous, 'liberated' existence was immoral and unworthy, and so changes her life profoundly by joining a radical religious movement, where she then marries and subjects herself to her husband's will, since a religious injunction dictates that she do so. She cannot leave home without her husband's escort and must go about almost entirely covered. She cannot work and has no say in the family's finances. The list could go on, but the crucial point to be made here is that this woman has decided to subject herself to her husband's will in all things. Nonetheless, she still satisfies the autonomy criteria, at least in the sense that she lives according to values that, upon reflection, she has decided to uphold. On the other hand, she has essentially dis-enfranchised herself and no longer lives her life according to her *own* will. Despite that fact, she still meets the requirements for minimal autonomy and is responsible for the life she has chosen. For example, we would still regard her as an agent with accountability, even though she has chosen an existence that significantly minimizes autonomy. Autonomy and self-realization are not necessarily synonymous ideals, because even though autonomy is a necessary condition for self-realization – realizing one's *own* self depends on it – self-realization is yet undetermined. It can take directions that either promote or hinder autonomy's further development.

Some people will also argue that a free life cannot be an immoral one. During our earlier discussion of autonomy theories, I mentioned that, in addition to hierarchical theories and authenticity-based theories, there are also Kantian theories that suggest that an action is completely autonomous only if it is motivated by whatever moral law an agent imposes on himself. A more recent representative for such a Kantian viewpoint is Christine M. Korsgaard.[44] She argues that autonomy entails universalizability: that is to say, in keeping with Kant's categorical imperative, that I only conduct myself according to those subjective principles of action that I can, at the same time, will that they should become universal law.[45] Roughly speaking, that means that one should only do things that one could also will that everyone else does too. Korsgaard explicitly argues that such actions must be considered a form of heteronomy.[46] In my opinion, that is too strong a requirement for autonomy, and is actually more extreme than Kant's own viewpoint. We can say that Kant's thought contains two levels of autonomy. On the one hand, you are completely autonomous only if you allow reason to dictate your actions and your actions to be determined by moral law. On the other hand, the conscious choice not to follow moral law is also autonomously made. According to Kant, an impulse or drive can only determine an agent's faculty of choice if the agent has elected to make it a part of his subjective principle of action.[47] As such, an agent must voluntarily choose to be led by a desire if that desire results in an action. And if that desire happens to occasion an immoral action, the action is still expressive of an agent's autonomy. We can certainly argue that an action that has been dictated by a rational reason is freer than an action based on a less rational reason, but it does not thereby follow that the latter action cannot also be called free. It is sufficiently free, in any case, that we can still hold the agent responsible for it.

Susan Wolf takes a similar viewpoint, advocating for what she terms a 'Reason View' on freedom, which holds that freedom is 'the ability to act in accordance with Reason', and more specifically, 'the ability to act in accordance with the True and the Good'.[48] As Wolf herself points out, one peculiar result of her theory is the asymmetry it establishes between praise and censure. In accordance with the Reason View, a person who has mentally determined to perform good actions deserves moral praise, but a person who is mentally determined to perform evil actions does not deserve moral censure, since the former individual is free, whereas the latter is not.[49] If we return to the example of Walden Two and Walden Three that we saw in the book's introduction, we can now say that, according to Wolf's theory, the inhabitants of Walden Two are free and morally accountable, where the inhabitants of Walden Three are not. This conclusion seems rather counterintuitive. The difference between Walden Two and Walden Three is that they are governed, respectively, by a well-meaning manipulator and a malicious one, and it hardly seems plausible that this fact alone would have such extreme consequences for freedom and responsibility. Accordingly, I regard the symmetry between Walden Two and Walden Three as a striking counterexample to Wolf's theory and its resultant asymmetry. An additional problem with Wolf's theory is that it does not take into account the Aristotelian viewpoint that we can also be held accountable for the condition in which we put ourselves. Let us imagine that Paul knows that his reaction to alcohol is sometimes atypical. Instead of becoming social and cheerful, he can become extremely aggressive, lose all self-control and be unable 'to act in accordance with the True and the Good'. Nonetheless, Paul chooses to drink because he enjoys the positive side of inebriation. However, it all goes to hell: a trifle causes him to explode and he injures another person for life. Paul tries to defend himself by saying that he was not rationally in control of himself at the time of the action. As far as I can determine, Wolf would accept this defence and believe that Paul could be held neither morally nor legally accountable, because at the time he was mentally determined to act as he did. In terms of widespread moral intuitions – or reactive attitudes, if you will – and just about every viable legal framework, Paul would, in fact, be held morally and legally responsible because he freely chose to put himself in that state. We can also imagine an example where an individual cultivates a disposition that becomes increasingly brutal and sadistic over time, so that eventually moral corruption suffuses him and he is no longer in a position 'to act in accordance with the True and the Good'. According to Wolf's theory, that person, too, would seem to lack all moral and legal responsibility for his actions, whereas general intuitions – and most ethical theories – would indicate that the person is responsible for being the way he is, and is accordingly responsible for all actions springing from that character. It is difficult to regard Wolf's theoretical arguments as so persuasive that they outweigh such prevailing intuitions. In my opinion, the same objection can be directed at Wolf as at Korsgaard. We can choose action alternatives that are unreasonable or immoral simply because we want to act in that way, and we can also regard these actions as free. Of course, we can always tie freedom to rational control and argue that the more rational the action, the freer it is, but unreasonable actions will still be sufficiently free for the agent to be responsible for them.

Much of what we do does not happen explicitly *because* it will give our lives meaning. Meaning is more of an implicit than an explicit motivation – or a side-effect, if you prefer. In philosophical discussions surrounding life's meaning, there is significant disagreement between subjectivists and objectivists. Subjectivists, as the name implies, regard meaning in life as subjective: that is, as utterly dependent on an individual's, or the subject's, attitudes. Objectivists, in contrast, believe that the standards for establishing life's meaning are subject-independent: for example, of a moral nature. Subjectivism has undoubtedly dominated twentieth-century philosophy, but that picture has somewhat altered in the last decade. One point in objectivism's favour is that there are indeed lives that appear meaningless, independent of the subjects who may value them. However, the issue here is whether we can ever fully explain meaning in life without taking a subject's evaluation of such as our springboard.

Susan Wolf argues that life's meaning is the product of an encounter between subjective attraction and objective attractiveness.[50]

For Wolf, life's meaning must in part originate in something whose worth exists independent of a given subject's valuation of it. Meaning must have an objective anchor. The issue then becomes how to determine that something has objective value. Who has the authority to make such an evaluation? Wolf concedes that there is no ultimate authority here, but nonetheless argues that we can distinguish between what has intrinsic value and what does not.[51]

This distinction has an intuitive appeal. Say that person X devotes his life to writing a masterpiece, which provides many people with a new and better life understanding, while person Y spends their existence filling page after page with the exact same sentence, perhaps 'All work and no play makes Jack a dull boy.' We can further imagine that X and Y both receive equal subjective satisfaction from their respective tasks. Nonetheless, there seems to be a significant distinction here, which stems from the fact that X is doing something genuinely valuable, while Y's project appears to be completely meaningless. That would suggest that meaning can and should be rooted in something beyond the subject's valuation of it.

At this point, Wolf touches on Hegel's critique of the Romantics for permitting objective criteria to fall away and the subjective experience of the world to assume absolute validity. As Hegel points out, however, such subjectivity, which implicitly becomes meaning's source, must also be empty: 'Whatever is, is only by the instrumentality of the *ego*, and what exists by my instrumentality I can equally well annihilate again. Now if we stop at these absolutely empty forms which originate from the absoluteness of the abstract *ego*, nothing is treated *in and for itself* and as valuable in itself, but only as produced by the subjectivity of the *ego*.'[52] The problem is that if it is completely up to the subject to ascribe or deny meaning to all things, then everything actually loses significance; meaning is no longer a property of things in themselves, and accordingly those things turn up empty.

As Wolf further formulates the point, life lacks meaning if it is thoroughly egocentric, if it is solely devoted to the subject's well-being and not to implementing values outside of the subject's own good.[53] However, that is an exceptionally strong requirement for meaning, since it holds that achieving meaning in your own life is possible only if you add value to other people's lives. Expressed in these terms, I believe that the requirement is too strong, and I do not see why a hermit in a cave, who is cut off from all human contact, and who, for example, devotes his life to the worship of his god, cannot achieve genuine meaning in life. However, Wolf formulates the idea in a less extreme way when she observes that, ultimately, we should focus on 'living in a way that connects positively with objects, people, and activities that have value independent of oneself'.[54] Put like this, the idea paves the way for a hermit's life to be considered meaningful, even if he does not add any value to other people's lives. As such, it seems sufficient to argue that some meaning must exist that is recognizable by others outside of oneself.

The next question is whether this idea requires *actual* recognition or whether it is enough that *in principle* others could recognize it. Both alternatives are problematic. It seems highly unreasonable to require that the meaning of a given activity or life hinges on other people's actual recognition of it. Say that Paul spends his whole life creating a great literary masterpiece, which he is convinced will prove a milestone in literary history (and whose quality, we might further suppose, warrants this evaluation), but that he also does it in secret without ever letting anyone glimpse even a page. Unfortunately, a fire claims both Paul and the manuscript before anyone can read the finished work. If we demand *actual* recognition from other people, Paul's existence must now be termed meaningless. However, it seems unreasonable to argue that Paul's life is meaningless simply because he was never able to show anyone his manuscript. The other alternative, meanwhile, is problematic as well, because it is essentially synonymous with dismissing the objectivity requirement. There is no activity, after all, which another person *in principle* could not recognize, even if it is the lifelong activity of repeatedly writing 'All work and no play makes Jack a dull boy.'

Every human life is rich in insignificance, but some ways of life appear to be more meaningless overall. Take Sisyphus, for example, who has been sentenced by the gods to roll a boulder up a mountain, only to watch it roll back down the other side – and so on for all eternity. Sisyphus' action seems to be indisputably meaningless. Indeed, if some lives are more meaningful than others, then Sisyphus is at the nether end of the meaning continuum. Being compelled to perform such a task day in and day out, after all, is the exact opposite of all that is essentially meaningful in human life. Along these same lines, Dostoevsky writes in *The House of the Dead*: 'The idea has occurred to me that if one wanted to crush, to annihilate a man utterly, to inflict on him the most terrible of punishments so that the most ferocious murderer would shudder at it and dread it beforehand, one need only give him work of an absolutely, completely useless and irrational character.'[55] Let us imagine, however, that Sisyphus eventually begins to find particular gratification in boulder rolling, and considers it to be an extremely meaningful activity. Objectively speaking, the activity will be just as meaningless as before, but on a subjective level the picture has changed entirely. The question now is whether we can say that Sisyphus lives a meaningful life simply because he experiences it as such.

What if we turn from Sisyphus to a chess player who has spent his whole life on chess? Or to a philosopher who devotes, so to speak, every waking moment to philosophy? What is the difference between these examples? What makes chess playing or philosophy a more meaningful pursuit than boulder rolling? The answer is anything but obvious. If someone holds an activity to be extremely meaningful, if it is something they really care about, I typically assume there is something to the activity that makes it meaningful. And I can recognize that fact, even if I am absolutely convinced that the activity would hold no significance for me. Let me take so-called scrapbooking as an example. This is a hobby in which individuals, mostly women, design albums, cards and other things, and purchase cardboard, patterned paper, stamps, glitter, markers and so on for decoration. Often a photo will prove the centre of the design. Countless websites, blogs and discussion forums have grown up around this activity, and some enthusiasts are so absorbed in it there seems to be no real limit to the time – and money – they will spend on it. And yet nothing seems more foreign to me than the thought of devoting time and money to scrapbooking. That does not prevent me, however, from recognizing that the hobby is deeply meaningful to others. On the other hand, the typical scrapbooker would probably fail to understand why I find wristwatches so absorbing and spend so much time – and money – orienting myself in the watch world. Nonetheless, I assume that the typical scrapbooker would also recognize the fact that others might find watches appealing. One could, of course, object here that a lone watch is not too significant, but social communities have also grown up around these objects – there are Internet discussion groups and social get-togethers – and a single watch takes on a great deal of meaning in a broader context. Indeed, certain watch brands, like Panerai, have supporters who follow them with the enthusiasm of football fans.

No matter how much significance can be associated with scrapbooking or watch collecting, however, it still seems insufficient here.

When all is said and done, *everything* probably falls short. On the other hand, there can be a constellation of objects, pursuits and relationships that, taken together, are sufficient to live with and for. Perhaps there is no final goal to which all other goals tend, no ultimate meaning, but simply a constellation of component goals and component meanings, which can either underpin or undermine each other. No single thing alone can give life sufficient meaning. Life's meaning is instead comprised of a network of component meanings, which are typically the relationships we have to our family and friends, to a girlfriend or boyfriend, a home, a job, a hobby and, not least, to our various goals. First and foremost, a person must attempt to establish such a constellation of component meanings that works for him. Of course, we can also argue, along with Aristotle, that the one and only thing we pursue for its own sake is happiness, and that everything I am here describing as objects with meaning and worth attached will be subordinated to this great, overarching goal.[56] Aristotle's take on happiness as being something general and objective, however, will not seem very convincing to the late modern individualist attempting to realize his *own* happiness. In the liberal tradition, happiness is undetermined, something left to the individual to define.

There is a multitude of potentially and actually meaningful lives, and which is relevant to you will depend on the person you are and the circumstances in which you live. However, it is generally true that, in order to have a meaningful life, a person must *care* about what he fills his life with. You must be committed to something, because commitment gives life substantial meaning. Aside from that, there is no universal – and informative – answer as to what makes life meaningful. What provides *your* life with meaning, what *you* care about, is something you alone can determine.

One problem the late modern individual faces, however, is in accepting the pockets of meaninglessness that lie between the elements of meaning in life. We live with a *horror vacui*, a fear of empty spaces, and so demand absolute significance, total happiness. When the unrealistic expectation of total happiness goes unfulfilled, that in itself makes us unhappy.[57] We increasingly interpret happiness to be not merely something the individual has a right to *pursue*, as the u.s. Declaration of Independence has it, but rather as a *right* to which the individual is entitled. And the state readily assumes the role of an agent designed to meet that need. There is yet a clear conflict with the liberal tradition here, because the struggle for happiness is shifted from the private sphere to the political domain. Some people will certainly argue that government authorities ought to promote people's happiness, since it is obvious that all citizens would prefer happiness to unhappiness. The problem is that happiness is individually based, and government authorities are not granted a privileged insight into what happiness entails on the individual's part. Happiness is undetermined, and no one can claim to dispense truth on what true happiness might be.

We must also learn to accept that certain obstacles in life are not freedom's antitheses, but rather its requirements. We do not liberate an individual by removing every duty and tie that binds him, allowing the person to devote himself to himself fully, such that his whole life becomes one of navel gazing. To become oneself, to realize oneself, is to also learn to take responsibility for more than oneself. A significant problem here is that we have largely shifted the concept of negative freedom from the political sphere, where it ought to play a significant role, to the personal one, where its place is not equally so obvious – at least not to the same extent. In his pursuit of happiness, modern man appears to be caught in a paradox that desires both unlimited freedom and belonging.[58] Resolving this dilemma requires that we redefine our understanding of personal freedom. Indeed, freedom today is often understood in a purely negative sense, as a liberation from all responsibilities to others. Entering into these committed relationships, however, can also be construed as a form of positive freedom – a freedom of a less solitary kind.

Negative freedom is crucial in a political context, of course, and personal freedom ought to retain a measure of it, but the matter becomes substantially more problematic when we make negative freedom our life's ideal rather than letting it remain a political ideal. If negative freedom is set on a pedestal as freedom's highest incarnation – and not just in the political domain, but also in the personal – then both freedom and the subject are emptied of all substance.

As Hegel views it, it is only my awareness of being obliged by something, and my acting in accordance with that commitment, that I can realize my freedom. He formulates it thus:

A binding duty can appear as a limitation only in relation to indeterminate subjectivity or abstract freedom, and to the drives of the natural will or the moral will which arbitrarily determines its own indeterminate good. The individual, however, finds his *liberation* in duty. On the one hand, he is liberated from his dependence on mere natural drives, and from the burden he labors under as a particular subject in his moral reflections on obligation and desire; and on the other hand, he is liberated from that indeterminate subjectivity which does not attain existence or the objective determinacy of action, but remains *within itself* and has no actuality. In duty, the individual liberates himself so as to attain substantial freedom.[59]

Hegel also describes the freedom to be gained by being with oneself in another. 'Love means in general the consciousness of my unity with another, so that I am not isolated on my own, but gain my self-consciousness only through the renunciation of my independent existence and through knowing myself as the unity of myself with another and of the other with me.'[60] According to Hegel, the need to love and be loved is the most fundamental of all our needs, and its place is in a family context, where one is conscious of being part of a unity. All individuals in the family are free, furthermore, even if they do not always feel free. This sense of unfreedom originates from the duty one has to *stay put*, even if it has been a bad day, week or month. Hegel's point, however, is that entering into such obligations is a realization of freedom, rather than a submission to unfreedom – it gives personal freedom content, it is the freedom to become someone.

Living together with others teaches a person about himself – it becomes clear to the individual who is is, and so he *becomes himself*. From this point of view, we can also regard a permanent commitment to another person as the freedom to become ourselves. And this idea is obviously not limited to romantic relationships. It applies anytime one takes on a care-giving role. When my father contracted cancer, I chose to set aside philosophy and nurse him until he died eighteen months later. According to a negative conception of freedom, my freedom was severely restricted during that time, as I had to put my regular life on hold, moving in with him and caring for him full-time. Yet, I would argue that it was rather a realization of my freedom, since I *chose* to nurse him during that period. It was an expression of what truly mattered to me. Such choices impose limits on one's conduct and demands self-discipline. Yet if freedom, in contrast, is interpreted as the absence of limitations, and self-discipline saddles us with such limitations, then self-discipline itself becomes an obstacle to freedom. As such, only a resolute and unbridled unrestraint will meet the freedom criteria. This conclusion, however, is erroneous. If I discipline myself, and choose to repudiate certain desires and behaviours, the very fact that I myself have set these boundaries eliminates any attendant unfreedom. When it comes down to it, the crucial issue is not whether personal freedom has its limits – these will be present in any case – but whether these limits are self-imposed.

Self-imposed limits are a realization of personal freedom. For what in the world is freedom for, if not to enable us to choose to exert ourselves for those who mean the most to us when they need us the most? In essence, personal freedom is not the absence of all burdens, but instead the freedom to devote ourselves fully to what *means* the most us, to things in life we hold the most dear.

Afterword

This book has addressed many different aspect of human freedom. I have attempted to establish a connection between them, from the basic ontological conditions for human action, where I tried to demonstrate that, within the frame of a naturalistic worldview, it is entirely possible to champion a relatively robust form of freedom of action, via the political framework where such freedom should have its place, before finally concluding with freedom's personal dimension, which concerns how our personal freedom should be used.

This book essentially culminates with the insight contained in David Foster Wallace's adage: 'The really important kind of freedom involves attention, and awareness, and discipline, and effort, and being able to truly care about other people and to sacrifice for them, over and over, in myriad petty little unsexy ways, every day.'[1] We should be thankful for our freedom, for it is what separates us from the other animals. And probably the best way to express our gratitude is to use our freedom for something more substantial than navel gazing.

The book's ontological discussion concluded with an account of autonomy that established some guidelines for the kind of society in which a being capable of such autonomy ought to live. The political discussion chiefly focused on the rights problematic, as it was broadly interpreted, on having a defined space for free self-development. It would have certainly been suitable here to have explored more extensively the different institutional and material conditions for freedom, but an author must take into account available time and space, and accordingly, make pragmatic choices about what to leave out. This choice, though free, is made in the awareness that every human action has its restrictions, including the task of writing a book.

Translating freedom to practice – for what good is our freedom if left unused – is simply to participate in the world with all the limitations the act entails. In other words, there is no such thing as unlimited freedom – all true freedom will have its boundaries. The boundaries on freedom, however, are not uniform in nature. Some limits are absolute and immutable, and others can be transformed through social or personal processes; some are legitimate, others are illegitimate.

The free self is always situated, but it nonetheless has the ability to reflect upon and alter itself and its surroundings. For example, the self is not completely at the mercy of the values with which it grew up and is surrounded. Being situated is not synonymous with being determined; it simply means that, when it comes to our orientation in the world and in ourselves, we never start from scratch – we are already located within a horizon of values and conceptions. This horizon, however, is also open to change. One can traverse it by experiencing the world and reflecting upon that experience, thereby establishing new horizons for personal freedom.

Freedom is a lifelong skill we hone as we continue to work on ourselves.

REFERENCES

Foreword

1 Regarding books on the history of freedom, the following, for example, can be recommended: David Schmidtz and Jason Brennan, *A Brief History of Liberty* (Oxford, 2010); Orlando Patterson, *Freedom*, vol. 1: *Freedom in the Making of Western Culture* (New York, 1991); Ben Wilson, *What Price Liberty?* (London, 2009); A. C. Grayling, *Towards the Light: The Story of the Struggles for Liberty and Rights* (London, 2007). The specific concern of these books is political freedom. However, an anthology comprised of philosophical texts from across philosophical history with an emphasis on freedom's ontology is Thomas Pink and Martin Stone, eds, *The Will and Human Action: From Antiquity to the Present Day* (London, 2003). Some good anthologies that exhibit much breadth in terms of more recent philosophical discussions of freedom are Robert Kane, ed., *The Oxford Handbook of Free Will* (Oxford, 2002); Gary Watson, ed., *Free Will*, 2nd edn (Oxford, 2003); Joseph Keim Campbell, Michael O'Rourke and David Shier, eds, *Freedom and Determinism* (Cambridge, MA, and London, 2004); Laura Waddell Ekstrom, ed., *Agency and Responsibility: Essays on the Metaphysics of Freedom* (Boulder, CO, 2000); Ian Carter, Matthew H. Kramer and Hillel Steiner, eds, *Freedom: A Philosophical Anthology* (Oxford and Malden, MA, 2007).
2 Daniel C. Dennett, *Elbow Room: Varieties of Free Will Worth Wanting* (Cambridge, MA, 1984), p. 3. For Dennett's viewpoint on freedom, see also his *Freedom Evolves* (London, 2003).

Introduction

1 B. F. Skinner, *Walden Two* [1948] (Indianapolis, IN, and Cambridge, 2005), p. 247.
2 Colin Turnbull, *The Mountain People* (New York, 1972). In this context, it should be mentioned that Turnbull's book has been the subject of extensive critique and has, for the most part, been discredited. However, that fact is irrelevant for my use of the book in the example with Niles.
3 Skinner, *Walden Two*, p. 247.
4 W. B. Gallie, 'Essentially Contested Concepts', *Proceedings of the Aristotelian Society*, 167 (1956).

5 Montesquieu, *The Spirit of the Laws*, trans. and ed. Anne M. Cohler, Basia C. Miller and Harold S. Stone (Cambridge, 2005), Book XI/2, p. 154.

6 Abraham Lincoln, 'Address at Sanitary Fair, Baltimore, Maryland, Apr. 11, 1864', in *Collected Works of Abraham Lincoln*, ed. Roy P. Basler (New Brunswick, NJ, 1953), vol. VII, pp. 301f.

7 Isaiah Berlin, 'Two Concepts of Liberty', in Berlin, *Four Essays on Liberty* (Oxford, 1969), p. 2.

8 It also depends upon one's basic metaphysical assumptions. Often sweeping categorizations of philosophical positions, such as 'naturalism' and 'pragmatism', are of little use, since they contain a variety of mutually incompatible positions. However, at least they give some indication of the philosophical landscape in which one finds oneself. Should anyone demand my personal 'faith statement', I would categorize myself as a 'naturalist' in the broadest sense of the word. That is, I assume that nothing exists outside of the natural universe (or that if anything does exist, it cannot influence the natural universe whatsoever and therefore cannot be used to explain it). Most contemporary philosophers would agree with such a broadly conceived naturalism. Meanwhile, I do not believe that the sciences in general, or that the natural sciences in particular, can tell us everything that is worth knowing about human life. I am also not a reductionist and do not think that different ontological levels are fully reducible to lower levels, until everything that exists can be explained in terms of elementary physical objects. On the contrary, I am a pluralist who believes that we can better understand a phenomenon by explaining it on many different levels through a variety of theoretical lenses.

9 John Dewey, *Human Nature and Conduct* (New York, 1922), p. 303.

10 Isaiah Berlin, *Liberty* (Oxford, 2002), pp. 4–12, 16ff., 29f., 16off., 265–70, 322ff.

11 Cf. Kathleen D. Vohs and Jonathan W. Schooler, 'The Value of Believing in Free Will: Encouraging a Belief in Determinism Increases Cheating', *Psychological Science*, 1 (2008).

12 Another relevant terminological detail here is that the English language, and hence the Anglophone literature, contains two different words for freedom: *liberty* and *freedom*. This does not occur in any other European language. In the literature, it is common to regard these two words as synonyms and that is what I will also do. An exception to this rule is Hannah Arendt, who draws a significant distinction between the two terms. However, I will not discuss her viewpoint here. For a good representation of Arendt's position, as well as the etymology of both expressions, see Hanna Fenichel Pitkin, 'Are Freedom and Liberty Twins?', *Political Theory*, 4 (1988). Bernard Williams also distinguishes between *freedom* and *liberty*. In his case, however, it is more of a pragmatic move designed to differentiate between an ontological and a political thematic. He does not appear to think there is a difference between the two expressions in normal language usage (Bernard Williams, 'From Freedom to Liberty: The Construction of a Political Value', *Philosophy and Public Affairs*, 1 (2001)).

13 For a discussion of the relationship between liberalism and libertarianism that draws a significantly sharper distinction than I believe is necessary, see Samuel Freeman, 'Illiberal Libertarians: Why Libertarianism Is Not a Liberal View', *Philosophy and Public Affairs*, 2 (2002). An anthology with a number of texts that, broadly speaking, belong to the political libertarian tradition is David

Boaz, ed., *The Libertarian Reader* (New York, 1997). A reference work that offers short articles on central thinkers and concepts is Ronald Hamowy, ed., *The Encyclopedia of Libertarianism* (Thousand Oaks, CA, and London, 2008). A good discussion can also be found in Norman P. Barry, *On Classical Liberalism and Libertarianism* (New York, 1987). A quite entertaining account of libertarianism's history in the USA is Brian Doherty, *Radicals for Capitalism: A Freewheeling History of the Modern American Libertarian Movement* (New York, 2007).

14 From this we can deduce that the concept of 'anarcho-capitalism' is also not a form of liberalism. At this point, anarcho-capitalism is a rather marginal ideology. If one were to name any of its theorists, Murray Rothbard and David Friedman, for example, would prove central. An anarcho-capitalist believes that the only desirable relationships are those voluntarily established between individuals, and that this idea is incompatible with the individual's being subject to a government that holds a force monopoly and such. Anarcho-capitalism further believes that a fully unregulated market is the only acceptable option, and that, for instance, protection from violence – or even from the law itself – are products individuals can either choose or neglect to buy from competing providers on the market. At this point, we are nowhere near what can rationally be called 'liberalism'. Liberalism, that is, does not consider government to be an unacceptable monopoly, as anarcho-capitalism does. At the same time, anarcho-capitalism tends to be regarded as a libertarian position.

15 The combined literature on different aspects of liberalism amounts to several thousand volumes. However, one has to begin somewhere and the following works can be used as springboards for further study: Hans Blokland, *Freedom and Culture in Western Society* (London, 1997); Alfonso J. Damico, ed., *Liberals on Liberalism* (Totowa, NJ, 1986); Katrin Flikschuh, *Freedom: Contemporary Liberal Perspectives* (London, 2007); Gerald F. Gaus, *Contemporary Theories of Liberalism* (London, 2003); John Gray, *Liberalism* (Buckingham, 1995); John Gray, *Post-liberalism* (London, 1993); John Gray, *The Two Faces of Liberalism* (Cambridge, 2000); Stephen Holmes, *Passions and Constraint* (Chicago, 1995); Paul Kelly, *Liberalism* (London, 2005); Pierre Manent, *An Intellectual History of Liberalism*, trans. Rebecca Balinski (Princeton, NJ, 1995); Ellen Frankel Paul et al., eds, *Natural Rights Liberalism from Locke to Nozick* (Cambridge, 2005); Ellen Frankel Paul et al., eds, *Liberalism: Old and New* (Cambridge, 2007); Paul Starr, *Freedom's Power. The True Force of Liberalism* (New York, 2007); Alan Wolfe, *The Future of Liberalism* (New York, 2009).

16 Some people will distinguish between freedom of will and freedom of action, where freedom of will consists in willing what one chooses and freedom of action means acting as one chooses, but this type of distinction will not play an important role in my discussion. I regard these ideas as two aspects of one and the same phenomenon. In this interpretation, one cannot have freedom of will without freedom of action and certainly not freedom of action without freedom of will. Other people will also distinguish between freedom of will and voluntariness, where one can act voluntarily without having freedom of will, but I do not accept this distinction either. Instead, I will argue that freedom of will is fundamental to voluntary actions.

I

To Act Voluntarily

1 A comprehensive historical overview, which holds countless fascinating court documents from such animal trials, can be found in Edward Payson Evans, *The Criminal Prosecution and Capital Punishment of Animals* (London, 1906). A more recent account and discussion of this subject is Jen Girgen, 'The Historical and Contemporary Prosecution and Punishment of Animals', in *Animal Law Review*, IX (2003).

2 Girgen, 'The Historical and Contemporary Prosecution and Punishment of Animals', p. 110.

3 Charles Darwin, *The Descent of Man and Selection in Relation to Sex* (Princeton, NJ, 1981), vol. I, p. 70.

4 Ibid., p. 88f.

5 Aristotle, *Politics*, trans. Ernest Barker (Oxford, 1995), 1253a.

6 Aristotle, *Aristotle's Nicomachean Ethics*, trans. Robert C. Bartlett and Susan D. Collins (Chicago, 2011), Book III, 1110a.

7 Cf. Dominic Streatfeild, *Brainwash: The Secret History of Mind Control* (London, 2006).

8 John Stuart Mill, *On Liberty*, ed. Elizabeth Rapaport (Indianapolis, IN, 1978), p. 56.

9 Ibid., p. 67.

10 Immanuel Kant, 'Lectures on Pedagogy', in *Anthropology, History, and Education*, trans. Mary Gregor, ed. Günter Zöller and Robert B. Louden (Cambridge, 2007), p. 454f. Cf. Immanuel Kant, 'Anthropology from a Pragmatic Point of View', ibid., p. 261.

11 Cf. Maurice Merleau-Ponty, *Phenomenology of Perception*, trans. Colin Smith (London, 1989), p. 146.

12 G.W.F. Hegel, *The Encyclopedia Logic: Part 1 of the Encyclopaedia of Philosophical Sciences*, trans. T. F. Geraets et al. (Indianapolis, IN, 1991), § 410.

13 Jonathan Jacobs, *Choosing Character: Responsibility for Virtue and Vice* (Ithaca, NY, and London, 2001), p. 19.

14 Fyodor Dostoevsky, 'Environment', *A Writer's Diary*, trans. Kenneth Lantz (Evanston, IL, 1994), vol. I, p. 136.

2

Freedom and Determinism

1 Letter to Molyneux, 20 January 1963, in John Locke, *The Correspondence of John Locke* (Oxford, 1979), vol. IV.

2 James Boswell, *The Life of Johnson* (London, 2008), p. 681 (15 April 1778).

3 Edward O. Wilson, *Consilience: The Unity of Knowledge* (London, 1999), p. 131; Edward O. Wilson, *On Human Nature* (Harmondsworth, 1995), p. 195.

4 Boswell, *The Life of Johnson*, p. 681 (15 April 1778).

5 Arthur Schopenhauer, *Schopenhauer: Prize Essay on the Freedom of the Will*, trans. Eric F. J. Payne, ed. Günter Zöller (Cambridge, 1999), p. 37.

6 For a discussion of this idea, see for example John R. Searle, *Intentionality: An Essay in the Philosophy of Mind* (Cambridge, 1983), p. 130.

7 Daniel M. Wegner, *The Illusion of Conscious Will* (Cambridge, MA, and London, 2002), p. 317f.

8 Colin Blakemore, *The Mind Machine* (London, 1988), p. 270.

9 For a very interesting discussion of this problem, see Jürgen Habermas, 'The Language Game of Responsible Agency and the Problem of Free Will: How Can Epistemic Dualism Be Reconciled with Ontological Monism', *Philosophical Explorations*, 10 (2007), pp. 13–50. See also Thomas Nagel, *The View from Nowhere* (Oxford, 1986).

10 William James, *The Will to Believe and Other Essays* (New York, 1956), p. 151.

11 It is notoriously difficult to explain what is meant by 'cause'. For a broad and thorough discussion of different perspectives and theories on causality, see Helen Beebee, Christopher Hitchcock and Peter Menzies, eds, *The Oxford Handbook of Causation* (Oxford and New York, 2009).

12 Ludwig Wittgenstein, *Philosophical Occasions, 1912–1951* (Indianapolis, IN, and Cambridge, 1993), pp. 429–44.

13 Ibid., p. 431.

14 Ibid., p. 433.

15 Ludwig Wittgenstein, *Culture and Value*, trans. Peter Winch (Chicago, 1984), p. 37.

16 Nancy Cartwright, *How the Laws of Physics Lie* (Oxford, 1983).

17 Denis Noble, *The Music of Life: Biology Beyond Genes* (Oxford and New York, 2006), chap. 5.

18 Cf. Helen Steward, *A Metaphysics for Freedom* (Oxford, 2012).

19 Lucretius, *On the Nature of Things*, trans. Frank O. Copley (New York, 1977), Book II, 216–93.

20 Patrick Suppes, 'The Transcendental Character of Determinism', *Midwest Studies in Philosophy*, 18 (1993), p. 254.

21 Libet has explained these experiments and their interpretation in a number of works. For our purposes, the following works are particularly central, 'Unconscious Cerebral Initiative and the Role of Conscious Will in Voluntary Action', *Behavioural and Brain Sciences*, 8 (1985); 'Consciousness, Free Action and the Brain', *Journal of Consciousness Studies*, 8 (2001); 'Do We Have Free Will?', in *The Oxford Handbook of Free Will*, ed. Robert Kane (Oxford, 2002). Libet has also made his research more accessible to a broader audience in the book *Mind Time: The Temporal Factor in Consciousness* (Cambridge, MA, and London, 2004). An anthology with many good discussions of Libet's work is Walter Sinnott-Armstrong and Lynn Nadel, ed., *Conscious Will and Responsibility: A Tribute to Benjamin Libet* (Oxford, 2011). For this interpretation of Libet, see for example Wegner, *The Illusion of Conscious Will*.

22 Chun Siong Soon et al., 'Unconscious Determinants of Free Decisions in the Human Brain', *Nature Neuroscience*, 13 April 2008; John-Dylan Haines, 'Beyond Libet: Long-term Prediction of Free Choices from Neuroimaging Signals', in *Conscious Will and Responsibility: A Tribute to Benjamin Libet*, ed. Walter Sinnott-Armstrong and Lynn Nadel (Oxford, 2011).

23 See for example Libet, 'Consciousness, Free Action and the Brain', p. 63; Libet, 'Do We Have Free Will?', pp. 562f.; Libet, *Mind Time*, pp. 154ff.

24 Libet, 'Do We Have Free Will'?, p. 563.

25 Davide Rigoni et al., 'Inducing Disbelief in Free Will Alters Brain Correlates

of Preconscious Motor Preparation: The Brain Minds Whether We Believe in Free Will or Not', *Psychological Science*, 5 (2011).

26 Raymond Tallis, *Aping Mankind: Neuromania, Darwinitis and the Misrepresentation of Mankind* (Durham, 2011), p. 248f.

27 My interpretation of Libet's experiments here is similar to that found in Dennett, *Freedom Evolves*, p. 239f.

28 For a good discussion of this viewpoint, see for example Alva Noë, *Out of Our Heads: Why You are Not Your Brain, and Other Lessons from the Biology of Consciousness* (New York, 2009).

29 Michael S. Gazzaniga, *Who's in Charge? Free Will and the Science of the Brain* (New York, 2011), p. 190.

30 Ibid.

31 The role that such up-on-down causality plays in the free will discussion is a matter of debate. An anthology that makes many good contributions to this topic is Nancey Murphy, George F. R. Ellis and Timothy O'Connor, eds, *Downward Causation and the Neurobiology of Free Will* (Berlin and Heidelberg, 2009). See also Nancey Murphy and Warren S. Brown, *Did My Neurons Make Me Do It? Philosophical and Neurobiological Perspectives on Moral Responsibility and Free Will* (Oxford and New York, 2006).

32 Cf. Carl Gustav Hempel, *Philosophy of Natural Science* (Inglewood Cliffs, NJ, 1966), p. 78.

33 Immanuel Kant, *Dreams of a Spirit-seer Elucidated by Dreams of Metaphysics*, in *Theoretical Philosophy, 1755–1770*, trans. and ed. David Walford (Cambridge, 1992), pp. 312f.

34 Many more positions are logically possible when we also take into account the fact that numerous philosophers take an 'agnostic' stance toward either determinism's truth and/or freedom's existence. If we expand the table to also include these possible combinations, we end up with the following:

	DETERMINISM	FREEDOM	TERM
1.	Yes	No	Hard determinism
2.	No	Yes	Libertarianism
3.	Yes	Yes	Compatibilism
4.	No	No	Scepticism
5.	Yes	?	
6.	?	Yes	
7.	No	?	
8.	?	No	
9.	?	?	

As previously stated, however, I will limit myself to a discussion of positions (1), (2) and (3) in the present work.

35 As a result, it would conceivably be better to characterize the two as 'exclusive' and 'inclusive' determinism, where exclusive determinism moves to exclude freedom from natural necessity's realm, while inclusive determinism wants to include it. However, I do not think much will be gained by introducing new terminology here, and have, therefore, chosen to continue with the established term: 'compatibilism'.

36 One of the best discussions of this position, which also attempts to show its ethical and existential implications, is Derk Pereboom, *Living without Free Will* (Cambridge, 2001).

37 See especially Galen Strawson, *Freedom and Belief* (Oxford, 1991).

38 See for example Saul Smilansky, *Free Will and Illusion* (Oxford, 2000).

39 Cf. Hagop Sarkassian et al., 'Is Belief in Free Will a Cultural Universal?', *Mind and Language*, 3 (2010). See also Shaun Nichols and Joshua Knobe, 'Moral Responsibility and Determinism: The Cognitive Science of Folk Intuitions', *Noûs*, 4 (2007).

40 Peter van Inwagen, *An Essay on Free Will* (Oxford, 1983), p. 16.

41 There is a large number of different libertarian positions. For a good, systematic discussion of these positions, which places emphasis on more recent analytical philosophy, see Randolph Clarke, *Libertarian Accounts of Free Will* (Oxford, 2003).

42 Perhaps the person who has used such examples most effectively to defend/ justify libertarian freedom is Robert Kane, *The Significance of Free Will* (Oxford and New York, 1996).

43 Aristotle, *Aristotle's Nicomachean Ethics*, trans. Robert C. Bartlett and Susan D. Collins (Chicago, 2011), Book III, 1110a17f.

44 Ibid., 1113b6.

45 Aristotle, *Physics*, trans. R. P. Hardie and R. K. Gaye, in *The Complete Works of Aristotle*, ed. Jonathan Barnes (Princeton, NJ, 1984) , vol. I, 256a6–8.

46 Roderick M. Chisholm, 'Human Freedom and the Self', in *Free Will*, ed. Gary Watson, 2nd edn (Oxford, 2003).

47 Gary Watson, 'Introduction', in *Free Will*, ed. Watson, p. 10.

48 A. J. Ayer, *Philosophical Essays* (London, 1954), p. 275.

49 As John McDowell writes: 'And judging, making up our minds what to think, is something for which we are responsible – something we freely do, as opposed to something that merely happens in our lives. Of course a belief is not always, or even typically, a result of our exercising this freedom to decide what to think. But even when a belief is not freely adopted, it is an actualization of capacities of a kind, the conceptual, whose paradigmatic mode of actualization is in the exercise of freedom that judging is.' John McDowell, 'Having the World in View: Lecture One', *Journal of Philosophy*, 95 (1998), p. 434.

50 John Dupré, *The Disorder of Things: Metaphysical Foundations of the Disunity of Science* (Cambridge, MA, and London, 1993), p. 215. See also John Dupré, *Human Nature and the Limits of Science* (Oxford, 2001), chap. 7.

51 Wittgenstein, *Philosophical Occasions, 1912–1951*, p. 431.

52 John Stuart Mill underscores the same thing: 'Though we cannot emancipate ourselves from the laws of nature as a whole, we can escape from any particular law of nature, if we are able to withdraw ourselves from the circumstances in which it acts. Thought we can do nothing except through laws of nature, we can use one law to counteract another.' 'Nature', *Collected Works of John Stuart Mill*, vol. x (Toronto and London, 1974), p. 379.

53 Bernard Williams, 'Practical Necessity', in *Moral Luck: Philosophical Papers, 1973–1980* (Cambridge, 1981), p. 130.

54 David Hume, *A Treatise of Human Nature*, ed. David Fate Norton and Mary J. Norton (Oxford, 2007), vol. I, B2.3.2.

55 Perhaps the best discussion of this viewpoint in a compatibilistic framework is given by John Martin Fischer and Mark Ravizza, *Responsibility and Control: A Theory of Moral Responsibility* (Cambridge, 1999).

56 Harry G. Frankfurt, 'Alternate Possibilities and Moral Responsibility', in *The Importance of What We Care About* (Cambridge, 1988). Frankfurt's article has resulted in its own academic industry of commentary, objection and defence, and this is not the place to outline this whole debate. A selection of works on Frankfurt's theory can be found in David Widerker and Michael Mckenna, eds, *Moral Responsibility and Alternative Possibilities: Essays on the Importance of Alternative Possibilities*, revd edn (Aldershot, 2006).

57 In addition, there are other objections to the requirement that a free action requires the agent to be able to act otherwise. For example, Dana Kay Nelkin argues that when it comes to the ability to act otherwise, there is an asymmetry between good and bad actions. She argues that this particular ability is required for free actions that are not characterized as good or were not performed for good reasons, whereas the requirement does not exist for good actions performed for good reasons (Dana Kay Nelkin, *Making Sense of Freedom and Responsibility* (Oxford, 2011)).

58 At the same time, there is no need for a compatibilist to regard a fear-occasioned action as unfree. For example, Hobbes would view an action prompted by fear to be as free as an action caused by any other emotion or inclination. The crucial point for Hobbes is whether or not a person is being physically prevented from acting as he or she desires. However, Hobbes's freedom concept will be outlined and discussed at greater length at the beginning of chapter Six.

59 For an interesting discussion that ends with this same viewpoint, see Mark Balaguer, *Free Will as an Open Scientific Problem* (Cambridge, MA, and London, 2010), chap. 4.

60 It bears pointing out here that the question of whether responsibility actually presupposes freedom is a matter of extensive debate. John Martin Fischer and Mark Ravizza argue in *Responsibility and Control: A Theory of Moral Responsibility* that freedom entails an ability to act otherwise, that several future options remain open, while responsibility does not require this, and therefore responsibility is possible even if freedom is not. However, I will not pursue their controversial argument in this context.

61 This viewpoint is related to Alfred Mele's 'agnostic autonomism', in Mele, *Autonomous Agents: From Self-control to Autonomy* (Oxford and New York, 1995).

3
Reactive and Objective Attitudes

1 Peter F. Strawson, *Freedom and Resentment and Other Essays* [1974] (London, 2008). Strawson's article has been the object of much debate. A solid anthology that covers many of the most central perspectives is Michael McKenna and Paul Russell, eds, *Free Will and Reactive Attitudes: Perspectives on P. F. Strawson's 'Freedom and Resentment'* (Farnham, 2008).

2 Strawson, *Freedom and Resentment*, p. 6.

3 Ibid., p. 8f.

4 Ibid., p. 9.

5 Jean-Jacques Rousseau, *The Reveries of the Solitary Walker*, trans. Charles E. Butterworth (Indianapolis, IN, 1992), p. 114.

6 Samuel Butler, *Erewhon* (London, 1985), pp. 102f.

7 Galen Strawson, *Freedom and Belief* (Oxford, 1991), pp. 88f.

8 This is no uncontroversial assertion, and Shaun Nichols among others argues that reactive attitudes will not be significantly influenced by an acceptance of determinism. Shaun Nichols, 'After Incompatibilism: A Naturalistic Defense of Reactive Attitudes', *Philosophical Perspectives*, 21 (2007).

9 Strawson, *Freedom and Resentment*, p. 12.

10 Michael S. Gazzaniga, *Who's in Charge? Free Will and the Science of the Brain* (New York, 2011), p. 194.

11 For an informative discussion of the exemption from guilt, which focuses more on the strict legal aspects than on the moral one, see Lawrie Reznek, *Evil or Ill? Justifying the Insanity Defense* (London and New York, 1997).

12 Galen Strawson, 'The Impossibility of Moral Responsibility', *Philosophical Studies*, 75 (1994).

13 Aristotle, *Aristotle's Nicomachean Ethics*, 1114a13–22.

14 For a modern version of the Aristotelian theory that holds one's character to be voluntary in many significant respects, and the individual to be accordingly responsible for the actions that follow from that character, see Jonathan Jacobs, *Choosing Character: Responsibility for Virtue and Vice* (Ithaca, NY, and London, 2001).

4
Autonomy

1 In this context, it should be mentioned that this precise connection between freedom and responsibility is disputed by John Martin Fischer and Mark Ravizza, *Responsibility and Control: A Theory of Moral Responsibility* (Cambridge, 1999), who argue that we can have responsibility without having freedom. However, their 'semi-compatibilistic' position will not be pursued further.

2 There is an extensive literature on autonomy and within it there are a variety of positions. For anthologies that contain the most relevant theoreticians and perspectives in contemporary philosophy, see John Christman, ed., *The Inner Citadel: Essays on Individual Autonomy* (Oxford and New York, 1989); John Christman and Joel Anderson, eds, *Autonomy and the Challenges to Liberalism: New Essays* (Cambridge, 2005); Ellen Frankel Paul et al., eds, *Autonomy* (Cambridge, 2003); James Stacey Taylor, ed., *Personal Autonomy: New Essays on Personal Autonomy and Its Role in Contemporary Moral Philosophy* (Cambridge and New York, 2005).

3 For a more comprehensive discussion of the concept's history, see for example Joachim Ritter and Karlfried Gründer, eds, *Historisches Wörterbuch der Philosophie* (Darmstadt, 1980), vol. I, pp. 701–19.

4 At this point, the description of autonomy seems to correspond with that of freedom. Gerald Dworkin, however, argues that autonomy is not synonymous with freedom, and justifies this by pointing out that one can interfere with a

patient's autonomy by lying to him or deceiving him, but that this will not limit the patient's freedom. (Gerald Dworkin, *The Theory and Practice of Autonomy* (Cambridge, 1988), p. 14.) That argument is only tenable if such encroachment does not actually violate the patient's freedom. Dworkin is on safe ground when it comes to a Hobbesian freedom concept. However, as I will demonstrate in the context of negative and positive liberty in chapter Six, his freedom concept is, in reality, untenable, and manipulation, threat and deception must also be said to violate an agent's freedom. If we return to the Aristotelian criteria for voluntariness, furthermore, it is clear that both lying and deception undermine the agent's possibility for voluntary action, since the knowledge criteria cannot be fulfilled under such conditions.

5 Perhaps the most influential explanation for this type of viewpoint is Harry Frankfurt, 'Freedom of the Will and the Concept of the Person', in *The Importance of What We Care About* (Cambridge, 1988).

6 There are many representatives for this type of viewpoint, but Charles Taylor, for example, has made an important contribution to the debate with Charles Taylor, *Sources of the Self: The Making of Modern Identity* (Cambridge, MA, 1989); *The Ethics of Authenticity* (Cambridge, MA, 1992); and 'What's Wrong with Negative Liberty?' in *Philosophy and the Human Sciences* (Cambridge, 1985), vol. II. Taylor's position, however, will be further discussed in chapters Six and Thirteen.

7 Christine M. Korsgaard, *The Sources of Normativity* (Cambridge, 1996) and *Self-constitution: Agency, Identity and Integrity* (Oxford and New York, 2009).

8 Harry G. Frankfurt, *The Reasons of Love* (Princeton, NJ, and New York, 2004), p. 97.

9 Ortwin de Graef et al., 'Discussion with Harry G. Frankfurt', *Ethical Perspectives*, 5 (1998), p. 33.

10 Harry G. Frankfurt, *Taking Ourselves Seriously and Getting It Right* (Stanford, CA, 2006), p. 14.

11 Harry G. Frankfurt, *The Importance of What We Care About* (Cambridge, 1988), p. 20.

12 Ibid., p. 18.

13 Ibid., p. 25.

14 Frankfurt, *Taking Ourselves Seriously and Getting It Right*, p. 7.

15 Harry G. Frankfurt, *Necessity, Volition, and Love* (Cambridge, 1999), p. 114.

16 John Stuart Mill, *A System of Logic Ratiocinative and Inductive*, vol. VIII of *Collected Works of John Stuart Mill* (Toronto and London, 1974), p. 840.

17 Aristotle, *Aristotle's Nicomachean Ethics*, trans. Robert C. Bartlett and Susan D. Collins (Chicago, 2011), 1114b22.

18 Mill writes that our freedom consciousness is comprised of the fact that 'I feel (or am convinced) that I could, and even should, have chosen the other course if I had preferred it, that is, if I had liked it better; but not that I could have chosen one course while I preferred the other'. (John Stuart Mill, *An Examination of Sir William Hamilton's Philosophy*, vol. VIII of *Collected Works of John Stuart Mill*, p. 450.) This is not meant to deny that we often do what we know we should not, but that such actions must be explained by saying, for example, that the reason to act immorally in a given situation outweighs the reason to act morally.

19 Mill, *An Examination of Sir William Hamilton's Philosophy*, p. 452f.

20 Cf. Gary Watson, 'Free Agency', *Journal of Philosophy*, 72 (1975), pp. 205–20.

21 Dworkin, *The Theory and Practice of Autonomy*, p. 15f.

22 The most comprehensive presentation of his viewpoint on autonomy can be found in John Christman, *The Politics of Persons: Individual Autonomy and Socio-historical Selves* (Cambridge, 2009).

23 Luke Rhinehart, *The Dice Man* (New York, 1971).

24 Henry E. Allison, *Kant's Theory of Freedom* (Cambridge, 1990), p. 40; Immanuel Kant, *Religion within the Limits of Reason Alone*, trans. Theodore M. Greene and Hoyt H. Hudson (New York, 1960), p. 14.

25 See for example Daniel Kahneman, *Thinking, Fast and Slow* (New York, 2011).

26 Stuart Hampshire, *Thought and Action* (London, 1959), p. 177.

27 Cf. Michael Frede, *A Free Will: Origins of the Notion in Ancient Thought* (Berkeley, CA, 2011), p. 75.

5
The Liberal Democracy

1 Francis Fukuyama, *The End of History and the Last Man* (New York, 1992).

2 G.W.F. Hegel, *Phenomenology of Spirit*, trans. A. V. Miller, ed. J. N. Findlay (Oxford, 1977); Alexandre Kojève, *Introduction to the Reading of Hegel: Lectures on The Phenomenology of Spirit*, trans. James H. Nichols, Jr., ed. Allan Bloom (Ithaca, NY, 1980).

3 Francis Fukuyama, *The Origins of Political Order: From Prehuman Times to the French Revolution* (London, 2011), p. 4.

4 See especially ibid., chap. 5.

5 Francis Fukuyama, 'The Future of History: Can Liberal Democracy Survive the Decline of the Middle Class?', *Foreign Affairs*, 1/91 (2012).

6 This can be found at www.freedomhouse.org.

7 I shall not engage here in an extensive discussion of the elements of democracy, because that would take us too far off course. A good collection of texts central to the theme can be found in Robert A. Dahl, Ian Shapiro and Jose Antonio Cheibub, eds, *The Democracy Sourcebook* (Cambridge, MA, and London, 2003). On the history of democracy, see for example John Dunn, *Democracy: A History* (New York, 2005) and John Keane, *The Life and Death of Democracy* (London, 2009).

8 Wilhelm Röpke, *Das Kulturideal des Liberalismus* (Frankfurt am Main, 1947), p. 17.

9 It must be underscored that, given his defence of absolutism, Hobbes is far removed from the liberal tradition. In opposition to more democratically inclined theorists, who argue that there is less freedom in absolute monarchy than in democracy, Hobbes claims that man will be subject to laws under both forms of government, and that one form of government must by no means have more numerous and stricter laws than the other. All laws adopted by the sovereign are regarded as God's laws, yet the sovereign determines what God's laws are.

10 Wilhelm von Humboldt, *The Limits of State Action*, ed. J. W. Burrow (London, 1969), p. 44.

11 John Locke, *The Second Treatise of Government*, in *Two Treatises of Government*, ed. Ian Shapiro (New Haven, CT, and London, 2003), §27.

12 John Locke, *The First Treatise of Government*, in *Two Treatises of Government*, ed. Shapiro, §42.

13 Montesquieu, *The Spirit of the Laws*, trans. and ed. Anne M. Cohler, Basia C. Miller and Harold S. Stone (Cambridge, 2005), Book 23.

14 Cf. Adam Smith, *An Inquiry into the Nature and Causes of the Wealth of Nations*, (Indianapolis, IN, 1981), Book 3, chap. 3.

15 Alexis de Tocqueville, *The Ancien Régime and the French Revolution*, trans. Arthur Goldhammer, ed. Jon Elster (Cambridge, 2011), p. 151.

16 John Stuart Mill, *Principles of Political Economy with some of their Applications to Social Philosophy*, vol. III of the *Collected Works of John Stuart Mill* (Toronto and London, 1974), p. 938.

17 This must be emphasized, since there are a number of representatives of *perfectionistic* liberalism, which is a theory of the good. See for example Joseph Raz, *The Morality of Freedom* (Oxford, 1986), and Steven Wall, *Liberalism, Perfectionism and Restraint* (Cambridge, 1998). In this context, a discussion of perfectionistic liberalism would take us too far off course.

18 Thomas Hobbes, *Leviathan* (Cambridge, 1991), p. 152.

19 In *Leviathan*, for example, Hobbes suggests that religious freedom should exist in society. The fundamental, inalienable rights with which Hobbes operates, in addition to religious freedom, include the right to defend oneself against attacks (both against one's body and one's honour), to not incriminate oneself and to neither take one's own life or another's life (and accordingly to refuse military service).

20 Edmund Burke, *On Empire, Liberty, and Reform. Speeches and Letters* (New Haven, CT, and London, 2000), p. 170.

21 It should also be observed here that economic freedom in present-day China is substantially less than many people have argued. In the Frazer Institute's *Economic Freedom of the World Index* for 2011, China ranks 92nd. (James Gwartney, Robert Lawson and Joshua Hall, *Economic Freedom of the World: 2011 Annual Report*, Vancouver: Frazer Institute 2011). In the Heritage Foundation's *Index of Economic Freedom 2012*, China ranks 138th (Terry Miller, Kim R. Holmes and Edwin J. Feulner, *2012 Index of Economic Freedom*, Washington and New York, The Heritage Foundation/ *Wall Street Journal* 2012).

22 Indra de Soysa and Hanne Fjelde, 'Is the Hidden Hand an Iron Fist? Capitalism and Civil Peace, 1970–2005', *Journal of Peace Research*, 3 (2010).

23 Milton Friedman, *Capitalism and Freedom* [1962] (Chicago, 2002), p. 10.

24 Stein Ringen, *What Democracy is For: On Freedom and Moral Government* (Princeton, NJ, and Oxford, 2009), p. 70.

25 Cf. Gwartney, Lawson and Hall, *Economic Freedom of the World: 2011 Annual Report* and Miller, Holmes and Feulner, *2012 Index of Economic Freedom*; http://hdr.undp.org.

26 At http://data.worldbank.org/indicator/SI.POV.GINI.

6
Positive and Negative Freedom

1 Isaiah Berlin, 'Two Concepts of Liberty', in Berlin, *Four Essays on Liberty* (Oxford, 1969), p. 2.

2 Thomas Hobbes, *Leviathan* (Cambridge, 1991), p. 91.

3 Thomas Hobbes, 'Selection from *The Questions concerning Liberty, Necessity, and Chance*', in *Hobbes and Bramhall on Liberty and Necessity*, ed. Vere Chappell (Cambridge, 1999), p. 81.

4 Hobbes, *Leviathan*, p. 146.

5 See also Thomas Hobbes, *Of Liberty and Necessity*, in *Hobbes and Bramhall on Liberty and Necessity*, ed. Chappell, p. 38.

6 Hobbes, *Leviathan*, p. 152.

7 Ibid., p. 206.

8 On this point, Hobbes differentiates, for example, from Kant, who distinguishes between fear of and respect for the law as determinant reasons for our actions, before arguing that respect is preferable simply because it does not deprive us of our freedom. (Immanuel Kant, *Groundwork of the Metaphysics of Morals*, trans. and ed. Mary Gregor (Cambridge, 1997), p. 14n.)

9 Hobbes, *Leviathan*, p. 239f.

10 Thomas Hobbes, *On the Citizen*, ed. and trans. Richard Tuck and Michael Silverthorne (Cambridge, 1998), p. 111.

11 Berlin, 'Two Concepts of Liberty', p. 3.

12 Isaiah Berlin, *Liberty* (Oxford, 2002), p. 32; cf. Berlin, 'Two Concepts of Liberty', p. 3.

13 Cf. Frank Dikötter, *Mao's Great Famine: The History of China's Most Devastating Catastrophe* (London, 2010).

14 Amartya Sen, *Poverty and Famines: An Essay on Entitlement and Deprivation* (Oxford, 1981).

15 Berlin, 'Two Concepts of Liberty', p. 3.

16 Ibid., p. 4f. Berlin, *Liberty*, p. 38.

17 Berlin, 'Two Concepts of Liberty', p. 13. See also Berlin, *Liberty*, p. 31.

18 John Rawls, *A Theory of Justice* (Cambridge, MA, 1971), p. 143.

19 This assumption can be problematized, since every increase in options does not necessarily result in more actual freedom of choice. Certainly not if we interpret freedom as something to be exercised. Indeed, too many alternatives can be hard to handle, though what constitutes 'too many' is up to the individual. Having four alternatives instead of two will normally increase one's freedom of choice, but having 100 alternatives does not necessarily imply greater freedom of choice than ten, since 100 will often appear paralysing. In *The Paradox of Choice*, Barry Schwartz argues that having the ability to choose is invaluable, but that the sheer number of possibilities in our society is so extreme as to be overwhelming. As a result, the variety of possible choices is no longer liberating; instead, we are 'tyrannized' by them. (Barry Schwartz, *The Paradox of Choice: Why More is Less* (New York, 2004, p. 2.) Among other things, Schwartz mentions one study that shows that customers who were offered six different jam samples were much more likely to decide to buy one than customers who were offered 24 samples (ibid, pp. 19f.). Initially, this seems strange, because

more alternatives would ostensibly increase the likelihood that one would find a favourite. In contrast, the large number of alternatives obviously makes it more difficult to decide on just one. According to Schwartz, having too many alternatives is injurious to freedom, because it requires time and energy that we ought to spend on other things. Of course, we all have different ways of dealing with a flood of choices. A common strategy is to stick to the same old thing and ignore other possibilities. For example, an individual might repeatedly purchase the same brand of car without evaluating any other. Another strategy is to 'outsource' the evaluation to another person, to a reviewer or an advisor, and simply follow their suggestion. That is a *voluntary* reduction of choice possibilities, and is clearly different from externally imposed limitations, for example, from a source of authority. As a consumer, there are many choices I deliberately avoid, such as switching electric and telephone providers, since I consider any potential savings I might incur to be less important than the time it would take me to to inform myself on prices and make that change. The trouble is simply not worth my while. However, I appreciate the fact that the possibilities are out there. I also assume that, for me as a consumer, competition between different providers will positively affect the price and quality of service.

20 We can further posit that the content of each alternative is known – or can be made known – to the agent. As a result, we cannot postulate cases of uncertainty, such as when an agent must swallow a pill from a bowl and every pill but one is deadly: in such a situation, the agent would obviously prefer to choose between a smaller number of pills.

21 Amartya Sen, *Rationality and Freedom* (Cambridge, 2002), chaps. 20–22.

22 Amartya Sen, *Inequality Reexamined* (Cambridge, MA, 1992), p. 51.

23 Berlin, 'Two Concepts of Liberty', p. 4.

24 Berlin, *Liberty*, p. 273.

25 Berlin, 'Two Concepts of Liberty', p. 8.

26 Berlin, *Liberty*, p. 39.

27 Jean-Jacques Rousseau, *The Social Contract*, trans. and ed. Victor Gourevitch (Cambridge, 1997), p. 53. My italics.

28 Ibid., p. 124.

29 Ibid., p. 104f.

30 Berlin, 'Two Concepts of Liberty', p. 9.

31 To observe such a development in positive freedom, we do not need to turn, for example, to Rousseau, or to communist or fascist regimes. The so-called 'new liberalism' at the end of the 1800s and beginning of the 1900s, which had Thomas Hill Green and Leonard Hobhouse as its most important representatives, tended in that same direction. (For a discussion of the different aspects of this variety of liberalism, see Avital Simhony and David Weinstein, eds, *The New Liberalism: Reconciling Liberty and Community* (Cambridge, 2001).) In 'Liberal Legislation and Freedom of Contract', Green writes: 'But when we thus speak of freedom, we should consider carefully what we mean by it. We do not mean merely freedom from restraint or compulsion. We do not mean merely freedom to do as we like irrespectively of what it is that we like . . . When we speak of freedom . . . we mean a positive power or capacity of doing or enjoying something worth doing or enjoying.' (Thomas Hill Green, 'Liberal Legislation and Freedom of Contract' [1881], in *Lectures on the Principles of Political*

Obligations and Other Writings (Cambridge, 1986).) As Green understands it, true freedom presupposes a person will do the 'right' things. Furthermore, the government has an obligation to facilitate such freedom. Green defines freedom as acting from the 'conception of a common good'. By making the conception of a common good central to his thought, Green moves away from what he considers to be liberalism's previous self-centred individualism. Individual freedom now becomes a particular type of self-determination where our capacities are used in pursuit of goals that are not only self-chosen, but also morally valuable. More particularly, individual self-realization should be more or less identical with altruism, where the individual makes the promotion of other people's well-being their primary focus. Hobhouse largely follows Green in his understanding of both individual self-realization and the state's role. As they both see it, genuine freedom requires the individual to realize himself in a certain way, namely, one that is best for the community. According to Hobhouse, the good life for an individual must form a rational whole. At the same time, the individual is so starkly woven into a social context that his self-realization is inextricably bound up with the self-realization of everyone else. Communal interests, therefore, trump those individual rights that were central to earlier liberalism. Whereas classical liberalism, furthermore, operated with a strong, but limited state, Hobhouse supports a strong state without those same limitations. As a result, new liberalism's endeavour to realize people's freedom poses a threat to that selfsame freedom.

32 Gerald C. MacCallum Jr, 'Negative and Positive Freedom', *Philosophical Review*, 76 (1967). Berlin has commented on and dismissed MacCallum's objections in Berlin, *Liberty*, p. 36n, 326.

33 Berlin, 'Two Concepts of Liberty', p. 5. Cf. Berlin, *Liberty*, p. 326.

34 Berlin, *Liberty*, p. 36n, 326.

35 Cf. Tim Baldwin, 'MacCallum and the Two Concepts of Freedom', *Ratio*, 2 (1984), p. 141.

36 Berlin, *Liberty*, p. 35.

37 Ibid., p. 32.

38 Immanuel Kant, 'On the Common Saying: "This May Be True in Theory, But It Does Not Apply in Practice"', trans. N. B. Nisbet, in *Kant's Political Writings*, ed. Hans Reiss (Cambridge, 2003), p. 74.

39 Taylor, 'What's Wrong with Negative Liberty?', p. 219.

40 Taylor, 'What Is Wrong with Negative Freedom?', p. 215f.

41 Ibid., p. 216.

42 Berlin, *Liberty*, p. 50f.

43 Ibid., p. 38.

44 Ibid., p. 38.

45 Berlin, 'Two Concepts of Liberty', p. 30.

46 Berlin, *Liberty*, p. 48.

47 Ibid., p. 172, 285.

48 Ibid. p. 41.

49 Berlin, 'Two Concepts of Liberty', p. 31.

50 John Gray, *Two Faces of Liberalism* (Cambridge, 2000), p. 6.

51 See for example Isaiah Berlin, 'The Bent Twig', in *The Crooked Timber of Humanity* (Princeton, NJ, 1998), p. 259.

52 Cf. Berlin, *Liberty*, p. 50n, 216f.

53 Ramin Jahanbegloo, *Conversations with Isaiah Berlin* (London, 1992), p. 44;
    Isaiah Berlin and Beata Polanowska-Sygulska, *Unfinished Dialogue* (Amherst,
    NY, 2006), p. 213.

54 Berlin and Polanowska-Sygulska, *Unfinished Dialogue*, p. 93.

55 John Gray, *Isaiah Berlin* (Princeton, NJ, 1996), chap. 6. See also John Gray,
    'Where Pluralists and Liberals Part Company', *International Journal of
    Philosophical Studies*, 6 (1998).

56 Cf. Michael Stocker, *Plural and Conflicting Values* (Oxford, 1990).

57 Isaiah Berlin, 'Reply to Robert Kocis', *Political Studies*, 31 (1983), pp. 390f.

58 Jahanbegloo, *Conversations with Isaiah Berlin*, p. 37.

59 Ibid., p. 108.

60 Isaiah Berlin, 'The Pursuit of the Ideal', in *The Crooked Timber of Humanity*, p. 11.

61 I am not going to embark on a comprehensive discussion here about the extent
    to which moral realism is convincing. One of moral realism's best-known critics
    is John Mackie, who has formulated what is known as an 'argument from
    queerness' (John Mackie, *Ethics: Inventing Right and Wrong* (Oxford, 1977)).
    Roughly speaking, he posits from the outset that values are ontologically 'queer'
    entities that simply do not fit into our ontology of physical entities. Moral values
    are unlike anything else we encounter in the world – they are presumably non-
    physical, and we do not know how they arose or how they can causally affect
    events. The moral realist can answer that it is certainly true that values are
    ontologically separate from physical entities. However, we are talking about
    two distinct ontological frameworks, and we should not eliminate values from
    ontology simply because they do not constitute physical entities, just as we
    should not eliminate physical entities from ontology because they do not
    constitute values. That would be a strictly dualist approach, but a moral realist
    need not be a dualist. He can, for example, argue that values are quite real and
    natural, that they are only accessible on a higher ontological level than that of
    physics, that they certainly are not explainable through a reduction to physical
    objects, but that this is also the case with a host of other phenomena. That
    would be called a non-reductionist naturalism. In the end, the moral realist can
    simply say that the world is considerably richer than what science is capable of
    discovering, and that we accordingly ought to operate with a richer objective
    conception than what, for example, the physicalistic world-view allows.

62 Jahanbegloo, *Conversations with Isaiah Berlin*, p. 39.

63 Stuart Hampshire, *Morality and Conflict* (Cambridge, MA, 1984), p. 155.

64 Berlin, *Liberty*, p. 52f.

65 Ibid., p. 41.

7
A Republican Concept of Freedom

1 To what extent the newer republican theories give a correct interpretation of
   classic republican viewpoints is a matter of debate (cf. John Charvet, 'Quentin
   Skinner and the Idea of Freedom', *Studies in Political Thought*, 2 (1993)), but I
   will not take the time to address that question here. In addition, I will not give a
   comprehensive presentation of the different elements contained in republicanism,

and will instead limit myself to its critique of liberalism's freedom concept and the alternative it provides.

2 For example, John Rawls writes that there is no fundamental difference between political liberalism and classical republicanism. (John Rawls, *Political Liberalism,* expanded edn (New York, 2005), p. 205f.)

3 Maurizio Viroli, *Republicanism*, trans. Antony Shugaar (New York, 2002), p. 61.

4 See especially Philip Pettit, *Republicanism: A Theory of Freedom and Government* (Oxford, 1989); Philip Pettit, *A Theory of Freedom: From the Psychology to the Politics of Agency* (Oxford, 2001); Quentin Skinner, *Vilkårlig makt: Essays om politisk frihet* (Oslo, 2009); Quentin Skinner, *Liberty Before Liberalism* (Cambridge, 1998).

5 Pettit maintains that a significant difference between himself and Skinner is that he equates freedom with non-dominance, while Skinner requires both non-dominance and non-interference (Philip Pettit, 'Keeping Republican Freedom Simple: On a Difference with Quentin Skinner', *Political Theory*, 30 (2002), p. 342). Pettit is correct that Skinner's freedom concept is not as clear-cut as his own, but, if anything, that makes Skinner's position more plausible, because he is not as severely burdened with a number of the difficulties that, I will subsequently argue, plague a pure republican position.

6 Benjamin Constant, 'The Liberty of the Ancients Compared with That of the Moderns', in *Political Writings*, ed. Biancamaria Fontana (Cambridge, 1988), pp. 307–28.

7 Ibid., p. 326.

8 Skinner, 'Freedom as the Absence of Arbitrary Power', in *Republicanism and Political Theory*, ed. Cécile Laborde and John Maynor (Malden, MA, 2008), pp. 96f.

9 Philip Pettit, 'The Instability of Freedom as Noninterference: The Case of Isaiah Berlin', *Ethics*, 4 (2011), p. 709.

10 Pettit, *Republicanism*, p. 56.

11 Pettit, *A Theory of Freedom*, p. 137.

12 Cited from Amartya Sen, *The Idea of Justice* (London, 2009), p. 352.

13 Pettit, *A Theory of Freedom*, p. 139.

14 Pettit, 'The Instability of Freedom as Noninterference: The Case of Isaiah Berlin', p. 707, n. 35.

15 Skinner, *Vilkårlig makt*, p. 206.

16 Pettit, *Republicanism*, p. 291.

17 Viroli, *Republicanism*, p. 10.

18 Skinner, *Vilkårlig makt*, p. 46.

19 Philip Pettit, *The Common Mind: An Essay on Psychology, Society and Politics* (Oxford, 1996), p. 310.

20 John Locke, *The Second Treatise of Government*, in *Two Treatises of Government*, ed. Ian Shapiro (New Haven, CT, and London, 2003), §22. For more relevant passages, see §§136f., 143ff.

21 Friedrich Hayek, *The Constitution of Liberty*, ed. Ronald Hamowy (Abingdon, 2011), p. 59.

22 Immanuel Kant, 'Remarks in the *Observations on the Feeling of the Beautiful and the Sublime*', in *Observations on the Feeling of the Beautiful and Sublime and Other Writings*, trans. and ed. Patrick Frierson and Paul Guyer (Cambridge, 2011).

8
Freedom and Equality

1 Norberto Bobbio, *Liberalism and Democracy*, trans. Martin Ryle and Kate Soper (London and New York, 1990), p. 32.

2 Indeed, the philosophical literature on the equality concept is so comprehensive that it is difficult to know where to begin, but many of the most fundamental texts are collected in Louis P. Pojman and Robert Westmoreland, eds, *Equality: Selected Readings* (New York and Oxford, 1997). Other useful anthologies are Andrew Mason, ed., *Ideals of Equality* (Oxford, 1998) and Matthew Clayton and Andrew Williams, eds, *The Ideal of Equality* (New York, 2000). A good overview of many of the most important themes and positions can be found in Stuart White, *Equality* (Cambridge, 2007). A book that has proven central to the debate surrounding equality and inequality in the last few years is Richard Wilkinson and Kate Pickett, *The Spirit Level: Why More Equal Societies Almost Always Do Better* (London, 2009); the subtitle in later editions has changed. However, any adequate discussion of Wilkinson's and Pickett's book would require a description of the extensive objections from various quarters that have been levelled at the book's empirical foundations, as well as at the quality of its statistical analysis, and that is both beyond my field of expertise and would take us too far off course.

3 Cf. Will Kymlicka, *Contemporary Political Philosophy* (Oxford, 1990), p. 4.

4 Karl Marx, *Critique of the Gotha Program*, in *Karl Marx: Selected Writings*, ed. Lawrence H. Simon (Indianapolis, IN, 1994).

5 Ibid., p. 315.

6 Amartya Sen, *Inequality Reexamined* (Cambridge, MA, 1992), p. 12f.

7 Michel Houellebecq, *The Elementary Particles*, trans. Frank Wynne (New York, 2000), p. 27.

8 Kurt Vonnegut, 'Harrison Bergeron', in *Welcome to the Monkey House* (New York, 1950). The text is also printed in Louis P. Pojman and Robert Westmoreland, eds, *Equality: Selected Readings* (New York and Oxford, 1997).

9 See especially Friedrich A. Hayek, *Law, Legislation and Liberty*, vol. I: *Rules and Order* (Chicago, 1973); vol. II: *The Mirage of Social Justice* (Chicago, 1976); and vol. III: *The Political Order of a Free People* (Chicago, 1979).

10 Robert Nozick, *Anarchy, State, and Utopia* (New York, 1974), p. 169.

11 François-Noël Babeuf and Sylvain Marechal, 'The Manifesto of Inequality', in *Equality: Selected Readings*, ed. Pojman and Westmoreland.

12 Harry G. Frankfurt, *The Importance of What We Care About* (Cambridge, 1988), pp. 134–58.

13 Harry G. Frankfurt, *Necessity, Volition, and Love* (Cambridge, 1999), p. 146n.

14 Cf. Ronald Dworkin, *Sovereign Virtue* (Cambridge, MA, 2000), chap. 2.

15 Ibid., p. 323.

16 Cf. John Rawls, *A Theory of Justice* (Cambridge, MA, 1971), p. 74, 104.

17 We can also observe that Rawls seems to later abandon this position when he maintains that people who choose free time over work should not have the right to the minimum income that would otherwise follow from his so-called difference principle. (John Rawls, *Justice as Fairness: A Restatement* (Cambridge, MA, 2001), p. 179.) Only those who are willing to work, he

argues, should receive anything. This brings him much closer to Dworkin's position.

18 Aristotle, *Aristotle's Nicomachean Ethics*, trans. Robert C. Bartlett and Susan D. Collins (Chicago, 2011), Book v.2–4.
19 That is especially significant when it comes to an understanding of Adam Smith. When Smith writes about 'distributive justice' and directs critical remarks at the idea, he is using the term in the older, Aristotelian sense. If one overlooks that fact, one will also be in danger of believing that Smith is either inconsistent or will fail to see that there are legitimate questions concerning distributive justice in the phrase's modern sense. For a discussion that clarifies these points – and to which the following discussion of Smith is indebted – see Samuel Fleischacker, *A Short History of Distributive Justice* (Cambridge, MA, 2004).
20 Adam Smith, *Lectures on Jurisprudence* (Indianapolis, IN, 1982), p. 9.
21 Adam Smith, *Theory of Moral Sentiments* (Indianapolis, IN, 1976), p. 81.
22 Ibid., pp. 79, 81.
23 Adam Smith, *An Inquiry into the Nature and Causes of the Wealth of Nations*, (Indianapolis, IN, 1981), p. 785.
24 Ibid., p. 725.
25 Ibid., p. 842.
26 Arthur Young, *The Farmer's Tour through the East of England* (London, 1771), vol. IV, p. 361.
27 Smith, *Wealth of Nations*, p. 100.
28 Cf. ibid., p. 96
29 Thomas Paine, *Rights of Man, Part II*, in *Political Writings*, ed. Bruce Kuklick (Cambridge, 2000), p. 235.
30 Ibid., p. 233f.
31 Ibid., p. 235.
32 Ibid., p. 244.
33 Thomas Paine, *Agrarian Justice*, in *Political Writings*, ed. Kuklick, pp. 327, 331.
34 Ibid., p. 332.
35 Smith, *Wealth of Nations*, pp. 869f.
36 Theodor W. Adorno, 'Über Statik und Dynamik als soziologische Kategorien', in *Gesammelte Schriften*, Book 8 (Frankfurt am Main, 1972), p. 220.
37 Martha Nussbaum and Amartya Sen, eds, *The Quality of Life* (Oxford, 1993).
38 Martha Nussbaum, *Creating Capabilities: The Human Development Approach* (Cambridge, MA, and London, 2011), p. x, cf. p. 18.
39 Martha Nussbaum, *Frontiers of Justice: Disability, Nationality, Species Membership* (Cambridge, MA, 2006), pp. 75, 274; Nussbaum, *Creating Capabilities*, p. 40.
40 Amartya Sen, *The Idea of Justice* (London, 2009), pp. 5f.
41 Ibid., p. 15.
42 A related viewpoint can be found in Michael Walzer, who has described this kind of political philosophy as 'heroic', although he certainly does not mean that as a compliment. The heroic philosopher brackets out the prevailing ideas in the society in which he lives, and on the basis of reason alone he attempts to establish political principles which have 'universal' validity. The philosopher then wishes to see these principles directly translated into political practice. According to Walzer, this political philosopher is doomed to disappointment,

because when he returns from the realm of abstraction to the society in which he lives, the citizens will be ignorant of these supposedly universal principles, which are unconnected to their local traditions, as well as their way of thinking about politics. (Michael Walzer, *Thinking Politically: Essays in Political Theory* (New Haven, CT, 2007).)

43 Sen, *The Idea of Justice*, p. 56f.

44 Ibid., p. 102.

45 Ibid., p. 106.

46 Amartya Sen, *Development as Freedom* (Oxford, 1999), p. 75.

47 Ibid., p. 288.

48 A hunger strike is a demonstration of powerlessness transformed into an instrument of power. What is power, after all, but the ability to enforce one's will? If you have power, you can make a person do what he would not otherwise choose to do. Powerlessness can be defined as the absence of power, as the inability to enforce your will, as being unable to make others act in a certain way, even though you may desire it. At the same time, powerlessness can also become an instrument of power. In *Senchus Mor*, a collection of ancient Irish laws that, according to legend, was compiled by order of St Patrick, there is a regulation describing how an individual might fast in order to compel a more powerful debtor to pay what he owes. A poor man who did not have the means, for example, to seize his debtor's property in order to enforce payment could instead sit outside the debtor's door and fast until the debt was settled. In this case, the creditor is powerless because he cannot actualize his will by forcing the debtor to pay what he owes. Indeed, one might well imagine that it would be no major problem for the debtor if his creditor starved to death. The fact of the matter is, however, that the presence of the faster on his doorstep brings shame, and so the debtor will pay in order to avoid that shame. A line can be drawn from this scenario to modern hunger strikes, which usually have a political purpose. The point here is that making one's powerlessness visible can prove a source of substantial power.

49 For a further discussion of this, see Sen, *Development as Freedom*, chap. 4.

50 It is worth remarking here that 600 million people under ten years old live with severe disabilities, and 400 million of these live in developing countries where the living conditions are quite difficult even for those without disabilities. Cf. Sen, *The Idea of Justice*, p. 258.

51 Sen, *Development as Freedom*, p. 284.

52 Sen also uses the expression 'positive freedom' in another sense, as in 'the person's ability to do the things in question taking everything into account (including external restraints as well as internal limitations)' (Amartya Sen, *Rationality and Freedom* (Cambridge, 2002), p. 586). This definition, however, will not be pursued further here.

53 Sen, *Rationality and Freedom*, p. 587.

54 Sen, *The Idea of Justice*, p. 295.

55 Nussbaum, *Frontiers of Justice*, p. 70.

56 Nussbaum, 'The Future of Feminist Liberalism', *Proceedings and Addresses of the American Philosophical Association*, 74 (2000), p. 56.

57 This list was first published in Martha Nussbaum, *Women and Human*

Development: The Capabilities Approach (Cambridge, 2000), pp. 78ff., and it has since appeared in a number of her later works.

58 Nussbaum, *Creating Capabilities*, pp. 62f.

59 Nussbaum, *Frontiers of Justice*, pp. 75, 281.

60 Ibid., p. 76; Nussbaum, *Creating Capabilities*, pp. 36, 108.

61 Nussbaum, *Creating Capabilities*, p. 42.

62 Sen, *The Idea of Justice*, p. 295. Sen, *Inequality Reexamined*, p. 45.

63 Plato, *The Republic of Plato*, 2nd edn, trans. and ed. Allan Bloom (New York, 1991), 501a.

64 Ibid., 370a–b.

65 Ibid., 433a.

66 Plato, *The Laws of Plato*, trans. and ed. Thomas L. Pangle (Chicago, 1988).

67 John Gray, *Black Mass: Apocalyptic Religion and the Death of Utopia* (London, 2007), p. 1.

68 Norman Cohn, *The Pursuit of the Millennium: Revolutionary Millenarians and Mystical Anarchists of the Middle Ages* [1957] (London, 1970).

69 Regarding the establishment of the theocracy in Münster, my most important source has been Cohn, *The Pursuit of the Millennium*, chaps 12 and 13.

70 G.W.F. Hegel, *Lectures on the Philosophy of History*, trans. J. Sibree (Mineola, NY, 2004), p. 33.

71 Ibid., p. 21.

72 Ibid., p. 37.

73 Cited from Paul Hollander, 'Revisiting the Banality of Evil: Political Violence in Communist Systems', *Partisan Review*, 1 (1997), p. 56.

74 Karl Marx, 'From *The German Ideology*', trans. D. Easton and Kurt H. Guddat, in *Writings of the Young Marx on Philosophy and Society*, *The German Ideology* (Indianapolis, IN, 1997), p. 424f.

75 Vladimir I. Lenin, *The State and Revolution*, trans. and ed. Robert Service (London, 1993).

76 Gray, *Black Mass*, p. 66f.

77 What follows is based especially on David R. Shearer, *Policing Stalin's Socialism: Repression and Social Order in the Soviet Union, 1924–1953* (New Haven, CT, and London, 2009). Another important source is J. Arch Getty and Oleg V. Naumov, *The Road to Terror: Stalin and the Self-destruction of the Bolsheviks, 1932–39* (New Haven, CT, and London, 1999).

78 One of the starkest descriptions of the extreme conditions under which those who had been forcibly deported could live – and die – is found in Nicholas Werth, *Cannibal Island: Death in a Siberian Gulag*, ed. Steven Randall (Princeton, NJ, and Oxford, 2007).

79 Karl R. Popper, *The Open Society and Its Enemies*, vol. I: *The Spell of Plato* (London, 2005), chap. 9.

80 Karl R. Popper, *Conjectures and Refutations* (London, 1989), p. 361.

81 Karl R. Popper, *The Open Society and its Enemies*, vol. II: *The High Tide of Prophecy* (London, 2005), p. 442.

82 Oscar Wilde, *Lady Windermere's Fan*, in *Complete Works of Oscar Wilde* (London, 1966), p. 417.

9
Liberal Rights

1 This assertion is not without its controversy. For example, Ronald Dworkin argues that the ideal of equality is more fundamentally linked to liberalism than the ideal of freedom (Ronald Dworkin, 'Liberalism', in *A Matter of Principle* (Oxford, 1985)). However, this viewpoint strikes me as rather eccentric. The term's etymology, as well as mainstream liberalism, supports the idea that freedom is the most central element here.

2 For a more comprehensive discussion of the conceptual history, see for example Joachim Ritter and Karlfried Gründer, eds, *Historisches Wörterbuch der Philosophie* (Darmstadt, 1980), vol. v, pp. 256–72.

3 Mill, *Principles of Political Economy*, p. 938.

4 An exceptional presentation of this idea can be found in Orlando Patterson, *Freedom*, vol. 1: *Freedom in the Making of Western Culture* (New York, 1991).

5 I have discussed Aristotle's viewpoint on slavery in Lars Fr. H. Svendsen, *Work* (Durham, 2008), pp. 51f.

6 John Dillon and Tania Gergel, eds, *The Greek Sophists* (London, 2003), p. 293.

7 Kevin Bales, *Disposable People: New Slavery in the Global Economy*, 3rd revd edn (Berkeley, CA, 2012). See also E. Benjamin Skinner, *A Crime So Monstrous: Face-to-face with Modern-day Slavery* (New York, 2009).

8 See for example Joel Feinberg, *Harm to Self* (Oxford and New York, 1986), pp. 83–7, and Robert Nozick, *Anarchy, State, and Utopia* (New York, 1974), p. 331.

9 John Stuart Mill, *On Liberty*, ed. Elizabeth Rapaport (Indianapolis, IN, 1978), p. 101.

10 See for example Peter Garnsey, *Thinking about Property: From Antiquity to the Age of Revolution* (Cambridge, 2008).

11 The literature on human rights is so extensive that it cannot be done justice here. A collection of a number of important texts from antiquity until the present day can be found in Madeline R. Ishay, ed., *The Human Rights Reader*, 2nd edn (London and New York, 2007). An accessible introduction to the human rights problematic can also be found in Michael Freeman, *Human Rights* (Cambridge, 2002). Among the contemporary philosophical discussions on human rights, I especially recommend James Griffin, *On Human Rights* (Oxford, 2008), and Charles R. Beitz, *The Idea of Human Rights* (Oxford and New York, 2009).

12 See especially Karl Marx, 'On the Jewish Question', in *Early Political Writings*, trans. and ed. Josef O'Malley (Cambridge, 1994), pp. 44–50.

13 Ronald Dworkin, 'Rights as Trumps', in *Theories of Rights*, ed. Jeremy Waldron (New York, 1985).

14 I give a brief discussion of this in Svendsen, *Work*, pp. 55f.

15 Cf. Will Kymlicka, *Multicultural Citizenship* (Oxford, 1995), chap. 3.

16 William. J. Talbott, *Which Rights Should Be Universal?* (Oxford and New York, 2005), p. 11.

17 In this context, it can be mentioned that Friedrich Hayek, who is restrictive in terms of welfare rights for adults, grants children considerably broader welfare rights. See especially Friedrich A. Hayek, *Law, Legislation and Liberty*, vol. II:

The Mirage of Social Justice (Chicago, 1976), pp. 87 and 101; and vol. III: *The Political Order of a Free People* (Chicago, 1979), p. 61.

18 One of the more curious arguments for the establishment of human rights comes from E. O. Wilson, who argues that human rights ought to be based on the fact that we are mammals! (Edward O. Wilson, *On Human Nature* (Harmondsworth, 1995), p. 199.) Yet mammal rights, to the extent they should even be addressed, will not coincide with human rights. Most human rights would make no sense as mammal rights, such as, for example, the right to education. Rights must stand in reasonable relation to the right-holder's attributes and desires.

19 This definition was launched in 1946 by Karl Evang, among others, and it appears in the first paragraph of the WHO's constitution (1948), which was subsequently adopted by all the organization's member countries. This definition is not particularly intuitive, since most people immediately associate health with the absence of disease and so on. In this respect, we can say that the World Health Organization's positive description of health as 'a state of complete physical, mental and social well-being' represents a strict departure from normal language usage. Indeed, one thing that immediately strikes us is that this definition, in one sense, is exceedingly narrow, since it indicates an empty set: there is not a single person on earth who meets the criteria for good health, simply because no human being has *complete* physical, mental and social well-being. At the same time, the definition is also extremely broad in the sense that there is no aspect of human life that can be said to be non-health-related. This alone gives us reason to doubt that the WHO's definition is particularly useful.

20 This point can also be found on a list in Talbott, *Which Rights Should Be Universal?*, pp. 137 and 163. Talbott discusses this right more extensively in William J. Talbott, *Human Rights and Human Well-being* (Oxford and New York, 2010), chaps 12 and 13.

10

Paternalism

1 Immanuel Kant, 'On the Common Saying: "This May Be True in Theory, But It Does Not Apply in Practice"', trans. N. B. Nisbet, in *Kant's Political Writings*, ed. Hans Reiss (Cambridge, 2003), p. 74.

2 Isaiah Berlin, 'Two Concepts of Liberty', in Isaiah Berlin, *Four Essays on Liberty* (Oxford, 1969), pp. 11, 23.

3 John Stuart Mill, *On Liberty*, ed. Elizabeth Rapaport (Indianapolis, IN, 1978), p. 12.

4 For an overview of this subject, see for example Gerald Dworkin, 'Paternalism', in *Stanford Encyclopedia of Philosophy*, http://plato.stanford.edu.

5 For this interpretation of soft paternalism, see for example Joel Feinberg, *Harm to Self* (Oxford and New York, 1986), p. 126. At the same time, Feinberg does not clearly outline what makes an action 'essentially involuntary', and seems to think that the boundaries here will actually fluctuate with the amount of risk involved and whether any potential damage can be remediated afterwards, as well as other factors (pp. 118–22).

6 Mill, *On Liberty*, p. 95.

7 See for example Georg Høyer et al., 'Paternalism and Autonomy: A Presentation of a Nordic Study on the Use of Coercion in the Mental Health Care System', *International Journal of Law and Psychiatry*, xxv/2 (2002).

8 Richard H. Thaler and Cass R. Sunstein, 'Libertarian Paternalism', *American Economic Review*, 2 (2003); Cass R. Sunstein and Richard H. Thaler, 'Libertarian Paternalism Is Not an Oxymoron', *University of Chicago Law Review*, 4 (2003); and Richard H. Thaler and Cass R. Sunstein, *Nudge: Improving Decisions about Health, Wealth, and Happiness* (New Haven, CT, 2008).

9 Thaler and Sunstein also discuss 'libertarian benevolence', which involves the same nudge-mechanism as libertarian paternalism, though this time it is directed at others, for example, toward inducing people to donate organs to a greater extent than they do today (ibid., chap. 11). Since this is not a form of paternalism, however, it shall not be further discussed in this context.

10 Thaler and Sunstein, 'Libertarian Paternalism Is Not an Oxymoron', p. 1160.

11 For broader presentations and discussions of Kahneman's and Tversky's work, see Daniel Kahneman, Paul Slovic and Amos Tversky, eds, *Judgment under Uncertainty: Heuristics and Biases* (Cambridge, 1982); Daniel Kahneman and Amos Tversky, eds, *Choices, Values and Frames* (Cambridge, 2000); and Thomas Gilovich, Dale Griffin and Daniel Kahneman, eds, *Heuristics and Biases: The Psychology of Intuitive Judgment* (Cambridge, 2002).

12 For relatively accessible discussions, see Dan Ariely, *Predictably Irrational: The Hidden Forces that Shape Our Decisions* (New York, 2008) and Nick Wilkinson, *An Introduction to Behavioral Economics: A Guide for Students* (New York and Basingstoke, 2007). For a more comprehensive and in-depth overview, see for example George Loewenstein, *Exotic Preferences: Behavioral Economics and Human Motivation* (Oxford, 2008). A number of the most central articles on the subject are collected in Colin F. Camerer, George Loewenstein and Matthew Rabin, eds, *Advances in Behavioral Economics* (Princeton, NJ, 2003).

13 Thaler and Sunstein, 'Libertarian Paternalism Is Not an Oxymoron', p. 1199.

14 Ibid., p. 1167. Cf. Thaler and Sunstein, *Nudge*, p. 6.

15 Daniel Kahneman, *Thinking, Fast and Slow* (New York, 2011), pp. 408–18.

16 Friedrich A. Hayek, 'Individualism: True and False', in *Individualism and Economic Order* (Chicago, 1980), pp. 8f.

17 Ibid., p. 11.

18 Cf. Nava Ashraf, Colin F. Camerer and George Loewenstein, 'Adam Smith, Behavioral Economist', *Journal of Economic Perspectives*, 3 (2005). The article is also published in Loewenstein, *Exotic Preferences*.

19 Hayek, 'Individualism: True and False', p. 15.

20 Friedrich Hayek, *The Constitution of Liberty*, ed. Ronald Hamowy (Abingdon, 2011), p. 82.

21 Thaler and Sunstein, 'Libertarian Paternalism Is Not an Oxymoron', p. 7n19.

22 Thaler and Sunstein, 'Libertarian Paternalism', p. 175. Thaler and Sunstein, 'Libertarian Paternalism Is Not an Oxymoron', p. 3.

23 Amartya Sen, 'Rational Fools: A Critique of the Behavioral Foundations of Economic Theory', *Philosophy and Public Affairs*, 4 (1977).

24 Thaler and Sunstein, *Nudge*, p. 5. Italics in the original.

25 Ibid., p. 249.

26 Thaler and Sunstein, 'Libertarian Paternalism', p. 177; Thaler and Sunstein, 'Libertarian Paternalism Is Not an Oxymoron', p. 1164.

27 Thaler and Sunstein, *Nudge*, p. 5.

28 Ibid., p. 11.

29 Ibid., p. 5f. Cf. Thaler and Sunstein, 'Libertarian Paternalism Is Not an Oxymoron', p. 1162.

30 Mill, *On Liberty*, p. 99.

31 Thaler and Sunstein, *Nudge*, p. 47.

32 A similar objection to Thaler and Sunstein is made by Steven Wu, 'When is a Nudge a Shove? The Case for Desire-Neutrality', Columbia Law School (2009), http://papers.ssrn.com.

33 Thaler and Sunstein, 'Libertarian Paternalism', p. 175.

34 Thaler and Sunstein, 'Libertarian Paternalism Is Not an Oxymoron', p. 3.

35 Thaler and Sunstein, *Nudge*, p. 5.

36 Ibid., p. 5.

37 Yet another problem here concerns the timetable for welfare maximization. Is achieving a greater good in the far distant future necessarily preferable to achieving a lesser good in the here and now? Thaler and Sunstein seem to make this assumption – at least, their discussion of retirement savings would seem to indicate that this is the case. However, can we actually do anything more than conclude that people are different, that some have more short-term and others more long-term rationales for their actions?

38 Mill, *On Liberty*, p. 5f.

39 See especially Thaler and Sunstein, *Nudge*, chap. 3.

40 Cf. John Rawls, *A Theory of Justice* (Cambridge, MA, 1971), p. 133; John Rawls, *Political Liberalism,* expanded edn (New York, 2005), pp. 66ff; Thaler and Sunstein, *Nudge*, p. 244f.

41 Ibid., p. 245.

42 Ibid., p. 36; Thaler and Sunstein, 'Libertarian Paternalism Is Not an Oxymoron', p. 1165.

43 Cf. Edward L. Glaeser, 'Paternalism and Psychology', *University of Chicago Law Review*, 1 (2006).

44 Thaler and Sunstein, 'Libertarian Paternalism Is Not an Oxymoron', p. 1165.

45 Thaler and Sunstein, 'Libertarian Paternalism', p. 175; Thaler and Sunstein, 'Libertarian Paternalism Is Not an Oxymoron', p. 1162.

46 Alexis de Tocqueville, *Democracy in America*, trans. Arthur Goldhammer (New York, 2004), p. 818f.

11

Informational Privacy

1 A similar viewpoint can also be found in Charles Fried, 'Privacy', *Yale Law Journal*, 3 (1968).

2 Friedrich Hayek, *The Constitution of Liberty*, p. 61.

3 Cf. Maeve Cook, 'A Space of One's Own: Autonomy, Privacy, Liberty', *Philosophy and Social Criticism*, 1 (1999).

4 For a well-ordered presentation of the different philosophical attempts to

define 'privacy', see H. J. McCloskey, 'Privacy and the Right to Privacy', *Philosophy*, 55 (1980).

5 For a similar approach, see for example Daniel J. Solove, *Understanding Privacy* (Cambridge, MA, and London, 2008), chap. 3.

6 Cf. Philippe Ariès and Georges Duby, eds, *A History of Private Life,* 5 vols (Cambridge, MA, 1992); Jeff Weintraub and Krishan Kumar, eds, *Public and Private in Thought and Practice: Reflections on a Grand Dichotomy* (Chicago, 1997). Cf. Barrington Moore Jr, *Privacy: Studies on Social and Cultural History* (Armonk, NY, 1984).

7 Samuel D. Warren and Louis D. Brandeis, 'The Right to Privacy', *Harvard Law Review*, 5 (1890).

8 Judith Jarvis Thompson, 'The Right to Privacy', *Philosophy and Public Affairs*, 4 (1975).

9 *Katz v. United States*, 389 U.S. 347 (1967). http://supreme.justia.com.

10 James Rachels, 'Why Privacy is Important', *Philosophy and Public Affairs*, 4 (1975).

11 Erving Goffman, *The Presentation of Self in Everyday Life* (New York, 1959).

12 T. S. Eliot, *The Complete Poems and Plays* (London and Boston, 1969), p. 14.

13 Jeremy Bentham, *Panopticon*, in *The Panopticon Writings*, ed. Miran Bozovic (London, 1995), p. 31.

14 Torbjörn Tännsjö, *Privatliv* (Lidingö, 2010).

15 Cf. Daniel J. Solove, *Nothing to Hide: The False Tradeoff Between Privacy and Security* (New Haven, CT, and London, 2011), chap. 2.

16 FORSA, 'Meinungen der Bundesbürger zur Vorratsdatenspeicherung', FORSA: Gesellschaft für Sozialforschung und statistische Analysen mbH, Berlin 2008. www.vorratsdatenspeicherung.de.

17 Brendan O'Neill, 'The Truth about the "Surveillance Society"', *Spiked*, 8 May 2008, www.spiked-online.com.

18 Steven Swinford and Nicola Smith, 'Word on the Street . . . They're Listening', *Sunday Times*, 26 November 2006.

19 Ben Wilson, *What Price Liberty?* (London, 2009), p. 5, 330.

20 Isaiah Berlin, 'Two Concepts of Liberty', in Isaiah Berlin, *Four Essays on Liberty* (Oxford, 1969), p. 7.

12
Freedom of Expression

1 John Milton, *Areopagitica*, in *Complete Poems and Major Prose*, ed. Merritt Y. Hughes (Indianapolis, IN, 2003), p. 720.

2 Ronald Dworkin, 'Rights as Trumps', in *Theories of Rights*, ed. Jeremy Waldron, (New York, 1985).

3 For a discussion of this idea, see for example Rawls, *Political Liberalism*, pp. 340–56.

4 *Brandenburg v. Ohio*, 395 U.S. 444 (1969), at http://supreme.justia.com.

5 John Stuart Mill, *On Liberty*, ed. Elizabeth Rapaport (Indianapolis, IN, 1978), chap. 2.

6 Ibid., p. 11.

7 Ibid., p. 16.

8 Ibid., pp. 16, 61.

9 Ibid., pp. 34, 61.

10 Ibid., pp. 36f., 61.

11 Ibid., p. 9.

12 Cf. ibid., p. 76f.

13 Ibid., p. 53.

14 I have explored this question further in the context of a sense of fear in Lars Fr. H. Svendsen, *A Philosophy of Fear* (London, 2008).

15 Though Voltaire never actually spoke these words, they so accurately represent his thoughts that he might as well have.

16 For a good discussion of this development, see Frank Furedi, *On Tolerance: A Defense of Moral Independence* (London and New York, 2011).

17 John Locke, *A Letter Concerning Toleration*, in *Two Treatises of Government and A Letter Concerning Toleration*, ed. Ian Shapiro (New Haven, CT, and New York, 2003).

13
Realizing Freedom

1 Charles Taylor, *Sources of the Self: The Making of Modern Identity* (Cambridge, MA, 1989), p. 14.

2 Viktor E. Frankl, *The Will to Meaning*, revd edn (New York, 1998), p. ix.

3 Ibid., p. 38.

4 Friedrich Nietzsche, *The Gay Science*, trans. Josefine Nauckhoff, ed. Bernard Williams (Cambridge, 2001), §270, cf. §335.

5 Cf. Anthony Giddens, *Modernity and Self-identity: Self and Identity in the Late Modern Age* (Cambridge, 1991), p. 5 and Anthony Giddens, *The Transformations of Intimacy* (Oxford, 1992), p. 30.

6 Michel Foucault, *Ethics: Subjectivity and Truth: Essential Works of Michel Foucault, 1954–1984* (New York, 1997), vol. I, p. 262.

7 Michel Foucault, *The Use of Pleasure: The History of Sexuality*, trans. Randy Hurley (New York, 1985), vol. II, pp. 72–7.

8 Michel Foucault, *Ethics: Subjectivity and Truth*, pp. 137f.

9 Ibid., p. 318.

10 Cf. Michel Foucault, *Power: The Essential Works of Michel Foucault, 1954–1984* (New York, 2000), vol. III, p. 241f.

11 Paul Ricoeur, *The Conflict of Interpretations*, trans. Kathleen McLaughlin et al., ed. Don Ihde (Evanston, IL, 1974).

12 Harry G. Frankfurt, *The Importance of What We Care About* (Cambridge, 1988), p. 170.

13 Harry G. Frankfurt, *The Reasons of Love* (Princeton, NJ, and New York, 2004), pp. 55f.

14 Ibid., p. 59.

15 Bernard Williams, *Ethics and the Limits of Philosophy* (Cambridge, MA, 1985), p. 11.

16 Martin Heidegger, *Being and Time*, trans. Joan Stambaugh (Albany, NY, 1996), §39–43, 57, 61–6, 69 and 79f. *Sorge* is one of the most important concepts in *Being and Time*, and I have only highlighted the most central paragraphs here.

17 Harry G. Frankfurt, *Necessity, Volition, and Love* (Cambridge, 1999), p. 114f.

18 Frankfurt, *Taking Ourselves Seriously and Getting It Right*.

19 Frankfurt, *Necessity, Volition, and Love*, p. 114.

20 Frankfurt, *The Reasons of Love*, p. 44

21 For a good presentation of Eichmann's life and work, see David Cesarani, *Becoming Eichmann: Rethinking the Life, Crimes, and Trial of a 'Desk Murderer'* (Cambridge, 2007).

22 Ortwin de Graef et al., 'Discussion with Harry G. Frankfurt', *Ethical Perspectives*, 5 (1998), p. 18.

23 Frankfurt, *The Reasons of Love*, p. 97.

24 Graef et al., 'Discussion with Harry G. Frankfurt', p. 33.

25 Frankfurt, *Necessity, Volition, and Love*, p. 108.

26 Frankfurt, *The Reasons of Love*, p. 44.

27 Ibid., p. 25.

28 Ibid., p. 26.

29 Frankfurt, *Necessity, Volition, and Love*, p. 93.

30 Ibid., p. 162.

31 Ibid., p. 110.

32 Frankfurt, *Taking Ourselves Seriously and Getting It Right*, p. 24.

33 Frankfurt, *Necessity, Volition, and Love*, p. 94.

34 Ibid., p. 93.

35 Ibid., p. 94.

36 Aristotle, *Aristotle's Nicomachean Ethics*, 1114b22.

37 Frankfurt, *Taking Ourselves Seriously and Getting It Right*, p. 7.

38 Fyodor Dostoevsky, *Notes from the Underground*, trans. Constance Garnett, ed. Charles Guignon and Kevin Aho (Indianapolis, IN, 2009).

39 Charles Taylor, *The Ethics of Authenticity* (Cambridge, MA, 1992), p. 40.

40 Michel Foucault, *Ethics, Subjectivity and Truth*, p. 291.

41 Immanuel Kant, *The Metaphysics of Morals*, trans. and ed. Mary Gregor (Cambridge, 1996), pp. 191f.

42 Immanuel Kant, *Anthropology, History, and Education*, ed. Günter Zöller and Robert B. Louden (Cambridge, 2007), pp. 132, 244f.

43 Frankfurt, *The Reasons of Love*, p. 6f.

44 Christine M. Korsgaard, *The Sources of Normativity* (Cambridge, 1996) and *Self-constitution: Agency, Identity and Integrity* (Oxford and New York, 2009).

45 Korsgaard, *Self-constitution*, p. 180. For Kant's formulation of the categorical imperative, see Immanuel Kant, *Groundwork of the Metaphysics of Morals*, trans. and ed. Mary Gregor (Cambridge, 1997), p. 34.

46 Korsgaard, *Self-constitution*, p. 161.

47 Immanuel Kant, *Religion within the Limits of Reason Alone*, trans. Theodore M. Greene and Hoyt H. Hudson (New York, 1960), p. 23.

48 Susan Wolf, *Freedom Within Reason* (Oxford, 1990), pp. 68, 73.

49 Ibid., p. 79.

50 Susan Wolf, *Meaning in Life and Why it Matters* (Princeton, NJ, and London, 2010), pp. 9, 26.

51 Ibid., p. 40.

52 G.W.F. Hegel, *Hegel's Aesthetics: Lectures on Fine Art*, vol. 1, trans. T. M. Knox (Oxford, 1975), p. 64.

53 Wolf, *Meaning in Life*, p. 41.

54 Ibid., p. 42.

55 Fyodor M. Dostoevsky, *The House of the Dead*, trans. Constance Garnett (New York, 2004), p. 26.

56 Aristotle, *Aristotle's Nicomachean Ethics*, Book 1.

57 Cf. Pascal Bruckner, *Perpetual Euphoria: On the Duty to be Happy*, trans. Steven Rendall (Princeton, NJ, and Oxford, 2010).

58 Cf. Ziyad Marar, *The Happiness Paradox* (London, 2003).

59 G.W.F. Hegel, *Elements of the Philosophy of Right*, trans. H. B. Nisbet, ed. Allen W. Wood (Cambridge, 1991), §149.

60 Ibid., §158.

Afterword

1 David Foster Wallace, *This is Water: Some Thoughts on a Significant Occasion, about Living a Compassionate Life* (New York, Boston and London, 2009), p. 120.

BIBLIOGRAPHY

Adorno, Theodor W., 'Über Statik und Dynamik als soziologische Kategorien',
　　in *Gesammelte Schriften*, 8 (Frankfurt, 1972)
Allison, Henry E., *Kant's Theory of Freedom* (Cambridge, 1990)
Ariely, Dan, *Predictably Irrational: The Hidden Forces that Shape Our Decisions*
　　(New York, 2008)
Ariès, Philippe, and Georges Duby, eds, *A History of Private Life* (Cambridge, MA,
　　1992), vol. V
Aristotle, *Aristotle's Nicomachean Ethics*, trans. Robert C. Bartlett and Susan D.
　　Collins (Chicago, IL, 2011)
—, *Politics*, trans. Ernest Barker (Oxford, 1995)
—, *Physics*, trans. R. P. Hardie and R. K. Gaye, in *The Complete Works of Aristotle*,
　　vol. I, ed. Jonathan Barnes (Princeton, NJ, 1984)
Ashraf, Nava, et al., 'Adam Smith: Behavioral Economist', *Journal of Economic
　　Perspectives*, 3 (2005), pp. 131–45
Ayer, A. J., *Philosophical Essays* (London, 1954)
Babeuf, François-Noël, and Sylvain Marechal, 'The Manifesto of Inequality', in
　　Equality: Selected Readings, ed. Louis P. Pojman and Robert Westmoreland
　　(New York and Oxford, 1997)
Balaguer, Mark, *Free Will as an Open Scientific Problem* (Cambridge, MA, and
　　London, 2010)
Baldwin, Tim, 'MacCallum and the Two Concepts of Freedom', *Ratio*, 2 (1984)
Bales, Kevin, *Disposable People: New Slavery in the Global Economy*, 3rd revd edn
　　(Berkeley and Los Angeles, CA, and London, 2012)
Barry, Norman P., *On Classical Liberalism and Libertarianism* (New York, 1987)
Beebee, Helen, Christopher Hitchcock and Peter Menzies, eds, *The Oxford
　　Handbook of Causation* (Oxford and New York, 2009)
Beitz, Charles R., *The Idea of Human Rights* (Oxford and New York, 2009)
Bentham, Jeremy, *Panopticon*, in *The Panopticon Writings*, ed. Miran Božovič
　　(London, 1995)
Berlin, Isaiah, 'The Bent Twig', in *The Crooked Timber of Humanity* (Princeton, NJ,
　　1998)
—, *Liberty* (Oxford, 2002)

—, 'The Pursuit of the Ideal', in *The Crooked Timber of Humanity* (Princeton, NJ, 1998)

—, 'Reply to Robert Kocis', *Political Studies*, 31 (1983)

—, 'Two Concepts of Liberty', in Isaiah Berlin, *Four Essays on Liberty* (Oxford, 1969)

—, and Beata Polanowska-Sygulska, *Unfinished Dialogue* (Amherst, NY, 2006)

Blakemore, Colin, *The Mind Machine* (London, 1988)

Blokland, Hans, *Freedom and Culture in Western Society* (London, 1997)

Boaz, David, ed., *The Libertarian Reader* (New York, 1997)

Bobbio, Norberto, *Liberalism and Democracy*, trans. Martin Ryle and Kate Soper (London and New York, 1990)

Boswell, James, *The Life of Johnson* (London, 2008)

Bruckner, Pascal, *Perpetual Euphoria: On the Duty to be Happy*, trans. Steven Rendall (Princeton, NJ, and Oxford, 2010)

Burke, Edmund, *On Empire, Liberty and Reform: Speeches and Letters* (New Haven, CT, and London, 2000)

Butler, Samuel, *Erewhon* (London, 1985)

Camerer, Colin F., et al., *Advances in Behavioral Economics* (Princeton, NJ, 2003)

Campbell, Joseph Keim, et al., eds, *Freedom and Determinism* (Cambridge, MA, and London, 2004)

Carter, Ian, et al., eds, *Freedom: A Philosophical Anthology* (Malden, MA, and Oxford, 2007)

Cartwright, Nancy, *How the Laws of Physics Lie* (Oxford, 1983)

Cesarani, David, *Becoming Eichmann: Rethinking the Life, Crimes, and Trial of a 'Desk Murderer'* (Cambridge, 2007)

Charvet, John, 'Quentin Skinner and the Idea of Freedom', *Studies in Political Thought*, 2 (1993)

Chisholm, Roderick M., 'Human Freedom and the Self', in *Free Will*, 2nd edn, ed. Gary Watson (Oxford, 2003)

Christman, John, ed., *The Inner Citadel: Essays on Individual Autonomy* (Oxford and New York, 1989)

—, *The Politics of Persons: Individual Autonomy and Socio-historical Selves* (Cambridge, 2009)

—, and Joel Anderson, eds, *Autonomy and the Challenges to Liberalism: New Essays* (Cambridge and New York, 2005)

Clarke, Randolph, *Libertarian Accounts of Free Will* (Oxford, 2003)

Clayton, Matthew, and Andrew Williams, eds, *The Ideal of Equality* (New York, 2000)

Cohn, Norman, *The Pursuit of the Millennium: Revolutionary Millenarians and Mystical Anarchists of the Middle Ages* [1957] (London, 1970)

Constant, Benjamin, 'The Liberty of the Ancients Compared with that of the Moderns', in *Political Writings*, ed. Biancamaria Fontana (Cambridge and New York, 1988)

Cook, Maeve, 'A Space of One's Own: Autonomy, Privacy, Liberty', *Philosophy and Social Criticism,* xxv/1 (1999), pp. 22–53

Crick, Francis, *The Astonishing Hypothesis: The Scientific Search for the Soul* (New York, 1994)

Dahl, Robert A., Ian Shapiro and Jose Antonio Cheibub, eds, *The Democracy Sourcebook* (Cambridge, MA, and London, 2003)

Dallaire, Bernadette, et al., 'Civil Commitment Due to Mental Illness and
    Dangerousness: The Union of Law and Psychiatry Within a Treatment-control
    System', *Sociology of Health and Illness*, XXII/5 (2000), pp. 679–99
Damico, Alfonso J., ed., *Liberals on Liberalism* (Totowa, NJ, 1986)
Darwin, Charles, *The Descent of Man and Selection in Relation to Sex* (Princeton, NJ,
    1981)
Dennett, Daniel C., *Elbow Room: Varieties of Free Will Worth Wanting* (Cambridge,
    NJ, 1984)
—, *Freedom Evolves* (London, 2003)
Dewey, John, *Human Nature and Conduct* (New York, 1922)
Dikötter, Frank, *Mao's Great Famine: The History of China's Most Devastating
    Catastrophe, 1958–1962* (London, 2010)
Dillon, John, and Tania Gergel, eds, *The Greek Sophists* (London, 2003)
Doherty, Brian, *Radicals for Capitalism: A Freewheeling History of the Modern
    American Libertarian Movement* (New York, 2007)
Dostoevsky, Fyodor M., 'Environment', in *A Writer's Diary*, trans. Kenneth Lantz
    (Evanston, IL, 1994), vol. I
—, *The House of the Dead*, trans. Constance Garnett (New York, 2004)
—, *Notes from the Underground*, trans. Constance Garnett, ed. Charles Guignon
    and Kevin Aho (Indianapolis, IN, 2009)
Dunn, John, *Democracy: A History* (New York, 2005)
Dupre, John, *The Disorder of Things: Metaphysical Foundations of the Disunity
    of Science* (Cambridge, MA, and London, 1993)
—, *Human Nature and the Limits of Science* (Oxford, 2001)
Dworkin, Gerald, 'Paternalism', in *Stanford Encyclopedia of Philosophy*,
    http://plato.stanford.edu/entries/paternalism
—, *The Theory and Practice of Autonomy* (Cambridge, 1988)
Dworkin, Ronald, 'Liberalism', in *A Matter of Principle* (Oxford, 1985)
—, 'Rights as Trumps', in *Theories of Rights*, ed. Jeremy Waldron (New York, 1985)
—, *Sovereign Virtue* (Cambridge, MA, 2000)
Ekstrom, Laura Waddell, ed., *Agency and Responsibility: Essays on the Metaphysics
    of Freedom* (Boulder, CO, 2000)
Eliot, T. S., *The Complete Poems and Plays* (London and Boston, MA, 1969)
Evans, Edward Payson, *The Criminal Prosecution and Capital Punishment of Animals*
    (London, 1906)
Feinberg, Joel, *Harm to Self* (Oxford and New York, 1986)
Fischer, John Martin, and Mark Ravizza, *Responsibility and Control: A Theory
    of Moral Responsibility* (Cambridge, 1999)
Fleischacker, Samuel, *A Short History of Distributive Justice* (Cambridge, MA, 2004)
Flikschuh, Katrin, *Freedom: Contemporary Liberal Perspectives* (London, 2007)
FORSA, 'Meinungen der Bundesbürger zur Vorratsdatenspeicherung' (Berlin, 2008),
    www.vorratsdatenspeicherung.de
Foucault, Michel, *Ethics, Subjectivity and Truth: Essential Works of Michel Foucault,
    1954–1984* (New York, 1997)
—, *Power: The Essential Works of Michel Foucault, 1954–1984* (New York, 2000),
    vol. III
—, *The Use of Pleasure: The History of Sexuality*, trans. Randy Hurley (New York,
    1985), vol. II

Frankfurt, Harry G., *The Importance of What We Care About* (Cambridge, 1988)
—, *Necessity, Volition, and Love* (Cambridge, 1999)
—, *The Reasons of Love* (Princeton, NJ and New York, 2004)
—, *Taking Ourselves Seriously and Getting It Right* (Stanford, CA, 2006)
Frankl, Viktor E., *The Will to Meaning*, exp. edn (New York, 1998)
Frede, Michael, *A Free Will: Origins of the Notion in Ancient Thought* (Berkeley and Los Angeles, CA, and London, 2011)
Freeman, Michael, *Human Rights* (Cambridge, 2002)
Freeman, Samuel, 'Illiberal Libertarians: Why Libertarianism Is Not a Liberal View', *Philosophy and Public Affairs*, 2 (2002)
Fried, Charles, 'Privacy', *Yale Law Journal*, 3 (1968)
Friedman, Milton, *Capitalism and Freedom* [1962] (Chicago, 2002)
Fukuyama, Francis, *The End of History and the Last Man* (New York, 1992)
—, 'The Future of History: Can Liberal Democracy Survive the Decline of the Middle Class?', *Foreign Affairs*, XCI/1 (2012)
—, *The Origins of Political Order: From Prehuman Times to the French Revolution* (London, 2011)
Furedi, Frank, *On Tolerance: A Defense of of Moral Independence* (London and New York, 2011)
Gallie, W. B., 'Essentially Contested Concepts', *Proceedings of the Aristotelian Society*, 167 (1956)
Garnsey, Peter, *Thinking about Property: From Antiquity to the Age of Revolution* (Cambridge, 2008)
Gaus, Gerald F., *Contemporary Theories of Liberalism* (London, 2003)
Gazzaniga, Michael S., *Who's in Charge? Free Will and the Science of the Brain* (New York, 2011)
Getty, J. Arch, and Oleg V. Naumov, *The Road to Terror: Stalin and the Self-destruction of the Bolsheviks, 1932–39* (New Haven, CT, and London, 1999)
Giddens, Anthony, *Modernity and Self-identity: Self and Identity in the Late Modern Age* (Cambridge, 1991)
—, *The Transformations of Intimacy* (Oxford, 1992)
Gilovich, Thomas, et al., eds, *Heuristics and Biases: The Psychology of Intuitive Judgment* (Cambridge, 2002)
Girgen, Jen, 'The Historical and Contemporary Prosecution and Punishment of Animals', in *Animal Law Review*, IX (2003)
Glaeser, Edward L., 'Paternalism and Psychology', *University of Chicago Law Review*, LXXIII/1 (2006)
Goffman, Erving, *The Presentation of Self in Everyday Life* (New York, 1959)
Graef, Ortwin de, 'Discussion with Harry G. Frankfurt', *Ethical Perspectives*, V/1 (1998)
Gray, John, *Black Mass: Apocalyptic Religion and the Death of Utopia* (London, 2007)
—, *Isaiah Berlin* (Princeton, NJ, 1996)
—, *Liberalism*, revd edn (Buckingham, 1995)
—, *Post-liberalism* (London, 1993)
—, *The Two Faces of Liberalism* (Cambridge, 2000)
—, 'Where Pluralists and Liberals Part Company', *International Journal of Philosophical Studies*, VI (1998), pp. 17–36
Grayling, A. C., *Towards the Light: The Story of the Struggles for Liberty and Rights* (London, 2007)

Green, Thomas Hill, 'Liberal Legislation and Freedom of Contract' (1881), in
   Lectures on the Principles of Political Obligations and Other Writings (Cambridge,
   1986)
Griffin, James, *On Human Rights* (Oxford, 2008)
Gwartney, James, et al., *Economic Freedom of the World: 2011 Annual Report*
   (Vancouver, 2011)
Habermas, Jürgen, 'The Language Game of Responsible Agency and the Problem
   of Free Will: How Can Epistemic Dualism Be Reconciled with Ontological
   Monism', *Philosophical Explorations*, x (2007), pp. 13–50
Haines, John-Dylan, 'Beyond Libet: Long-term Prediction of Free Choices from
   Neuroimaging Signals', in *Conscious Will and Responsibility: A Tribute to
   Benjamin Libet*, ed. Walter Sinnott-Armstrong and Lynn Nadel (Oxford, 2011)
Hamowy, Ronald, ed., *The Encyclopedia of Libertarianism* (Thousand Oaks, CA, and
   London, 2008)
Hampshire, Stuart, *Morality and Conflict* (Cambridge, MA, 1984)
—, *Thought and Action* (London, 1959)
Hayek, Friedrich, *The Constitution of Liberty*, ed. Ronald Hamowy (Abingdon,
   2011)
—, 'Individualism: True and False', in *Individualism and Economic Order* (Chicago,
   1980)
—, *Law, Legislation and Liberty*, vol. I: *Rules and Order* (Chicago, 1973)
—, *Law, Legislation and Liberty*, vol. II: *The Mirage of Social Justice* (Chicago, 1976)
—, *Law, Legislation and Liberty*, vol. III: *The Political Order of a Free People*
   (Chicago, 1979)
Hegel, G.W.F., *Elements of the Philosophy of Right*, trans. H. B. Nisbet, ed. Allen W.
   Wood (Cambridge, 1991)
—, *The Encyclopedia Logic: Part 1 of the Encyclopaedia of Philosophical Sciences*,
   trans. T. F. Geraets et al. (Indianapolis, IN, 1991)
—, *Hegel's Aesthetics: Lectures on Fine Art*, trans. T. M. Knox (Oxford, 1975), vol. I
—, *Lectures on the Philosophy History*, trans. J. Sibree (Mineola, NY, 2004)
—, *Phenomenology of Spirit*, trans. A. V. Miller, ed. J. N. Findlay (Oxford, 1977)
Hempel, Carl Gustav, *Philosophy of Natural Science* (Inglewood Cliffs, NJ, 1966)
Hobbes, Thomas, *Leviathan* (Cambridge, 1991)
—, *Of Liberty and Necessity*, in *Hobbes and Bramhall on Liberty and Necessity*,
   ed. Vere Chappell (Cambridge, 1999)
—, *On the Citizen*, trans. and ed. Richard Tuck and Michael Silverthorne
   (Cambridge, 1998)
—, 'Selection from *The Questions concerning Liberty, Necessity, and Chance*', in
   Hobbes and Bramhall on Liberty and Necessity, ed. Vere Chappell (Cambridge,
   1999)
Hollander, Paul, 'Revisiting the Banality of Evil: Political Violence in Communist
   Systems', *Partisan Review*, LXIV/1 (1997)
Holmes, Stephen, *Passions and Constraint* (Chicago, 1995)
Houellebecq, Michel, *The Elementary Particles*, trans. Frank Wynne (New York,
   2000)
Humboldt, Wilhelm von, *The Limits of State Action*, ed. J. W. Burrow (London, 1969)
Hume, David, *A Treatise of Human Nature*, ed. David Fate Norton and Mary J.
   Norton (Oxford, 2007), vol. I

Høyer, Georg, et al., 'Paternalism and Autonomy: A Presentation of a Nordic Study on the Use of Coercion in the Mental Health Care System', *International Journal of Law and Psychiatry*, xxv/2 (2002)

Inwagen, Peter van, *An Essay on Free Will* (Oxford, 1983)

Ishay, Madeline R., ed., *The Human Rights Reader*, 2nd edn (London and New York, 2007)

Jacobs, Jonathan, *Choosing Character: Responsibility for Virtue and Vice* (Ithaca, NY, and London, 2001)

Jahanbegloo, Ramin, *Conversations with Isaiah Berlin* (London, 1992)

James, William, *The Will to Believe and Other Essays* (New York, 1956)

Kane, Robert, *The Significance of Free Will* (Oxford and New York, 1996)

—, ed., *The Oxford Handbook of Free Will* (Oxford, 2002)

Kahneman, Daniel, *Thinking, Fast and Slow* (New York, 2011)

—, and Amos Tversky, eds, *Choices, Values and Frames* (Cambridge, 2000)

—, et al., eds, *Judgment under Uncertainty: Heuristics and Biases* (Cambridge, 1982)

Kant, Immanuel, 'Anthropology from a Pragmatic Point of View', in *Anthropology, History, and Education*, trans. Mary Gregor, ed. Günter Zöller and Robert B. Louden (Cambridge, 2007)

—, *Dreams of a Spirit-seer Elucidated by Dreams of Metaphysics*, in *Theoretical Philosophy, 1755–1770*, trans. and ed. David Walford (Cambridge, 1992)

—, *Groundwork of the Metaphysics of Morals*, trans. and ed. Mary Gregor (Cambridge, 1997)

—, 'Lectures on Pedagogy', in *Anthropology, History, and Education*, trans. Mary Gregor, ed. Günter Zöller and Robert B. Louden (Cambridge, 2007)

—, *The Metaphysics of Morals*, trans. and ed. Mary Gregor (Cambridge, 1996)

—, 'On the Common Saying, "This May Be True in Theory, But It Does Not Apply in Practice"', in *Kant's Political Writings*, trans. N. B. Nisbet, ed. Hans Reiss (Cambridge, 2003)

—, *Religion within the Limits of Reason Alone*, trans. Theodore M. Greene and Hoyt H. Hudson (New York, 1960)

—, 'Remarks in the *Observations on the Feeling of the Beautiful and Sublime*', in *Observations on the Feeling of the Beautiful and Sublime and Other Writings*, trans. and ed. Patrick Frierson and Paul Guyer (Cambridge, 2011)

Keane, John, *The Life and Death of Democracy* (London, 2009)

Kelly, Paul, *Liberalism* (London, 2005)

Kojève, Alexandre, *Introduction to the Reading of Hegel: Lectures on the Phenomenology of Spirit*, trans. James H. Nichols Jr, ed. Allan Bloom (Ithaca, NY, 1980)

Korsgaard, Christine M., *Self-constitution: Agency, Identity and Integrity* (Oxford and New York, 2009)

—, *The Sources of Normativity* (Cambridge and New York, 1996)

Kymlicka, Will, *Contemporary Political Philosophy* (Oxford, 1990)

—, *Multicultural Citizenship* (Oxford, 1995)

Lenin, Vladimir I., *The State and Revolution*, trans. and ed. Robert Service (London, 1993)

Libet, Benjamin, 'Consciousness, Free Action and the Brain', *Journal of Consciousness Studies*, 8 (2001)

—, 'Do We Have Free Will?', in Robert Kane, ed., *The Oxford Handbook of Free Will* (Oxford, 2002)

—, *Mind Time: The Temporal Factor in Consciousness* (Cambridge, MA, and London, 2004)

—, 'Unconscious Cerebral Initiative and the Role of Conscious Will in Voluntary Action', *Behavioural and Brain Sciences*, VIII/4 (1985), pp. 529–39

Lincoln, Abraham, 'Address at Sanitary Fair, Baltimore, Maryland, Apr. 11, 1864', in *Collected Works of Abraham Lincoln*, ed. Roy P. Basler, vol. VII (New Brunswick, NJ, 1953)

Loewenstein, George, *Exotic Preferences: Behavioral Economics and Human Motivation* (Oxford, 2008)

Locke, John, *A Letter Concerning Toleration*, in *Two Treatises of Government and A Letter Concerning Toleration*, ed. Ian Shapiro (New Haven, CT, and New York, 2003)

—, *The Correspondence of John Locke* (Oxford, 1979), Book IV

—, *The First Treatise of Government*, in *Two Treatises of Government* (Cambridge, 2005)

—, *The Second Treatise of Government*, in *Two Treatises of Government* (Cambridge, 2005)

Lucretius, *On the Nature of Things*, trans. Frank O. Copley (New York, 1977)

MacCallum, Gerald C. Jr, 'Negative and Positive Freedom', *Philosophical Review*, LXXVI (1967)

McCloskey, H. J., 'Privacy and the Right to Privacy', *Philosophy*, LV/211 (1980), pp. 17–38

McDowell, John, 'Having the World in View: Lecture One', *Journal of Philosophy*, XCV (1998)

McKenna, Michael, and Paul Russell, ed., *Free Will and Reactive Attitudes: Perspectives on P. F. Strawson's 'Freedom and Resentment'* (Farnham and Burlington, VT, 2008)

Mackie, John, *Ethics: Inventing Right and Wrong* (London, 1977)

Manent, Pierre, *An Intellectual History of Liberalism*, trans. Rebecca Balinski (Princeton, NJ, 1995)

Marar, Ziyad, *The Happiness Paradox* (London, 2003)

Marx, Karl, *Critique of the Gotha Program* [1875] in *Karl Marx, Selected Writings*, ed. Lawrence H. Simon (Indianapolis, IN, 1994)

—, 'From *The German Ideology*', trans. D. Easton and Kurt H. Guddat, in *Writings of the Young Marx on Philosophy and Society: The German Ideology* (Indianapolis, IN, 1997)

—, 'On the Jewish Question', in *Early Political Writings*, trans. and ed. Josef O'Malley (Cambridge, 1994)

Mason, Andrew, ed., *Ideals of Equality* (Oxford 1998)

Mele, Alfred R., *Autonomous Agents: From Self-control to Autonomy* (Oxford and New York, 1995)

Merleau-Ponty, Maurice, *Phenomenology of Perception*, trans. Colin Smith (London, 1989)

Mill, John Stuart, *Collected Works of John Stuart Mill*, vol. VIII: *A System of Logic Ratiocinative and Inductive* (Toronto and London, 1974)

—, *Collected Works of John Stuart Mill*, vol. VIII: *An Examination of Sir William Hamilton's Philosophy* (Toronto and London, 1974)

—, 'Nature', *Collected Works of John Stuart Mill* (Toronto and London, 1974), vol. x

—, *Collected Works of John Stuart Mill*, vol. viii: *Principles of Political Economy with some of their Applications to Social Philosophy* (Toronto and London, 1974)

—, *On Liberty*, ed. Elizabeth Rapaport (Indianapolis, in, 1978)

Miller, Terry, et al., *2012 Index of Economic Freedom* (Washington and New York, 2012)

Milton, John, 'Areopagitica', in *Complete Poems and Major Prose*, ed. Merritt Y. Hughes (Indianapolis, in, 2003)

Montesquieu, *The Spirit of the Laws*, trans. and ed. Anne M. Cohler et al. (Cambridge, 2005)

Moore, Barrington Jr., *Privacy: Studies on Social and Cultural History* (Armonk, ny, 1984)

Murphy, Nancey, and Warren S. Brown, *Did My Neurons Make Me Do It? Philosophical and Neurobiological Perspectives on Moral Responsibility and Free Will* (Oxford and New York, 2006)

—, et al., eds, *Downward Causation and the Neurobiology of Free Will* (Berlin and Heidelberg, 2009)

Nagel, Thomas, *The View from Nowhere* (Oxford, 1986)

Nelkin, Dana Kay, *Making Sense of Freedom and Responsibility* (Oxford, 2011)

Nichols, Shaun, 'After Incompatibilism: A Naturalistic Defense of Reactive Attitudes', *Philosophical Perspectives,* xxi (2007)

—, and Joshua Knobe, 'Moral Responsibility and Determinism: The Cognitive Science of Folk Intuitions', *Noûs,* xli/4 (2007), pp. 663–85

Nietzsche, Friedrich, *The Gay Science*, trans. Josefine Nauckhoff, ed. Bernard Williams (Cambridge, 2001)

Noble, Denis, *The Music of Life: Biology Beyond Genes* (Oxford and New York, 2006)

Noë, Alva, *Out of Our Heads: Why You Are Not Your Brain, and Other Lessons From the Biology of Consciousness* (New York, 2009)

Nozick, Robert, *Anarchy: State and Utopia* (New York, 1974)

Nussbaum, Martha, *Creating Capabilities: The Human Development Approach* (Cambridge, ma, and London, 2011)

—, *Frontiers of Justice: Disability, Nationality, Species Membership* (Cambridge, ma, 2006)

—, 'The Future of Feminist Liberalism', *Proceedings and Addresses of the American Philosophical Association*, 74 (2000)

—, and Amartya Sen, ed., *The Quality of Life* (Oxford, 1993)

—, *Women and Human Development: The Capabilities Approach* (Cambridge, 2000)

O'Neill, Brendan, 'The Truth About the "Surveillance Society"', *Spiked* (8 May 2008)

Paine, Thomas, *Agrarian Justice*, in *Political Writings*, ed. Bruce Kuklick (Cambridge, 2000)

—, *Rights of Man, Part ii*, in *Political Writings*, ed. Bruce Kuklick (Cambridge, 2000)

Patterson, Orlando, *Freedom*, vol. i: *Freedom in the Making of Western Culture* (New York, 1991)

Paul, Ellen Frankel, et al., eds, *Autonomy* (Cambridge and New York, 2003)

—, ed., *Liberalism: Old and New* (Cambridge, 2007)

—, ed., *Natural Rights Liberalism from Locke to Nozick* (Cambridge, 2005)

Pereboom, Derk, *Living Without Free Will* (Cambridge, 2001)

Pettit, Philip, *The Common Mind: An Essay on Psychology, Society and Politics* (Oxford, 1996)

—, 'The Instability of Freedom as Noninterference: The Case of Isaiah Berlin', *Ethics*, 4 (2011)

—, 'Keeping Republican Freedom Simple: On a Difference with Quentin Skinner', *Political Theory*, xxx/3 (2002), pp. 339–56

—, *Republicanism: A Theory of Freedom and Government* (Oxford, 1989)

—, *A Theory of Freedom: From the Psychology to the Politics of Agency* (Oxford, 2001)

Pink, Thomas, and Martin Stone, eds, *The Will and Human Action: From Antiquity to the Present Day* (London, 2003)

Pitkin, Hanna Fenichel, 'Are Freedom and Liberty Twins?', *Political Theory*, xvi/4 (1988), pp. 523–52

Plato, *The Laws of Plato*, trans. and ed. Thomas L. Pangle (Chicago, IL, 1988)

—, *The Republic of Plato*, 2nd edn, trans. and ed. Allan Bloom (New York, 1991)

Pojman, Louis P., and Robert Westmoreland, eds, *Equality: Selected Readings* (New York and Oxford, 1997)

Popper, Karl R., *Conjectures and Refutations* (London, 1989)

—, *The Open Society and Its Enemies*, vol. 1: *The Spell of Plato* (London, 2005)

Rachels, James, 'Why Privacy is Important', *Philosophy and Public Affairs*, iv/4 (1975), pp. 323–33

Rawls, John, *Justice as Fairness: A Restatement* (Cambridge, MA, 2001)

—, *Political Liberalism* (New York, 2005)

—, *A Theory of Justice* (Cambridge, MA, 1971)

Raz, Joseph, *The Morality of Freedom* (Oxford, 1986)

Reznek, Lawrie, *Evil or Ill? Justifying the Insanity Defense* (London and New York, 1997)

Rhinehart, Luke, *The Dice Man* (New York and Woodstock, 1971)

Ricoeur, Paul, *The Conflict of Interpretations*, trans. Kathleen McLaughlin et al., ed. Don Ihde (Evanston, IL, 1974)

Rigoni, Davide, et al., 'Inducing Disbelief in Free Will Alters Brain Correlates of Preconscious Motor Preparation: The Brain Minds Whether We Believe in Free Will or Not', *Psychological Science*, xxii/5 (2011), pp. 613–18

Ringen, Stein, *What Democracy Is For: On Freedom and Moral Government* (Princeton, NJ, and Oxford, 2009)

Ritter, Joachim, and Karlfried Gründer, eds, *Historisches Wörterbuch der Philosophie* (Darmstadt, 1980)

Röpke, Wilhelm, *Das Kulturideal des Liberalismus* (Frankfurt, 1947)

Rousseau, Jean-Jacques, *The Reveries of the Solitary Walker*, trans. Charles E. Butterworth (Indianapolis, IN, 1992)

—, *The Social Contract,* trans. and ed. Victor Gourevitch (Cambridge and New York, 1997)

Sarkassian, Hagop, et al., 'Is Belief in Free Will a Cultural Universal', *Mind and Language*, xxv/3 (2010), pp. 346–58

Schmidtz, David, and Jason Brennan, *A Brief History of Liberty* (Oxford, 2010)

Schopenhauer, Arthur, *Prize Essay on the Freedom of the Will*, ed. Günter Zöller, trans. Eric F. J. Payne (Cambridge, 1999)

Schwartz, Barry, *The Paradox of Choice: Why More is Less* (New York, 2004)

Searle, John R., *Intentionality: An Essay in the Philosophy of Mind* (Cambridge, 1983)

Sen, Amartya, *Development as Freedom* (Oxford, 1999)

—, *The Idea of Justice* (London, 2009)

—, *Inequality Reexamined* (Cambridge, MA, 1992)

—, *Poverty and Famines: An Essay on Entitlement and Deprivation* (Oxford, 1981)

—, 'Rational Fools: A Critique of the Behavioral Foundations of Economic Theory', *Philosophy and Public Affairs*, VI/4 (1977), pp. 317–44

—, *Rationality and Freedom* (Cambridge, 2002)

Shearer, David R., *Policing Stalin's Socialism: Repression and Social Order in the Soviet Union, 1924–1953* (New Haven, CT, and London, 2009)

Simhony, Avital, and David Weinstein, eds, *The New Liberalism: Reconciling Liberty and Community* (Cambridge, 2001)

Sinnott-Armstrong, Walter, and Lynn Nadel, eds, *Conscious Will and Responsibility: A Tribute to Benjamin Libet* (Oxford, 2011)

Skinner, B. F., *Walden Two* [1948] (Indianapolis, IN, and Cambridge, 2005)

Skinner, E. Benjamin, *A Crime So Monstrous: Face-to-Face with Modern-day Slavery* (New York, 2009)

Skinner, Quentin, *Liberty Before Liberalism* (Cambridge, 1998)

—, *Vilkårlig makt: Essays om politisk frihet* (Oslo, 2009)

Smilansky, Saul, *Free Will and Illusion* (Oxford, 2000)

Smith, Adam, *An Inquiry into the Nature and Causes of the Wealth of Nations*, Glasgow Edition, vol. II (Indianapolis, IN, 1981)

—, *Lectures on Jurisprudence*, Glasgow Edition, vol. V (Indianapolis, IN, 1982)

—, *Theory of Moral Sentiments*, Glasgow Edition, vol. I (Indianapolis, IN, 1982)

Solove, Daniel J., *Nothing to Hide: The False Tradeoff Between Privacy and Security* (New Haven, CT, and London, 2011)

—, *Understanding Privacy* (Cambridge, MA, and London, 2008)

Soon, Chun Siong, et al., 'Unconscious Determinants of Free Decisions in the Human Brain', *Nature Neuroscience*, XI (2008), pp. 543–5

Soysa, Indra de, and Hanne Fjelde, 'Is the Hidden Hand an Iron Fist? Capitalism and Civil Peace, 1970–2005', *Journal of Peace Research*, XLVII/3 (2010), pp. 287–98

Starr, Paul, *Freedom's Power: The True Force of Liberalism* (New York, 2007)

Steward, Helen, *A Metaphysics for Freedom* (Oxford, 2012)

Stocker, Michael, *Plural and Conflicting Values* (Oxford, 1990)

Strawson, Galen, *Freedom and Belief* (Oxford, 1991)

—, 'The Impossibility of Moral Responsibility', *Philosophical Studies*, LXXV/1–2 (1994)

Strawson, Peter F., *Freedom and Resentment and Other Essays* [1974] (London, 2008)

Streatfeild, Dominic, *Brainwash: The Secret History of Mind Control* (London, 2006)

Suppes, Patrick, 'The Transcendental Character of Determinism', *Midwest Studies in Philosophy*, XVIII/1 (1993), pp. 242–57

Svendsen, Lars Fr. H., *A Philosophy of Fear* (London, 2008)

—, *Work* (Durham, 2008)

Swinford, Steven, and Nicola Smith, 'Word on the Street . . . They're Listening', *Sunday Times* (26 November 2006)

Talbott, William. J., *Which Rights Should Be Universal?* (Oxford and New York, 2005)

—, *Human Rights and Human Well-being* (Oxford and New York, 2010)

Tallis, Raymond, *Aping Mankind: Neuromania, Darwinitis and the Misrepresentation of Mankind* (Durham, 2011)

Tännsjö, Torbjörn, *Privatliv* (Lidingö, 2010)

Taylor, Charles, *Sources of the Self: The Making of Modern Identity* (Cambridge, MA, 1989)

—, *The Ethics of Authenticity* (Cambridge, 1992)

—, 'What's Wrong with Negative Liberty?', *Philosophy and the Human Sciences*, II (Cambridge, 1985)

Taylor, James Stacey, ed., *Personal Autonomy: New Essays on Personal Autonomy and Its Role in Contemporary Moral Philosophy* (Cambridge and New York, 2005)

Thaler, Richard H., and Cass R. Sunstein, 'Libertarian Paternalism', *American Economic Review*, 2 (2003)

—, and —, 'Libertarian Paternalism Is Not an Oxymoron', *University of Chicago Law Review*, 4 (2003)

—, and —, *Nudge: Improving Decisions about Health, Wealth, and Happiness* (New Haven, CT, 2008)

Thompson, Judith Jarvis, 'The Right to Privacy', *Philosophy and Public Affairs*, IV/4 (1975)

Tocqueville, Alexis de, *The Ancien Régime and the French Revolution*, trans. Arthur Goldhammer, ed. Jon Elster (Cambridge, 2011)

—, *Democracy in America*, trans. Arthur Goldhammer (New York, 2004)

Turnbull, Colin, *The Mountain People* (New York, 1972)

Viroli, Maurizio, *Republicanism*, trans. Antony Shugaar (New York, 2002)

Vohs, Kathleen D., and Jonathan W. Schooler, 'The Value of Believing in Free Will: Encouraging a Belief in Determinism Increases Cheating', *Psychological Science* XIX/1 (2008), pp. 49–54

Vonnegut, Kurt, 'Harrison Bergeron', in *Welcome to the Monkey House* (New York, 1950)

Wall, Steven, *Liberalism: Perfectionism and Restraint* (Cambridge, 1998)

Wallace, David Foster, *This Is Water: Some Thoughts on a Significant Occasion about Living a Compassionate Life* (New York and Boston, MA, and London, 2009)

Walzer, Michael, *Thinking Politically: Essays in Political Theory* (New Haven, CT, 2007)

Warren, Samuel D., and Louis D. Brandeis, 'The Right to Privacy', *Harvard Law Review*, IV/5 (1890)

Watson, Gary, 'Free Agency', *Journal of Philosophy*, LXXII/8 (1975), pp. 205–20

—, ed., *Free Will* (Oxford, 2003)

—, 'Introduction', in *Free Will*, ed. Gary Watson (Oxford, 2003)

Wegner, Daniel M., *The Illusion of Conscious Will* (Cambridge, MA, and London, 2002)

Weintraub, Jeff, and Krishan Kumar, eds, *Public and Private in Thought and Practice: Reflections on a Grand Dichotomy* (Chicago, 1997)

Werth, Nicholas, *Cannibal Island: Death in a Siberian Gulag*, ed. Steven Randall (Princeton, NJ, and Oxford, 2007)

White, Stuart, *Equality* (Cambridge, 2007)

Widerker, David, and Michael Mckenna, eds, *Moral Responsibility and Alternative Possibilities: Essays on the Importance of Alternative Possibilities* (Aldershot and Burlington, VT, 2006)

Wilde, Oscar, *Lady Windermere's Fan: Complete Works of Oscar Wilde* (London, 1966)

Wilkinson, Nick, *An Introduction to Behavioral Economics: A Guide for Students* (New York and Basingstoke, 2007)

Wilkinson, Richard, and Kate Pickett, *The Spirit Level: Why More Equal Societies Almost Always Do Better* (London, 2009)

Williams, Bernard, 'Practical Necessity', in *Moral Luck: Philosophical Papers, 1973–1980* (Cambridge, 1981)

—, *Ethics and the Limits of Philosophy* (Cambridge, 1985)

—, 'From Freedom to Liberty: The Construction of a Political Value', *Philosophy and Public Affairs*, xxx/1 (2001), pp. 3–26

Wilson, Ben, *What Price Liberty?* (London, 2009)

Wilson, Edward O., *Consilience: The Unity of Knowledge* (London, 1999)

—, *On Human Nature* (Harmondsworth, 1978)

Wittgenstein, Ludwig, *Culture and Value*, trans. Peter Winch (Chicago, 1984)

—, *Philosophical Occasions, 1912–1951* (Indianapolis, in, and Cambridge, 1993)

Wolf, Susan, *Freedom Within Reason* (Oxford, 1990)

—, *Meaning in Life and Why it Matters* (Princeton, nj, and London, 2010)

Wolfe, Alan, *The Future of Liberalism* (New York, 2009)

Wu, Steven, 'When is a Nudge a Shove? The Case for Preference-neutrality', Columbia Law School (2009), http://papers.ssrn.com

Young, Arthur, *The Farmer's Tour Through the East of England* (London, 1771)

ACKNOWLEDGEMENTS

My thanks to Gunnar C. Aakvaag, Kristin Clemet, Marius Doksheim, Pål Foss, Kirsten Rygh Kalleberg, Morten Kinander, Atle Ottesen Søvik and Erik Thorstensen for their comments on the text. I also want to thank the Norwegian Non-fiction Fund and the Liberal Research Institute for their economic support. Last but not least, I want to thank the Department of Philosophy at Bergen University and the Civita think tank for giving me the time to work on this book.